Older Women in the Criminal Justice System

of related interest

Geronticide
Killing the Elderly
Mike Brogden
ISBN 1 85302 709 X

Women Who Offend
Edited by Gill McIvor
ISBN 1 84310 154 8
Research Highlights in Social Work 44

Working Therapeutically with Women in Secure
Mental Health Settings
Edited by Nikki Jeffcote and Tessa Watson
Foreword by Jenni Murray
ISBN 1 84310 218 8
Forensic Focus 27

Ageing with a Lifelong Disability
A Guide to Practice, Program and Policy Issues for Human
Services Professionals
Chris Bigby
ISBN 1 84310 077 0

Older Women in the Criminal Justice System

Running Out of Time

Azrini Wahidin

Jessica Kingsley Publishers
London and Philadelphia

First published in the United Kingdom in 2004
by Jessica Kingsley Publishers
116 Pentonville Road
London N1 9JB, England
and
400 Market Street, Suite 400
Philadelphia, PA 19106, USA

www.jkp.com

Copyright © Azrini Wahidin 2004

Library of Congress Cataloging in Publication Data
Wahidin, Azrini, 1972-
  Older women in the criminal justice system : running out of time / Azrini Wahidin.
    p. cm.
  Includes bibliographical references and index.
  ISBN 1-84310-170-X (pbk.)
    1. Women prisoners—Great Britain. 2. Aged prisoners—Great Britain. 3. Aged offenders—Great Britain.
I. Title.
  HV9647.W336 2004
  365'.6'08460941—dc22

                    2004006410

British Library Cataloguing in Publication Data
A CIP catalogue record for this book is available from the British Library

ISBN 1 84310 170 X

Tables and charts in the Introduction (pages 9–42) and Appendix D (pages 205–214) were generated using data provided by the Research, Development and Statistics Directorate at the Home Office

Printed and Bound in Great Britain by
Athenaeum Press, Gateshead, Tyne and Wear

To Che-Mah

Acknowledgements

My first and biggest thanks go to the women I interviewed. Their stories are the heart of this book. I am grateful to the Centre for Gerontology, School of Social Relations University of Keele, for the award of the studentship which funded the research on which this book is based.

I am indebted to those colleagues and friends who have assisted my work over the years. There are too many to name them all individually but they will know who they are. However, I want to mention some people who went out of their way to help. In particular, Ron Aday, Caroline Stewart, Dr Mary Piper, Rachel Councell, Mark Judd, Mervyn Eastman, Simon Biggs, Chris Phillipson, Sue May, Olga Heaven, Angela Devlin, the governors, and officers at the various prisons I visited.

I wish to express my immense gratitude to the following: Wan-Nita Wahidin, Kate Rose, Judith Phillips and Brian Williams, for encouragement, criticism, extraordinary patience, and example. The Department of Social Policy, Sociology and Social Research at the University of Kent has been a stimulating intellectual home whilst I wrote this book.

Finally, I dedicate this book to Che-Mah Wahidin; mother, friend and mentor who otherwise has and continues to defy description.

Contents

List of Figures

List of Tables

Introduction

It is said that no one truly knows a nation until one has been inside its jails. A nation should not be judged by how it treats its highest citizens, but its lowest ones. (Mandela 1994:174)

As a society, we are unaccustomed to thinking about elderly people as criminal offenders. Usually, when the elderly receive publicity they are represented as the victims of crime, not its perpetrators. Common portrayals of the elderly offender in the media have been that of writing bad cheques, driving under the influence, engaging in disorderly conduct, or shoplifting in order to survive or to provoke attention. The public perception of women who commit offences such as shoplifting, violence against a person, drug-related offences is that they are younger and that they receive relatively short prison sentences. When a woman receives a long sentence, as in the case of Myra Hindley,[1] it is seen as an exception (and it is assumed that violence is a highly atypical crime for women).

A related problem is the stereotype that murders, drug offences and violence against the person are committed by young able-bodied males. This gives a distorted picture of the nature of these crimes where women are concerned, because their crimes rarely fall into this category. More especially, we are unlikely to associate elderly women with crime, or women in general with crime serious enough to result in prison sentences continuing into old age. Lately, however, elders are committing more serious offences that were at one time confined almost exclusively to the young. This book will show that some women in later life do commit crimes: some are arrested; some are convicted; some are sent to prison; and some grow old in prison.

Older Women in the Criminal Justice System: Running Out of Time focuses on the narratives of elders in prison by integrating gerontology and criminological theory in order to understand their needs and the challenges elders in prison pose to the criminal justice system. The neglect of research in this area is a latent form of ageism that says that the problems of this group can be disregarded, or that ageing criminals are simply not worth discussing. The explanation frequently given for the lack of statistical information on this topic is that at present the numbers involved are too small to yield significant information (Linda Jones, Head of the Women's Policy Group and Mrs Selfe, Women's Policy Group: personal communication, 2003), with the implication that this justifies excluding and ignoring the rights of elders in prison. Yet there has been no assessment of the implications of this, or recognition that Britain, like the USA, is facing an ageing prison population. This has become known as the 'geriatrification' of the prison population.

This book will be concerned with 'unsilencing' a group of prisoners who because of their age, gender and 'status' as older women in prison have been muted by the criminal justice system. Their experiences have remained marginalised in the debates around policy, and how the criminal justice system responds to the changes generated by the growing number of older offenders in the criminal justice system remains yet to be seen.

The recent shift towards mandatory sentencing, the war on drugs, and the greying of the UK population are the major turning points that unexpectedly escalated the need to address the issues raised in this book. It will be of interest to students of gerontology and criminology, and criminal justice professionals – lawyers, judges, police officers, social workers, medical staff, probation and prison staff who work directly with elders in prison. It will be a source for those responsible for the design and implementation of new programmes and policy, as it will pursue ways to improve guidelines for working with the elderly female prison population. Although the book is centred around the experiences of female elders, it will raise generic issues that are relevant to the elderly male prison population.

Facts and gaps: Demographic characteristics

Women in prison form only a very small proportion of the total prison population, 5.2 per cent,[2] and women over 50 represent only 4.6 per cent of the total female prison estate. Out of the total prison population 8.5 per cent are over the age of 50. On 31 December 2002 there were 176 women over the age of 50 and 4608 men over 50 years of age and in prison. The Home Office Prison Department has no overall policy or strategy for dealing with women who are in later life and in prison despite having policies in place for mothers and babies who constitute a similar group numerically (Her Majesty's Chief Inspector of Prisons (HMCIP) 1997, 2001a; Home Office (HO) 1995a).

Contrary to popular belief, the most common offence for the older age group is not perpetrated by the menopausal shop-lifter – that is, not theft and handling or fraud and forgery – but violence against the person and drug offences. In contrast, if we look at prisoners over the age of 50 by sentence length and offence group for 2003, what is noticeable is that there is only a slight variation in the most common offences for types of sentences.

Table 1.1 Prisoners over 50 by sentence length and offence group	
Up to and including 12 months	*Over 12 months and up to and including 5 years*
Violence against the person	Violence against the person
Others	Drug offences
Sexual offences	Sexual offences
Over 5 years and less than life	*Life*
Sexual offences	Sexual offences
Drug offences	Violence against the person
Violence against the person	Robbery

(© Crown Copyright. Data provided by the Research, Development and Statistics Directorate of the Home Office.)

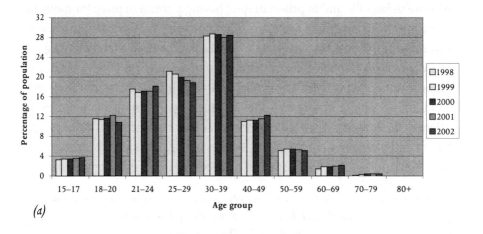

(a)

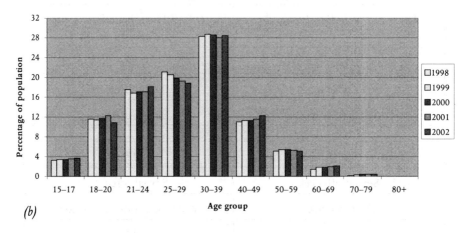

(b)

Figure 1.1(a) Percentage of female prison population by age category. **(b)** Percentage of male prison population by age category (© Crown Copyright. Data provided by the Research, Development and Statistics Directorate of the Home Office).

From the above graphs one can see that the underlying trend for the age demographics for both males and females in the prison estate is to increase almost linearly towards the 'middle-age' ranges, then showing a steep decline into older age. However, the 50 and above population in both males and females is higher than the 15–17 age range.

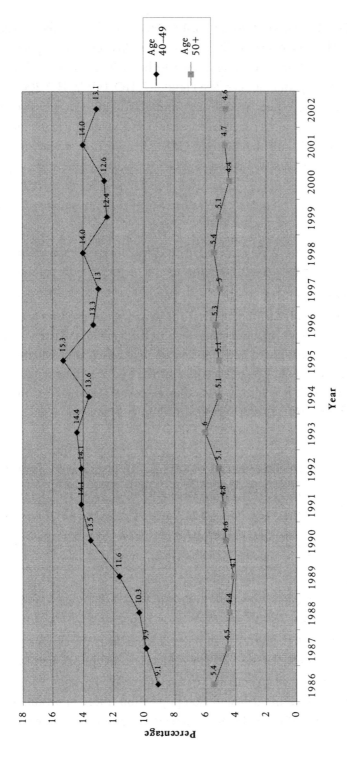

Figure 1.2 *Percentage of total female prisoners population for 'older' age groups* (© *Crown Copyright. Data provided by the Research, Development and Statistics Directorate of the Home Office.*)

Women in later life currently constitute 4.6 percent[3] of the total female prison population. This percentage is likely to increase because our population is ageing (Newman 1988:xvii), more women are being incarcerated and mandatory sentences are getting longer (See Figure I.2; HO 1997c; HO 2001a and b, NACRO 1992b; White, Woodbridge and Flack 1999). If more younger people are receiving longer mandatory sentences this means that some will remain imprisoned until they are old. This phenomenon is known as the 'stacking effect' (Aday 2003). A related fact is that 'lifers' are highly represented amongst the current older prison population. (See Stone 1997 and Table 1.2 and Figure 1.3 below). There are two types of life sentence for adult offenders:

- The mandatory life sentence. This is the only sentence available to the courts for persons over the age of 21 found guilty of murder.

- The discretionary life sentence. This may be imposed for a violent or sexual offence, the sentence for which is not fixed by law (for example, rape, manslaughter, arson). It is generally passed because it is not possible to determine at the time of sentence whether the prisoner would be safe to release at the end of a determinate sentence. It may also be passed to mark the seriousness of the offence (HMP Prison Service 1990: Lifer Manual).

Table 1.2 Mean time served of female lifers released by year

1970	1971	1972	1973	1974	1975	1976	1977	1978	1979	1980	1981	1982
2.75	–	3.75	7.32	3.91	–	5.26	6.00	7.62	8.77	6.53	8.81	8.74

1983	1984	1985	1986	1987	1988	1989	1990	1991	1992	1993	1994	1995
8.62	8.29	9.22	10.50	11.50	10.00	7.95	10.90	10.30	12.00	8.49	13.05	10.90

The population of women prisoners in England and Wales has features which distinguish it from that of men (HO 1991,1994, 1997c; HMIPP 2001; HMCIP 2001a, 2001b, 2002). Between 1993 and 2001 the average population of women in prison rose 140 per cent as against 46 per cent for men, reflecting sentencing changes at the courts (HO 1999: 4 Section 95; see also HO 2001c). In 2002 the female prison population (those in prison, not on remand) stood at 3396;[4] in 1999 the female prison population was 2436,

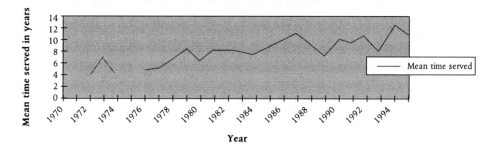

Figure 1.3 Mean time served of female lifers released by year (© Crown Copyright. Data provided by the Research, Development and Statistics Directorate of the Home Office.)

which represents a 39.4 per cent increase, and the long-term trend is for the population to continue to rise (HO 2001c; HMCIP 2001b; White *et al.* 1999).

Figure A11 (p.219) shows that the largest concentration of prisoners aged 50+ is at Holloway (Closed), followed by Send (Closed) and Morton Hall, New Hall (Semi-Open) and Styal (Closed). As numbers are predicted to increase (as a result of bifurcation and the Government's 'Get Tough on Crime Policy'), this will surely pose particular issues in terms of the kind of physical environment, health-care facilities, and resettlement programmes required to comply with the Human Rights Act (Article 8), and to fulfil the statement of purpose which may be seen displayed at the entrance of every prison:

> 'Her Majesty's Prison Service serves the public by keeping in custody those committed by the courts. Our duty is to look after them with humanity and help them lead law-abiding and useful lives in custody and after release'. (Phil Wheatley, Prison Service Director General 2003)

Age breakdown of prison population

Data collated on February 1997 and on April 2003 show that in 1997 from the total female prison population, there were 131 women who were over 50,[5] and only 21 were serving a life sentence. In 2003 there were 176 women over the age of 50, and 29 were serving a life sentence. This shows a slight increase from 16.03 per cent in 1997 to 16.48 per cent in 2003.

Table 1.3 Cross-tabulation of age against sentence length for female and male prisoners aged 50 and above					
Remand/ unsentenced	0<12 months	12 months <5 years	5>less than life	Life	All
	4784	1318	1791	964	8857

(© Crown Copyright. Data provided by the Research, Development and Statistics Directorate of the Home Office.)

Note: *See Table A2 and figure A11 for the number of women over 50 at each establishment.*

Doing prison research – 'Breaking in'

Researching the experiences of female elders in prison lends itself to a qualitative approach. This method allowed the elders to recount a form of history which not only told a personal story but also shed light on the changing social structure of the institution, the changes in their identity related to the ageing process, time passing and the prison environment. Such an approach incorporates time, place and the participant's frame of references (Marshall and Rossman 1989:49). As with participant observation (and its variants), these methods are designed to elicit qualitative data, which reflect and record the participants' diversity, their experiences and their emotions. In addition, this approach opens up the conduit of meanings that elders give to the situation in which they find themselves, rather than the quantitative expression of the relations between 'variables' (Denzin and Lincoln 1998a, b and c; Layder 1993:42).

The aim of this book is to construct a picture of prison life in which the women I interviewed can recognise their own voices, subjectivities and priorities – that is, their own acts of communication with the outside world (Denzin and Lincoln 1994a, 1998c). The construction of such a picture is inevitably and rightly, a dialogic transition, the product of which owes much to, but is also transformative of, the categories and modes of thought or feeling contributed by each party.

> Establishing and maintaining a field presence is not about gaining a season's, or even a lifetime pass to the exotic world of the 'other'. It is about creating and sustaining a world 'between' ourselves and those we study... Ideally, the knowledge that emerges from this encounter is a dialogic rather than monologic: it is knowledge produced in human interaction... (Maher 1997:213)

Locating the field

Sixteen prisons[6] were contacted, ranging from a maximum secure prison to young offender institutions, mother and baby units, remand units and open prisons. I visited both male and female prisons including the Elderly unit at HMP Kingston[7] and the only female prison in Northern Ireland. I was involved in various and lengthy discussions about the needs and experiences of elders in prison. The purpose of these preliminary visits to the institutions was three-fold:

- to discuss the proposed research
- to demonstrate the implications that the research might have for the women and the demands it would make on the institutions' time
- to negotiate future access
- to allow governors and senior officers, the 'gate-keepers' (see Goffman 1961), to contribute to the research idea.

The informality of these interactions and my identity as a non-Home Office researcher was an essential key to gaining access to conduct my research. Negotiating access is ongoing and a precarious process, which can be renego-tiated or revoked at any time when senior officers or governors move to other prisons or retire. Below is an example of a prison denying me access to conduct the research.

> You will no doubt be aware that we receive many requests for student visits and placements, which place a considerable burden upon both prisoner and staff resources.
>
> As a result of this we take the view that only those visits/placements which are 'Home Office Approved', or sponsored, should be proceeded with, and then only if there are clearly defined benefits for the service/prison popula-tion.
>
> I am sorry to say that I cannot agree to the visit sought.

The details of the conversations were therefore not recorded at the time but were noted after the conversations had taken place.

Following a lengthy series of access negotiations, the time in prison was used so that the officers and the women were able to develop a sense of the study's legitimacy, and to establish my credibility as a researcher. As an 'outsider', it was important that members of staff felt that they were more than just a source to be exploited (Opie 1992; Reinharz 1983; Renzetti and Lee 1993). One elder was initially reluctant to speak to me but then was told by an elder in the study that I was an independent researcher and a friend of — ; she then spent a great deal of time talking about her experiences. Prior to being in the field I was also informed by an elder (who was allowed out on day visits at time) about her experiences of research in prison from an insider's perspective. Many of the women she came across assumed she was a Home Office researcher and verbally abused her until she proved her status as an inmate. The critical point is that this lengthy period spent familiarising myself with the environment, listening to elders in prison, probation officers and prison inspectors, reinforced the idea that listening and hearing is a reflexive, on-going learning process (Daniels 1983; Fontana and Frey 1994; Reary 1996). This acknowledgment that listening is a continuous process enables one to work on learning to listen in different ways that are personal, professional, disciplined, and sensitive to differences (Adler and Adler 1993, 1994; Jayaratne and Stewart 1991; Liebling 1992).

The process of becoming familiar with the environment at both an abstract and a practical level provided substantial background knowledge which has prevented misunderstandings and allowed me to be sensitive to difference prior to, during and after the interviews (Mies 1993; Olesen 1994; Patai 1991). Figure I.4 demonstrates the recursive nature of the research process.

Aspects of gaining access – negotiating access

The process of obtaining permission from the 'gate-keepers' is in itself a process of deciphering the 'secret codes' of the prison bureaucracy. For example, it was a matter of deciding whether to gain access *only* through the Home Office, or through individual governors, deputy governors and other governor grades or both. In approaching individual institutions rather than the Home Office, access was contingent on the discretion of the governor. In order to access the appropriate pathway to the governor, one had to become familiar with the 'value' and occupational hierarchy within the prison estate and be aware of implications each pathway may have for the elders and the research. Each level in the establishment hierarchy contains its own currency, requiring a different approach, and has its own advantages and disadvantages in terms of the research process. In this context it was important to proceed as an independent researcher, allowing all ranks within this hierarchy to participate in the evolving research at its various stages of development, in the knowledge that at its best 'prison is not a comfortable place to live, to work, or to carry out research' (Dammer 1994:1).

The process of gaining, negotiating and maintaining access began in October 1996 and has been continually updated and developed to monitor changes in policy on both sides of the Atlantic and in Northern Ireland. Out of the 16 prisons, four were involved in the final study: Penjara (Main Stay Centre and Category A female prison), Avida (an open prison), Gefangis (a closed prison, to where the lifer progresses for the second stage of her lifer career) and Prigonie (an open prison).

The above prisons reflected a representative sample of the female prison estate, representing the various stages of the lifer career and in general the type of security, type of offence, sentence serving and the various stages required to rehabilitate women offenders, depending on offence and tariff.

The research field

The study focuses on 35 in-depth semi-structured interviews conducted at four female establishments. The prisons range from a maximum secure prison to an open prison, reflecting the various types of prison establishments and criminal careers found in the penal system in the UK which includes all of the following:

1. the older first-time offender currently serving a term of imprisonment

2. the older offender who has had previous convictions but not served a prison sentence previously

3. the older offender who has previously served a custodial term after conviction

4. prisoners fulfilling a life sentence and who have grown old in prison

5. Long-term prisoners.

Discussed ideas
with the
following:
Academics
Writers
Probation
Offenders
Ex-offenders
Members of the
Home Office
Activists
Prison Officers
Governors

● Led to contacts
● Visited various prisons in England, Wales and
  Northern Ireland
● Setting up meetings with various organisations
  such as National Association of Probation
  Officers (NAPO); Directorate of the female estate
● Visited the Home Office Library
● Prison Service Library
● Staffordshire Probation Library
● Put me in touch directly with prison governors/
  members of the Home Office

Explained the nature of the
study by letter which was
followed up by a phone call.

Arranged a time to visit with the intention to
discuss the thesis. This took the form of a
meeting with the Governor or Lifer Governor
or Principal Officer. This was then followed
by a tour of the prison.

Followed up the visit with a letter
requesting permission to conduct
fieldwork.

Once a date was arranged, posters went up around
the prison estate with details of who I was and the
nature of the study.

Officers, the Chair of the Board of Visitors at the
various female estates spoke informally to the
women about the study. These introductions were
supplemented by offenders who reinforced the
validity of the study via the prison grapevine. For
example, one women wrote to her friend who was
based at another prison explaining who I was and
the nature of the study.

Figure 1.4 The process of gaining access

The fieldwork for the main study involved visiting the four prisons, which varied from:

1. a maximum secure prison which holds Category A female prisoners[8]

2. a closed prison with a mother and baby unit attached

3. a closed prison which holds young offenders and remand prisoners

4. an open prison, which holds young offenders.

The elders participated on a voluntary basis; their availability and willingness determined the sample.

Gaining, negotiating and maintaining access as a non-Home Office researcher in prison

The experience of gaining, negotiating and maintaining access as a non-Home Office researcher in prison can be described as involving four parts:

1. having the credentials that count

2. finding a role

3. maintaining and negotiating access

4. passing tests.

The success of negotiating, gaining and maintaining access involves diplomacy and serendipity where unexpected avenues open up and anticipated obstacles disappear. This process of listening to the 'gate-keepers' provided the opportunity to observe and become familiar with the regime and the day-to-day realities of prison life.

Obtaining official permission, which was the first stage of the process, was followed by negotiations with individuals directly responsible for the running of the prisons. From this angle, access is on-going and a precarious process, which can be renegotiated or revoked at any time when senior officers or governors move to other prisons or retire.

Entering the field of qualitative research

The nature of the interviews, setting and the process of placing the woman at ease made me more inclined to use a tape recorder. This gave scope for eye contact, and the recordings allowed the older women's voices to be heard so that it would be their words, rather than an interpretation or summary of each interviewee's experiences. Tape recording provided the space 'to concentrate on the interview' in every sense (Moser and Kalton 1971:281). Following the respondent's approval, all interviews were taped and transcribed by me in full, word for word, to encapsulate the woman's style and emotions through syntax while allowing me to immerse myself in her 'voice'. As Bennett and Wright (1984:30) explain, 'As interviews can be tape recorded and transcribed verbatim, respondents' methods of describing and explaining their behaviour can be preserved.'

It is surprising that the research method of transcribing tape-recorded interviews receives so little attention in the literature (for one exception, see Kelly 1988). While transcribing the tapes one becomes aware of the problems involved in transposing the spoken to the written word. Meaning in the spoken word is often conveyed through gesture, tone of voice and emotional expression (Kelly 1988: preface). In terms of immersing yourself in the data, there is no substitute for transcribing the interviews oneself and in full, as the coding, writing and understanding of the research data requires a familiarity and an immersion in the data (Peralyla 1997). Listening to the interviews kept the women and the information 'alive' while working on the transcripts. The tapes reminded me of the cacophony of the prison, the constant jangling of keys, doors slamming and on a one-to-one level, the sound of distress, the non-lexical signs of the pain of imprisonment which are often lost on paper.

Relationships were created through these interactions, which went beyond the research, providing another dimension to the words on the page of the transcript. Each transcript, by virtue of its content, brings to the surface the *pain* and *fear* of the experience of prison.

The process of transcribing allows one to immerse oneself in the data, yet one is still unable to recreate on paper that passing of time. The transcripts were edited only to make sense of what had been said, into a form which could be read. These aspects of data collection played an important part in my understandings of the words finally given and inevitably contributed to the interpretations of the results, despite their absence from the 'analysis'. The transcripts represent a multi-dimensional lived experience, and illustrate how the elders come to constitute their 'self', 'identity', and 'experience' through language and through the here-and-now of the interview relationship.

One has to recognise that the researcher and the participants occupy different political and cultural positions in relation to the economies of time and space. The interviewing situation and the time-frame for the interviews creates a zone in which identities are continually in the process of being negotiated. Thus, these identities are partial and incomplete grounded in a purposeful conversation. This does not mean that researchers may not empathise or share common interests, experiences, objectives, or even prejudices with the participants. Rather, what is relevant when conducting ethnographic research is that the researcher acknowledges and reflects upon how diversity, differences and similarities can be shared and negotiated, and the implications of age, class, argot, gender, race and sexuality for the research process. The participants came from experiences, social backgrounds, historical moments which, in terms of past time, I cannot claim to share. The years spent working in a prison/as a practitioner (i.e. teaching in a prison), learning about the aetiology and ontological foundations of the prison estate, talking to elders served not only to raise my awareness of the issues relating to elders on the outside and in prison, but also to challenge pre-existing assumptions. It is cogently stated that 'prejudice' is an ontological condition of human existence in society and thus 'no researcher comes to her research a *tabula rasa*' (Roseneil 1993:179). A critical and feminist methodological approach, via the application of grounded theory (Corbin and Strauss 1990; Glaser and Strauss 1967; Strauss and Corbin 1990; Denzin and Lincoln 1994b; Strauss 1987), allowed the voices of elders in prison to be heard. The data produced were a response to how each woman saw me as a researcher, how I constructed the questions and responses and how she interacted with me. This approach is congruent with feminist thinking, that women are participants rather than just mere words on a transcript. This method is less prescriptive and opens the window into women's experiences (Strauss 1987).

Many of the quantitative studies on elder males in the USA have emphatically argued that further research in this unexplored territory is required and overall a more humane approach to the management of elders in prison is necessary to alleviate the pains of punishment in a system which is designed for the young, able-bodied person (Duffee 1984; Kerbs 2000; McCarthy 1988;

McCarthy and Langworthy 1988). This call is still relevant in 2003, since there are many gaps within the literature on older offenders, in particular of older women in prison. This book aims to fill at least one of the gaps by documenting the subjective experiences of women in later life who are in prison, and to initiate policy recommendations. Time is of the essence as we continue to fail to address the needs of this growing population. It is only by systematically addressing the needs of elders in prison rather than *reacting* to them, that we can then begin 'to look after them with humanity and help them lead law-abiding and useful lives in custody and after release' (see p.15).

While elders in prison have not reached endemic proportions as in the USA, this group will continue to increase because of changes in sentencing and demographic shifts in the population and with that bring particular issues which can no longer be ignored (HO 1997a, 1997b). Finally, I argue that it is only by integrating gerontological and criminological literature that, in the future, we can prevent yet another crisis from occurring.

Perhaps the title of this book *Older Women in the Criminal Justice System*[9] is misleading. This book is concerned with charting the experiences of older women in prison. The reader must remember that the penal system exists to punish and otherwise deal with people who have been convicted of a criminal offence (usually remand prisoners are in custody while awaiting trial[10]). What exists in England and Wales is a process of justice, typified by a network of closely linked organisations, each with its own role, aim, targets, culture and history. *Older Women in the Criminal Justice System* will look at one part of the penal system, as the older women move from court to prison.

> 'Where shall I begin, please your Majesty?' he asked. 'Begin at the beginning', the King said gravely, 'and go on till you come to the end: then stop'.
> (Lewis Carroll (1971) *Alice's Adventures in Wonderland*)

The chapters follow the elders' experiences of imprisonment from the beginning: from court to their initial reception, their experiences of imprisonment and how they 'make do' in a structure which is designed for the young, able-bodied male.

Homo criminalis: Old age and crime

In the foreseeable future, policymakers will have to make decisions at every point of the criminal justice system: from the time of apprehending older offenders to the time they are released. As Pollak (1941) so astutely observed approximately 60 years ago:

> Old criminals offer an ugly picture and it seems as if even scientists do not like to look at it for any considerable amount of time… On the other hand, if the thesis of the interrelationship between age and crime is to hold, an investigation of all its implications has to yield results, and with the tendency of our population to increase in the higher age brackets, a special study of criminality of the aged seem to meet a scientific as well as a practical need. (1941: 212)

In spite of the unique characteristics and problems, the ageing offender has been largely neglected by researchers. This situation may be attributed to several factors. Pollak (1941) mentioned that 'old criminals offer an ugly picture' resulting in less scientific appeal for researchers.

While there is a growing recognition of the female offender in criminological literature, there has been a significant lack of attention paid to the experiences of ageing women behind bars (Aday 1988, 1994a, 2003; Goetting 1983, 1984). The past decade has seen the publication of a growing body of work on women's prisons and women prisoners in the United Kingdom, and on elder abuse within institutions, but not specifically on female elders in prison (Brogden and Nijhar 2000; Carlen 1983; Penhale 1993). Phillips, Worrall and Brammer account for this omission by arguing that 'although there has now been considerable study of women in prison in the penal literature, older women are not separated out as a distinct category' (Phillips, Worrall and Brammer 2000:267).

The literature on older offenders has concentrated on male elders in prison in America. It has, in the main, identified that prison population is greying and with that service requirements will need to adapt and respond to the life-course needs that are beginning to confront the criminal justice system (Aday 1984, 2003; Gramling and Forsyth 1988; Phillips 1996; Rothman, Dunlop and Entzel 2000). There has been one study by me that specifically examines the experiences of older females in prison and their related service requirements. One problem confronting researchers in the field on both sides of the Atlantic is the definition – where does the elderly offender begin in gerontological criminological literature? Official statistics on the age breakdown of offences, and prison statistics (see HO 1997a, 1997b, 1999) describe 'older' offenders as anywhere between 21 and 59 or simply give figures for offenders aged 21 and above. A review of the literature suggests that previous researchers have defined elderly prisoners as those 65 years of age and older (Gramling and Forsyth 1988; Newman 1984), some 60 (Kratcoski 1990), some 55 (Goetting 1992; Roth 1992), and many 50 (Aday 2003; Flynn 1992). The majority of studies, however, have used the age 50 or 55 as the chronological age to define when one becomes an older offender. The literature on offenders does not provide definitive guidelines concerning the age at which an offender becomes an elder; however, the ages of 50, 55, 60 and 65 are often used in discussing arrest and incarceration figures (Goldsmith and Goldsmith 1975; Newman, Newman and Gewitz 1984). It is less easy to define or determine at what point in terms of chronological age one becomes 'older'. It appears in terms of prison-defined age, that one might say an older female offender is fifty and over.

Aday (1999) conducted a national survey of state correctional departments, and found that 50 years of age was the most common criterion for old age that correctional officials utilise. This study reported that correctional officials commonly agree that the typical offender in their 50s had the physical appearance and accompanying health problems of someone at least ten years older. Morton (1992) further stipulates that 50 is the ideal starting point to initiate preventative health care and the taking of other appropriate measures to reduce long-term medical costs for older offenders. Furthermore, the Corrections Yearbook for the United States includes in its annual profiles of older prisoners those who are 50 or older (Adams 1995:2).

However, the problem of defining age in terms of chronology is that it fails to take into account that the concept of ageing is relative to the role or activity under discussion. For example, professional athletes are old when they turn 30. Would a person committing a first offence at 40 be middle-aged or old, relative to that behaviour? For the purpose of this book the term 'elder' will be used to denote a person aged 50 or over. The age of 50 and above resonates with some of the Home Office cohort groupings which have also been influenced by gerontological literature and groupings used by Age Concern. Although there is no definitive, nationwide standard for what constitutes an 'elderly inmate', most researchers identify 50 as the threshold age. Prisoners are typically functionally older than their chronological age, a result of their lifestyle, lack of medical care, and environmental factors (http://www.fcc. state.fl.us.fcc.reports/final99/leld.html).

Legislation enacted in Florida in 2000 designated the age of 50 as the threshold for defining the term 'elderly inmate'. Research conducted in America has indicated that several states, such as Georgia, Texas, Tennessee and Florida, operate programmes specifically aimed at the elderly male offender, which defines elderly offenders as 50 and over (Aday 2003; Steffensmeier 1987; Steffensmeier and Moti 2000). In the UK we have no specific facilities for ageing female offenders although we have Unit for Men over 65 years of age at HMP Kingston (HMCIP 2001b) and another being built at HMP Norwich in 2003. It is also important to highlight the impact of using one cut-off point or another on policies for controlling crime or processing offenders, and it is only by further research into the needs and experiences of elderly offenders that one will find a suitable age cut-off point based on a subjective understanding of what it is to be an elder in prison (Johnson 1989; Johnson and Alozie 2001).

Because of the effect of ageing, the elderly inmate has very different needs, and places far more demands on the system, than the younger inmate. This is especially true of health-care needs. Prisoners over the age of 55 suffer, on average, three chronic health problems, such as hypertension, diabetes, alcoholism and emphysema (Acoca 1998; Adams and Vedder 1961). Although this debate is necessary, Flynn (1992) argues that the major issue for researchers is not so much a matter of identifying and verifying the exact chronological cut-off points as is the growing need to achieve consensus in this growing field for the purpose of comparative research and for planning purposes.

I will begin to address the absence in the British and American literature of older female offenders, and their experiences of the prison system. I will argue that the very nature of the prison-female estate demands research centralising the experiences of female elders. Through attending to and validating the voices of elders one can illustrate the techniques which subjectify the gendered self; this has implications not only for policymakers and practitioners within prisons but for theory, research and practice relating to elders in prison. By approaching this topic from a gerontological, sociological and criminological perspective, the book will show how the 'absences' of female elders from discourses of penal policy results in their material absence from the centre stage of prison life, sentencing them to live their lives in the shadows. The lack of facilities and awareness of the needs of female elders leads to a material 'absence' within the prison realm.

The problems that women in later life experience in the prison system largely result from the fact that prison is geared to the able-bodied young male. *Older Women in the Criminal Justice System: Running Out of Time* will bring to light the needs of elders and how, by failing to acknowledge this 'forgotten minority' (Ham 1976), we are compounding the pains of imprisonment far beyond the recognised intentions of sentencing. Women's prisons have not previously been designed with the disabled or elderly person in mind. It is imperative to understand how elders, once in prison, enter a zone of marginality where their needs become subsumed under the operational needs of the prison.

A historical view of older offenders

The literature available on elder offenders is restricted to predominantly US–based research (Newman 1984). The literature suggests that it was in the USA in the 1980s that there was a renewed interest in aging offenders (Ham 1976; Ruberstein 1984), locating the elderly offender in a medical and welfarist model (Aday 1994a; Aday and Webster 1979; Schichor 1984). However Pollock (cited in Gewerth 1988) argues that

> the problem of crime amongst the aged may be newly recognised, but it is certainly not new. Research interest in criminal behaviour among the elderly dates back to the early part of the century – the phenomenon was first discussed at a criminology conference in Budapest in 1899. (Pollack 1941:213 cited in Gewerth 1988).

The literature on offenders in later life ignores the experiences of elder female prisoners and makes no mention of the various stages and types of prisons through which the lifer progresses (HO 1993): in other words, the effects of institutional differences on those who grow old behind bars. The work of Aday (1994a, 1994b, 2003) has been ground-breaking in writing of the elderly male offender in the United States and, in particular, he identifies a void in the literature regarding the ageing prison population. To date, however, there has been no mention of females in later life who are in prison. In addition his research concentrates on the first-time, older offender rather than on a range of older prisoners such as those found in this book. A critique of Aday's work is that gender is omitted from his analysis. Furthermore, he posits the older offender in a medical discourse, thus pathologising the criminal act. He argues that the criminal act is the effect of a dysfunction in the brain (See Bennett, Parrot and Macdonald 1996; Prins 1980). His 1994 study is an exploratory piece based on 25 semi-structured interviews centred at one penal establishment, and throughout his work he suggests that 'there is some degree of cognitive dysfunction present among this group of first-time, elderly offenders' (Aday 1994a: 79). In 1989 Sally Swift, a prison chaplain in the UK, described her experiences of working in a prison and discussed the changing face of prisoners, recognising the emergence of an ageing prison population. Many of the above have suggested that, with the growing number of elders entering the criminal justice system, the Royal Commission on Criminal Justice should examine the vulnerability of older people, paying attention to all aspects of the process from arrest to imprisonment and release. To date, however, there has been no such far-reaching discussion or research on the above. Moreover, there are few available accounts of older people's own experiences of crime and the criminal justice system, which follows older offenders through imprisonment through to their life beyond the gates.

It is worth noting that the process of institutional infantilising of old people and the denial of their rights as adults is congruent both with the way women offenders are processed into the system of imprisonment and with the way elders experience residential homes (Booth 1985; Garland 1993; Willcocks 1986; Wilson 2000). One must be aware that, if these cohorts bypass imprisonment, it has much to do with paternalistic attitudes towards the elderly founded on ageist assumptions and patriarchal control. The discourse employed to divert elders from imprisonment depends on the nature of the offence, its seriousness and the degree of risk (Kercher 1987). It is obvious from the paucity of information in the UK that research on elders behind bars is still very much in its formative stage.

In her article, 'With Intent To Steal', Manthorpe (1983) was arguably the first British academic to acknowledge and distinguish between the different types of older offenders: the 'Thieves who grow old'; 'Those who honestly forget to pay'; 'The compulsive shop lifter'; and elders who suffer from a mental illness and find themselves in prison through circumstance. However, although these categories begin to differentiate the elder caught in the criminal justice system, they fail to distinguish between types of sentencing. In contrast, categories employed here differentiate the older offender into five types (see page 19) while acknowledging the different experiences that elder female offenders have in relation to the types of prisons in the female estate.

Types of offender

A salient feature of Manthorpe's work on elder offenders is that she identifies and describes the strain, fear and anxiety that they feel as they are being processed through the criminal justice system. Her article acknowledges the subjectivity of the offender. In contrast, Knight (1986) locates the aetiology of offence in the pathology of the individual, presenting the offender as the object of medical/criminological discourse. The article, entitled 'Geriatric Homicide' (further referred to in the article as 'The Darby and Joan Syndrome'), intimates an element of irony in the notion of an offender being in later life. What is particularly evident is how the author, via his own experience of working in the field, attempts to prescribe models and typologies of crimes by older people posited in a medical/biological discourse which is not in fact applicable, given that peak ages in his study are based not on the age of the offender at reception but on the age at the time of the interview. Knight argues that the absence of research on the older offender is indicative of society's view of older people as victims rather than perpetrators of heinous crimes. The main flaw in this article is the construction of classifications, which treat age as a significant variable, sensationalising this 'type' of murder by suggesting that it is characterised by particular savagery; whereas the literature concerning spousal murder in fact suggests that its characteristics are similar regardless of age group. He writes that as a 'forensic pathologist' he is used to all types and degrees of personal injury, but in some of these tragedies in the elderly, the 'savagery of the attack is surprising even to me'. 'It seems almost as if many years of frustrated and suppressed anger erupt into one final orgy of hatred, so gross are some of these attacks' (1986:298). But one can argue that his surprise is more a reflection of his own ageism.

Nevertheless, there is some indirect evidence that psychiatric or cognitive disturbance may play a statistically greater role in criminal behaviour within older than younger age groups. Taylor and Parrott's (1988) work examines the rate of schizophrenia among elderly male prisoners on remand at Brixton prison from June 1979 to May 1980. The data were collected from 1241 men, which amounted to 45 per cent of the total prison intake of 2743. Just over 2 per cent (63 men) were aged 55 or over, about one-third of them being over 65. They argued that the older men were more likely to show signs of psychiatric or physical illness than their younger peers. About half of those aged 55 and over showed active symptoms of psychiatric disorder and about half had physical disorders on entering the prison, which was approximately twice the rate among the younger men in both cases. Of course, it is important to be clear about the logic of these findings, which in no way demonstrate that offending as a result of mental disorder is more common amongst the elderly; rather, they probably reflect the diminished overall rate of offending in the older age groups, and in particular the diminished rate of offences motivated by cultural or economic factors associated with younger groups. Thus, while the care of cognitively or emotionally disabled offenders is clearly an issue in all age groups, there is no logical foundation for the construction of 'geriatric crime' as such. Their study tentatively draws a connection between growing old with crime and the socio-economic and past histories of men who at the time of the study were on remand.

As stated earlier, the prevalent view from the literature is that older people are victims rather than perpetrators of criminal activity. Contrary to this view, women offenders over 45 from all ethnic origins (see Appendix D) are involved in a broad spectrum of offences, excluding sexual ones. I would argue that the differential rate of offending between men and women is indeed a powerful cultural phenomenon, but that does not justify pathologising those who behave non-stereotypically for their age and sex. The differences stand as a testimony to the power of gender as a socio-cultural and psychological organiser. On the evidence of the literature, one cannot locate elders who commit crime in the medical model. Moreover, what the literature emphatically argues is that further research in this unexplored territory is required and that a more humane approach to the management of elders in prison is necessary to alleviate the pains of punishment in a system which is designed for the young able-bodied person (Duffee 1984; Kerbs 2000; McCarthy 1988; Fazel *et al.* 2001).

Women, old age and the criminal justice system – invisible women

The portrayal of old people as victims wins votes and sells newspapers; neither criminal activity nor the inhumane denial of the special needs of the elderly in prison are easily squared with this attitude of paternalistic concern. Elders behind bars are excluded from the media gaze, subsumed in the general accounts of female offenders (HMCIP 1997, 2001a). For comparable reasons, women are excluded from the little research there is on elderly offenders. Nevertheless, Aday (2003) argues that the number of persons over the age of 50 arrested for serious or violent crimes has been increasing in the USA. Stricter sentencing laws both in the States (ibid.) and in the UK will dramatically increase the elder prison population. Even before these changes in law, the sentencing procedures and the growing punitive obsession in both countries has led the American Department of Justice (1989) to project that 16 per cent of federal prisoners would be over 50 by 2005 (cited in James 1992). In the UK, although there is no research on elders over 50 in prison, there is a growing recognition in the Home Office, as demonstrated in their 1999 report entitled *Statistics on Women and the Criminal Justice System*, that the demographic age pyramid will change as a result of the increase in the numbers of elder offenders being processed by the criminal justice system.

From rocking chair to law breaking

Existing studies on older offenders including those on older female offenders, have not examined the subjective understandings of older offenders in prison. Moreover, it has been agued that 'there is still comparatively little empirical research, certainly in a British context, which attempts to make visible the lives of mid-life and older women' (Bernard and Phillips 2000:2) and this therefore is another specific gap that this book attempts to fill.

Many of the gerontological texts provide a historical understanding of the development of the gerontological field from the first demographic studies conducted in the mid-1940s to the most recent genre, that until now has omitted gender issues (Arber and Ginn 1995a; Bernard and Meade 1993; Ginn and Arber 1995). Throughout the gerontological literature of the last decade it is emphasised that the voices and needs of older persons have to be integrated into policy, and that such policy must not be steeped in the stereotypes of ageing but must acknowledge and assess diversity and difference.

Bengston, Burgess and Parrott (1997) argue that the study of ageing has lacked a strong theoretical core and until recently has tended to ignore an understanding of ageing identity, the body, cultural representations of ageing (to name a few), which are central features of an emerging post-modern paradigm in gerontological theory. However, as demonstrated above, the role of theory in gerontology and its growth as a discipline coincides with the post-war years; a growth in public awareness and interest in ageing issues – from 'Grey Power movements' to the ageing population, the crisis over pensions and the funding of the welfare state (Aiken 1995; Phillipson 1998). Nevertheless, the lack of theoretical integration in British gerontology has been a cause of some anxiety over the past 20 years (Biggs 1999). Fennell, Phillipson and Evers comment: 'Much more characteristic of British research is the lack of attention to theory of any kind. This failing has been a feature of the social gerontological tradition' (1993:42). The pressures on older people in the workplace combined with the rapid growth in early retirement have resulted in a significant shift in the way ageing is experienced and perceived (Achenbaum 1978; Bornat, Phillipson and Ward 1985; Fahey and Holstein 1993; Phillipson 1993).

Gubrium and Wallace (1990) seek to promote the development of gerontological theory by posing the question 'who theorises age?' Their focus suggests that it is not only professional social gerontologists who theorise age; we all are involved in constructing the 'other' in relation to ourselves. Critical gerontology, according to Baars (1991), is concerned with 'a collection of questions, problems and analyses that have been excluded by established [mainstream gerontology]'(cited in Fennell et al. 1993:13). These vary from questions about the role of the state in the management of old age (Phillipson 1982, 1998; Phillipson and Walker 1986; Townsend 1962, 1981) to issues about the purpose of growing old within the context of a post-modern life course (Cole et al. 1993; Coleman, Bond and Peace 1993; Featherstone 1995). Critical gerontology seeks to problematise the construction of ageing and to identify the conditions experienced by elders in society (Gregorio 1987; Bond, Briggs and Coleman 1993).

The two functionalist theories which dominated US gerontology in the 1950s and the 1960s, were known as 'disengagement theory' and 'activity theory'. Both theories reflect the culturally dominated views of what should be the appropriate way to analyse social phenomena (Turner and Champion 1989). Disengagement theory has been challenged for perpetuating discriminatory policies and attitudes towards older people (e.g. Estes 1979, 1993; Phillipson 1993; Phillipson and Walker 1986). It will become apparent within the following chapters that an enforced withdrawal by, or exclusion of, older prisoners can be erroneously interpreted by staff as reflecting an internal predisposition of the elder to 'disengage' and thus not cope with the prison regime. Cumming and Henry (1961), the main protagonists of disengagement theory, argued that the gradual withdrawal of older people from work roles and social relationships was both an 'inevitable' and 'natural process' (see Neugarten 1996):

> ...withdrawal may be accompanied from the outset by an increased preoccupation with himself: certain institutions may make it easy for him. (Cumming and Henry 1961: 14)

One can even argue that this discourse legitimises custodial forms of treatment in institutional care (Reed and Glamser 1979). In a similar vein, the proponents of acquiescent functionalism/liberal pluralism argue that the process of disengaging is a natural consequence of bodily decline, instead of analysing contemporary developments of the state, the economy and the social inequality, which permeate a capitalist society with the aim of excluding others. This school of thought legitimates the exclusion of elderly people from the labour market and from significant alternative social roles and fails to acknowledge the role of women as they enter later life and significant identity roles change. The condition of dependency of the elderly is not an inevitable outcome of the ageing process, but is both socially structured, and socially conditioned and thus is open to change (Dex and Phillipson 1986; Phillipson 1997).

Activity theory pre-dates disengagement theory. It suggests that successful ageing can only be achieved if social networks and occupational identity are maintained. In the 1950s Havighurst and Albrecht (1953 cited in Katz 1996), maintained that ageing and later life could be a lively and creative part of the life course. Nevertheless, both theories fail to address the issue of power, inequality and how the experiences of later life are gendered. Bond, Coleman and Peace (1993) argue that activity theory condones indifference towards old age and social problems. Second, disengagement theory underplays the role cultural and economic structures have in creating the withdrawal of elders from the workforce. If anything, both theories are couched in essentialising and ageist discourses that serve to posit the ageing body in a framework of medical and welfarist discourse (Bengsten and Schaie 1999).

The Political Economy approach to an understanding of old age draws on a Marxist tradition. It grew from a critical response to disengagement theory and argued that old age was socially constructed to support the needs of the capitalist economy (Estes 1979; Phillipson 1982). The main proponents of this theory were Estes, Swan and Gerand (1982) and in the UK, Townsend (1981).

As Phillipson argues (1998:17):

> Older people came to be viewed as a burden on western economies, with demographic change...seen as creating intolerable pressures on public expenditure.

Ageism not only relates to discrimination against older people, as Butler would have had us believe when he introduced the word 'ageism' in 1968.

> Ageism can be seen as a process of systematic stereotyping of and discrimination against people because they are old, just as racism and sexism accomplish this with skin colour and gender. Old people are categorised as senile, rigid in thought and manner, old-fashioned in morality and skills... Ageism allows the younger generation to see old people as different from themselves; thus they subtly cease to identify with their elders as human beings. (Butler 1975: 12 cited in Andrews 1991:2)

As Bytheway (1994) argues, ageism is not simply discrimination by dominant groups in society against one particular minority group; it is much more complex than that. Attempts have been made to construct a practical and comprehensive definition of 'ageism', which is much broader than the traditional 'narrow' definition, which focuses on old age, and which also embraces observations on the omnipresent nature of 'age' in our society (Johnson and Bytheway 1993). A useful working definition is that composed by Bytheway and Johnson (1990):

> Ageism is a set of beliefs originating in the biological variation between people and the ageing process. It is in the actions of corporate bodies, what is said and done by their representatives, and the resulting view that are held by ordinary ageing people, that ageism is made manifest.

In consequence it follows that:

> Ageism generates and reinforces a fear and denigration of the ageing process, and stereotyping presumptions, regarding competence and the need for protection. Ageism 'legitimates' the use of chronological age to mark out systematically denied resources and opportunities that others enjoy, and who suffer the consequences of such denigration, ranging from well meaning patronage to unambiguous vilification.

Thus, non-elders and elders need to abandon ageist language, behaviour and vocabulary and to recognise age realistically for what it is. Removing chronological age markers as a dominant indicator, then, perhaps means we are moving towards a more inclusive way of assessing individuals on the basis of need. Maggie Kuhn, founder and national convenor of the Grey Panthers in the USA, argues that the effect of stereotypes of ageing 'infects us all'.

> Ageism permeates our Western culture and institutions. It infects us, the ageing and aged, when we reject ourselves and despise our powerlessness, wrinkled skin, and physical limitations. It's revealed when we succumb to apathy and complacent acceptance of the things that society does to diminish us... Our image of ourselves reflects the image society has of us. Our self image is affected by a society that considers old people superfluous because they are not productive and useful. (Kuhn in Phillipson and Walker 1986)

It is this process of marginalisation, legitimised by ageist discourse, which leads to the exclusion of elders' needs. Macdonald and Rich poignantly write,

> Slowly, I begin to see that the fear of the stigma of age, and total ignorance of its reality in the lives of women, flow deep in myself, in other women I know, in the women's movement. That our society breeds ignorance and fear of both aging and death. That the old woman carries the burden of that stigma, and with remarkable, unrecorded courage. I begin to see that I myself am aging, was always aging, and that only powerful forces could have kept me from self interest alone – from working to change the social and economic realities of older women. That ageism is part of the air both Barbara and I have breathed since we were born, and that it is unthinkable that women should continue to be indifferent to the meaning of the whole of our lives, until we are old ourselves. (1984: 11–12)

This powerful statement sustains the distinctiveness of old women – their lives although remarkable go unrecognised and their stories unrecorded. It could be argued that the use of 'old' and 'older' emphasises not just difference but also a distinction between them and us. Be that as it may, it also asserts loudly that ageing is a shared experience, that we are all subject to the fear and ignorance of ageism, and that the power of ageism should be challenged in ways that promote a holistic and undivided view of the 'whole of our lives'.

In this whole process the state plays a large part, by determining choices, opportunities and the quality of life available to the elderly. This positing of elders in a dependency role creates what Estes (1979, 1993) argues is the 'Ageing Enterprise' of institutions and rules within which the general problems of the elderly are constructed, or indeed, are 'manufactured'.

One of the main flaws of gerontology is its gender blindness, although there is a growing body of literature that addresses female elders in society

(Arber and Ginn 1995a, 1995b; Bernard and Meade 1993). The important and distinctive contribution made by Arber and Ginn's edited collection is that it draws our attention, not only to a group which have been 'problematised' and pushed to the fringes of society, but to the prevalent discriminatory practices and ageist ideology. Furthermore, its most important message is that the level of care, quality of life and the idea of 'citizenship' in a stake-holding society are just as relevant to older people as for any section of society. The above authors challenge the 'old way of thinking', arguing that gender cannot be treated as a homogenous category, static over the life course. Arber and Ginn (1995b) emphasise that gender is a social construction in a state of fluidity which is culturally and historically specific. They demonstrate that class, socio-economic circumstances, ethnicity and sexuality are interwoven with women and men's roles and relationships (Friedan 1983, 1992). Furthermore, the authors sensitively draw out the feelings surrounding disengagement from the public to the private, new roles and new identities that are invented to deal with demands made upon elderly people by the lack of support afforded them (Victor 1987; Ford and Sinclair 1987). Key issues raised from the deconstruction of stereotypical images of masculinity and femininity include a challenge to the dichotomy created by the division of labour and the ramifications of this (Arber and Evandrou 1993; Twigg 2000).

In the late 1980s there was a growing interest in post-modernism and critical/social and cultural gerontology (Bytheway *et al.* 1983). It can be argued that the roots of 'post-modern gerontology' derive from Gubrium and Holstein's (1995) work on the 'mask' phenomena. He argues that the 'mask' operates as a way of depicting an aspect of the ageing self whilst simultaneously constructing/protecting the real self. This idea is encapsulated by J.B. Priestley when asked at the age of 79 to describe what it felt like to be old:

> It is as though, walking down Shaftsbury Avenue as a fairly young man, I was suddenly kidnapped, rushed into a theatre and made to don the grey hair, the wrinkles and the other attributes of age, then wheeled on stage. Behind the appearances of age I am the same person, with the same thoughts, as when I was younger. (Puner 1978:7)

It has been argued that in a post-modern culture the reinvention of the ageing body revived through consumer images of perpetual youth in turn leads to the blurring of traditional life-course boundaries (Achenbaum 1995; Featherstone 1991; Featherstone and Hepworth 1983, 1989, 1993;

Featherstone and Wernick 1995) challenging stereotypes of what it is to be old. This blurring of the life course problematises negative 'ageist' stereotypes and practices and in turn produces more accurate and positive images that imply that later life is a time of vitality, creativity, empowerment and resourcefulness all attainable in old age (Featherstone and Hepworth 1983, 1993). However, although some older people have the wealth and resources to lead a varied lifestyle, this is in stark contrast to the majority of impoverished elders in society (Victor and Evandrou 1983; Victor 1991). It can be argued that raised expectations, pressures to be youthful and fear-arousing images of poverty, sickness and victimhood make old age less acceptable, and lead people to re-affirm the boundary between themselves and the 'real' old 'other'. In my study, Molly Mossdale states, 'I don't feel old', and Rebecca Rose, one of the oldest women in the study, states, 'I'm young for my age' (Andrews 1999; Bytheway 1983a; Rosenthal 1990; Thompson 1992). In order to understand how the elderly offenders constitute themselves I will discuss the role of the 'absent body' (Öberg 1996) in gerontological literature and how the body and identity or the reinvention of identity are determined by the relationship between psychological factors, socio-economic realities, and societal norms (Bernard, Chambers and Granville 2000; Falk 1994, 1995). It is in the transition from concepts such as 'master status' (Goffman 1961, 1963a), 'the mask of ageing' (Featherstone and Hepworth 1989), 'the masquerade' (Tseëlon 1995; Woodward 1988) to a more complex understanding of the interplay between the social, economic and psychological variables in the process of ageing, that the concept of the 'persona' (Biggs, S. 1993, 1997, 1999) has developed. Each model illustrates that self-presentation of an ageing identity is subject to flux and multiple possibility. Biggs argues that 'there are very few direct empirical references to the mask phenomenon in social gerontology'(1997:553).

A new domain in ageing studies

> The theories of Foucault are not intended as permanent structures, enduring in virtue of their universal truth. They are temporary scaffoldings, erected for a specific purpose, which Foucault is happy to abandon. (Gutting 1989:16)

The integration of Foucauldian thought in the study of ageing is still very much in its formative stages (see Biggs and Powell 2001; Katz 1996; Wahidin and Powell 2001). These writers have been influenced by Foucault's interest in the way in which individuals are constructed as subjects and objects of a myriad of gazes. For example, professionals such as geriatricians and social workers are pivotal interventionists in their ability to classify, pathologise and reproduce types of knowledge and power and create surveillance in relation to the ageing person (Foucault 1980; Rabinow 1986). Moreover, Foucauldian theory allows one to move away from the strictures of Cartesian dualisms and analyse the coterminous flux of power, knowledge and the body. I will discuss the role of Foucauldian theory in greater depth in the following chapter.

As Gilleard and Higgs (2000) argue, post-modernism provides a cultural analysis of ageing and its relationship to the performativity of the body, identity and power. This school of thought deconstructs 'truth claims' behind ontological and epistemological generalisations based on the trimvirate of race, class and gender without slipping into traditional gerontological concerns that lends itself to purely structural dependency theories.

As the reader, you may be asking: why integrate the discipline of geron-tology and criminology? Gerontologists, as outlined above, have primarily dealt with health-care problems, retirement, housing, and the psychological effects of growing old in a capitalist and patriarchal society. Criminologists have been trying to answer the perplexing question, 'what are the causes of crime?' For many years both gerontologists and criminologists have concen-trated their attention exclusively in their respective fields (Malinchak 1980). This book has developed out of a desire to re-introduce this area of research from an interdisciplinary perspective as the ageing population begins to reach a crisis point. Both disciplines bring a richness to understanding the experi-ences of older men and women who find themselves lost in the criminal justice system. It is only by having an integrated approach that we can begin to fully understand the complexity of ageing in the criminal justice system and in turn to put their needs firmly on the penal policy agenda.

Conclusion

The book will attempt to counter the invisibility of elder female offenders in prison by analysing their subjective experiences of imprisonment. The voices of the women will demonstrate how discourses of the 'essential woman' maintain current typifications of femininity in prison. This will assist our understanding of how and why penal policy is adapted for women on the basis of essentialising discourse. In addition, I will examine the complex social processes that lie behind the categorisation of female confinement and how gender assumptions and stereotypes play a pivotal role in the experiences of elders in prison. In the literature on older offenders there has yet to be an analysis of the effects that secure settings/institutions have on the identity of elders. My research attempts to explore the whys and wherefores of growing old within a total institution and how the total institution excludes the needs of women who are in later life.

By engaging with Foucauldian theory one can illustrate how the capillaries of power, techniques of discipline, pervade all areas of life. The following chapter provides a rationale for the application and engagement of Foucauldian theory in unravelling the experiences of female elders in prison.

The book is divided into eight chapters. The chapters are intended to be read sequentially, although each chapter is relatively self-contained to allow readers and practitioners to dip into sections of the book.

Chapter 1 Women and the Criminal Justice System: Discipline and Punish

This chapter introduces the reader to the work of Michael Foucault (1926–1984) and examines how modern forms of knowledge and power produce distinctive forms of subjectivity. In the study of crime and punishment Foucauldian theory provides a new lens in exploring the development of punishment. This chapter will examine how punishment in prison becomes gendered.

Chapter 2 From Court to Prison: Women on the Edge of Time

This chapter provides a detailed account of prison life, from the initial reaction to imprisonment to existing on a day-to-day basis. Elders who are imprisoned find themselves on the edge of prison time but they are also placed on the edge of time in prison owing to the lack of appropriate facilities.

Chapter 3 Prison Life: Now You See Me Now You Don't

Chapter 3 discusses the way prison penalises women by denying them the roles and responsibilities which they have been used to occupying. Aspects of their identity (i.e. femininity and as an older woman in prison) are appropriated by techniques of discipline, which work upon the body to sever life threads to the outside world and assist the effacement of the self.

Chapter 4 Running Out of Time

This chapter examines the concept of time and time usage in prison. It is only by inserting the words of the women in prison into debates on time and agency that we come to understand the complexity and contradictions of temporal frames in prison. Prison time will be shown to be simultaneously experienced as further punishment while also being resisted.

Chapter 5 Health Care and the Cost of Imprisonment

Chapter 5 demonstrates how elders are further punished by the lack of adequate medical facilities and practices such as discontinuity of medication and batch treatment. Elders merely exist in prison, because of the lack of appropriate educational, recreational and medical provision made available to them.

Chapter 6 Within These Walls: Older Women in Custody

This chapter closes in on prison life by looking at how elders in prison are effaced by a system that is structured on the needs of the able-bodied male. In this chapter I will examine how the pains of imprisonment are multiplied by the lack of appropriate facilities adding to the general invisibility of elders in prison.

Chapter 7 Forget Me Not: Older Women in the Criminal Justice System

This chapter examines their fears as time passes on the outside and how aspects of their gender are denied to them in prison, e.g. role of motherhood and, in some cases, forced childlessness. This chapter will contextualise various forms of punishment and the discursive practices in prison. These techniques of control are contradictory in their aims, and in terms of outcomes have perverse, long-lasting effects on the elders' sense of self. It is by high-lighting the multi-dimensional nature of punishment that one can see how these techniques of control usurp the elder's identity by severing life threads to the outside world.

Chapter 8 Concluding Comments: Responses to Ageing – Women in the Criminal Justice System

The final chapter provides an evaluation of the case studies, the research findings and their implications. The book argues that because of the lack of facilities in prison, elders in prison find themselves running out of time. Elders in prison are not constituting an 'operational problem' in prison and in the criminal justice system. The practical difficulties of providing resources for elders in the prison system will be analysed, positive aspects outlined and alternatives suggested.

This book shows how, beyond the usual rigours of prison, older women are further punished by the system on the basis of their age. I will demonstrate that the homo-relational world of the prison is only an illusion. Contrary to the image of the passive older woman, the women in this book show that within prison they have carved out new spaces in their bid to survive institutional life.

Notes

1   In 1965 Myra Hindley was convicted with Ian Brady for what is now known as the 'Moors Murders'. It was the first time in British history that a woman had been involved in a killing partnership that had involved the serial sex murders of children.

2   © Crown Copyright. Data provided by the Research, Development and Statistics Directorate of the Home Office, 2003.

3   © Crown copyright. Data provided by the Research, Development and Statistics Directorate of the Home Office, 2003.

4   *Statistics On Women And The Criminal Justice System* – A Home Office Publication Under Section 95 of The Criminal Justice Act 1991. In 1998 the female prison population stood at 3110, nearly 70 per cent higher than it was in 1992.

5   © Crown copyright. Data provided by the Research, Development and Statistics Directorate of the Home Office, 2003.

6   At the time of writing there were 16 female prison establishments.

7   See HMP Kingston – Portsmouth, *An Introduction for Lifers to the Older Prisoner's Unit*, HMP Kingston (in-house document); and for further information see: HMCIP (2001b), *Report on a Full Announced Inspection of HMP Kingston* and HMIP England and Wales (2002c), *Report on an Unannounced Follow-up of Inspection of HM Prison Kingston*.

8   Male prisoners are placed in one of four security categories: A, B, C or D, and are allocated to prisons according to the nature of their offence. Women are categorised simply for open or closed conditions. The only exception is that a woman prisoner can be designated as category A (see Leech, M. 2003). The current categories were defined in the Mountbatten Report (Home Office 1966).

9   The term 'Criminal Justice System' is used extensively by the Home Office in its publications and at that department's website (www.homeoffice.gov.org).

10   The remand population is made up of those defendants awaiting trial and those who have been convicted but are awaiting sentence.

Chapter 1

Women and the Criminal Justice System: Discipline and Punish

This chapter will illustrate the relevance of Foucauldian theory in understanding the development of punishment, the use of power, and how capillaries[1] of punishment in prison are directed in a specific way at the female body. It is by understanding the techniques of discipline used in prison that we can demonstrate the gendered application of punishment. Furthermore, this section will illustrate how conventional typifications of femininity shape the history and current practices in women's penal establishments, but not as if it were a one-way process. Punishment applied to women's prisons is grounded not on what women are like but on how women 'ought' to behave (Howe 1994). The discussion will illustrate how prison becomes a place which is both *as* and *for* punishment.

It has been suggested that 'writ[ing] about punishment and classification without Foucault is like talking about the unconscious without Freud' (Cohen 1985:10). Garland considers that Foucault's work constitutes a 'central reference point in the sociology of punishment' (1990:131). Overall, Foucault's contribution to the production of social theory is 'one of the most important events of our century' (Veyne 1984 cited in Merquior 1985:33). However, Foucault is yet to have the same 'effect' on gerontology. The aim of this book is to integrate Foucauldian theory into the discipline of gerontology. This will be achieved by listening to the narratives of the elders and by examining how the elders make sense of their experiences of imprisonment and their ageing bodies. In addition, the use of his 'box of tools' (Katz 1996) will illustrate how and why elders live life in the shadows renegotiating the power of the total institution. A Foucauldian lens will make visible the multi-dimensional relationship and technologies of power used in a total institution by the women and by the structure itself (Hoy 1986). Secondly, Foucault allows for an exploration of the effects of architectural structures and hence spatial formations upon the subject (see also Markus 1993). Goffman averred:

> Many total institutions, most of the time, seem to function merely as storage dumps for prisoners...but they usually present themselves to the public as rational organisations designed consciously, through and through, as effective machines for producing a few officially avowed and officially approved ends. (Goffman 1961: 73)

The main difference between these two key theorists is that, for Goffman, total institutions were untypical for society as a whole, whereas for Foucault the carceral element of institutional life encapsulates a core feature of social life.

The work of Foucault is crucial in understanding the nature of power in prisons and how these capillaries affect the identities of elders in prison. The term 'capillaries' will be used throughout to reflect the finding that the power to shape the elderly subject is indeed dispersed; that it results from the whole spectrum of routines, forms of treatment, disciplines, attitudes of staff, other prisoners, the women themselves and the outside culture; and that the effect is very much the reconstruction of the subject as opposed to the mere punishment of the illegal act. Although Foucault does not locate age as a defining construct (constituent of identity), one can apply his theories to understand how ageist discourse is implicated in policing a particular cohort (Prior 1997; Smart 1985) and how power and knowledge combine to shape the experiences of adult ageing.

The relevant work of Foucault's is *Discipline and Punish – The Birth of the Prison* (1977b). It is a work of social theory, cultural criticism, penology, philosophy and history, which also constructs a perspective which stands outside these disciplines. Here Foucault succeeds in writing a 'genealogy of the modern soul, showing how the human sciences substituted for the Christian soul, a soul born under perpetual surveillance and subject to infinite discipline – to an interrogation without limits' (Miller 1990: 474). Foucault's insistence on the detail of disciplinary techniques is a key feature of his contribution to the analysis of prisons and other institutions (Armstrong 1992; Foucault

1971, 1976). His fascination with the detail of penal techniques leads Garland to claim that 'Foucault addresses himself to the minutiae of penal practice and the intricacies of institutional life in a way which recalls – and goes beyond – the classic studies of prison life' (Garland 1990: 100). However, he says relatively little about what prisons are like in practice, talking mainly about the theory behind imprisonment and the circumstances motivating people to argue for it rather than for physical punishment. As Garland comments:

> The principles of surveillance, observation, inspection and of disciplinary training, examination and normalisation – together with the physical, architectural, and organisational forms in which they are embodied – are presented to us so clearly and in such detail that we can begin to understand the material practices upon which modern penal institutions depend. (Garland 1990:152)

Thus, Foucault examines how under this new regime, the body of the condemned becomes the condemned body – a movement denoted by the transition from corporal to carceral punishments, techniques of discipline, normalisation and individualisation creating 'a whole domain of knowledge and types of power' (Foucault 1972, 1975, 1977b: 185). As Foucault (1977b: 16) states, punishment no longer addressed itself to the 'body of the criminal but to the soul'. Thus the use of power 'seems all the less "corporal" in that it is more subtly "physical"'(Rabinow 1986:193).

Foucault's work allows one to embrace the complex relationship between the nature of structuralism and agency through his understanding of power. His idea of power is central to understanding how and why 'power is everywhere, not because it embraces everything, but because it comes from everywhere' (Foucault 1990: 93). Power is not absolute; it is relational and cannot exist other than as a function of multiple points of resistance. The play of power relations is complex, unstable and self-transforming. It is argued that, 'we must cease once and for all to describe the effects of power in negative terms: it "excludes", it "represses", it "censors", it "abstracts", it "masks", it "conceals"' (Foucault 1980: 5). 'In fact, power produces; it produces reality; it produces domains of objects and rituals of truth [in discursive and non-discursive domains]. The individual and the knowledge that may be gained about him belong to this production' (Rabinow 1986: 205–206). His central topic is the way in which power is exercised in modern society; he is not primarily concerned with the constitution of moral authority, as is

Durkheim, or with the logic of the capitalist economy, as are 'the Marxists'. He poses law as a moral mythology, and treats the symmetry between economic relations and other elements of social structures as more or less self-evident; what Foucault is concerned with first and foremost are the internal workings of the institutions brought forth by the structural imperatives of capitalism (Donnelly 1982, 1986; Dreyfus and Rabinow 1982). It can be argued that punishment in modern society, 'from being an art of unbearable sensation, has become an economy of suspended rights' (Foucault 1977b:11).

In short, Foucault argues that power must be analysed as a micro-politics of social life, as an all-pervading phenomenon, which emerges everywhere. The lens applied allows one to problematise and deconstruct discourses, which constitute the identities of elders who are in prison (Foucault 1975, 1977b, 1978). Rouse (1994) argues that this approach allows for an examination of the relationship between power and knowledge, the dynamics of being the object and subject of knowledge/power relationships, which is central to understanding the subject through a Foucauldian lens. Moreover, the techniques used to create the obedient subject are techniques which are 'broken down into flexible methods of control, which may be transferred and adapted...[as] centres of observation disseminated throughout society' (Foucault 1977b:211–212) by the 'judges of normality' (Foucault 1977b: 304) and the elders themselves. Foucault makes it clear from the outset that, in describing penality, he is describing what he calls 'technologies of power'. These practices assist the process by which the subject is reconstituted under the juridical stare (Rose 1996). In the analysis of this reconstitution of the subject proffered by Foucault (1977b), he argues that therapeutic discourse is central to a power-knowledge complex which is directed towards creating forms of subjectivity that 'fit' a particular discourse of governance and citizenship (Hoy 1986; Foucault 1982c; Lash 1984; Lash and Urry 1994). There is a collage of diverse projects, programmes and agencies, all busily encouraging the production of appropriate emotions, desires and selves and for netting anybody who seems likely to 'escape', e.g. school dropouts, the homeless, the psychologically 'disturbed'. Concepts such as the genealogy of subjectification,[2] the role of discourse,[3] power, knowledge, resistance, disciplinary normalisation and surveillance describe characteristics of contemporary penal practices, and will be explored in order to understand the experiences of elders in later life who are in prison.

The power of prison

> It [is] a matter of analysing not behaviours or ideas, nor societies and their 'ideologies', but the problematisations through which being offers itself to be, necessarily, thought – and the practices on the basis of which these problematisations are formed. (Foucault 1981: 11)

Every elder female offender is placed under the custody of the 'carceral', 'juridical stare' and medical gaze. It can be argued that elder female offenders become institutionally fixed as a deviation from the 'norm' to be brought back to 'normality' through correctional regimes. Thus 'discipline', 'individualisation' and 'normalisation' are the cornerstone of prison, within which the emphasis is control and change through coercive treatment, invariably thwarting any notion of rehabilitation and reform (Cohen and Scull 1983; Cohen and Taylor 1978; Sim 2002). It is distinctive because of the absence of a 'private' space of individual freedom where private lives become public property (see Booth 1985; Peace 1986; Willcocks 1986; Willcocks, Peace and Kellaher 1987).

The structure of prisons in organisation, architecture and training fails to address the diversity of need of those who are other than able-bodied. This neglect provides a fertile space for the delivery of state-legitimated pain. The institution's neglect of diversity and difference within the prison estate operates on many levels and it is through further exclusion that the pains of imprisonment are multiplied by the lack of appropriate facilities. It has been well documented that women's prisons, children's homes, and residential communities are, no less than men's prisons, places of violence, where violence becomes a common currency that has to be learned, feared and used as part and parcel of resistance to a total institution (Carlen 1983; Carlen *et al.* 1985; Clough 1981; Cook 1998; McVicar 1974). This violence is symptomatic of the system itself rather than the system's victims or those responsible for the duty of care (Fleischer 1989). The geography of state-sanctioned exclusion creates a space for a world to emerge which requires a new survival code for elders. The severance of the world outside compounds and reminds the women of their estrangement and dislocation from the outside. It has been well documented that prison is not a panacea for society's ills but, instead, exacerbates the violence, prejudice and discrimination in society at large (Priestley 1989; Stern 1989, 1998; Sykes 1958; Toch 1992).

Women's prisons: Constructing the female offender

> If we cling to a unidimensional picture of penal institutions and their prisoners, we cannot begin to understand the nature of prison's power over the individual. By broadening the focus to include prisons for women, we immediately see that prisons function to control gender as well as crime. (Rafter 2000:xi)

Prior to the nineteenth century, the accounts of the physical conditions of prisons which housed men, women and children together was of unrelieved misery, disease, sexual abuse, squalor and extortion. It was only in 1853 that the first purpose-built prison for women was opened. Penal practice was underpinned by the notion that women were 'doubly deviant' (Dobash, Dobash and Gutteridge 1986; Smart 1981), not only for committing a crime but for offending against the nature of their sex. Women's criminogenic propensities were of *vitium* and *luxuria contra naturum*. The 1839 Penal Reform Act marked the beginning of official differences in the treatment of male and female offenders, creating two separate systems of imprisonment which reflected the ascendancy of a philosophy of 'rehabilitation of the person' (conceived differently for men and women) as opposed to mere 'retribution for a crime' (in theory applied indifferently as to gender). It has been documented in depth that the sentencing, the prison regimes and adaptations of penal policy applied to women continue today to be based upon assumptions about women's role in society and about the behaviour and needs of women in prison, founded on the notion of an 'essential woman' (Carlen 1983; Heidensohn 1987, 1989, 1994). In general, penal regulation of offending women, as argued by Carlen, serves to 'discipline, medicalise and feminise' (Carlen 1983:182). It is characterised by its 'invisibility, its domesticity and its infantilisation' (Carlen 1983:18).

The consequences of conventional typifications are that 'criminal women' are doubly excluded from personhood, rights and prerogatives: first, by being women, and second, by being excluded from the very status of femininity which would be their one claim to certain prerogatives. This probably underlies the apparent paradox whereby, on the one hand, the aim of punishment and rehabilitation is to restore women to 'appropriate' femininity (and this involves a paradox in itself, since women are to be restored therapeutically to a condition which is itself pathological by 'human' norms), yet on the other, there is an 'excess' of punishment (Allen 1987; Smart 1989, 1995) consisting of the removal (in addition to their liberty) of the very prerogatives associated with womanhood (Heidensohn 1987, 1996). By applying a Foucauldian approach, one can examine the 'juridical construction of the subject' (Rabinow 1986) in penal practice, which helps shape our definition of what women and men are. Because criminality has assumed a masculine, youthful status, elders are placed in an aggregation of conflicting discourses, which serve to further the pains of imprisonment. The contradictions in penal practice in relation to women mean that elders are assumed to be 'other' – yet parallel to this is the imposition of an age-neutral rule which subsumes them in the general category of women prisoners, in practice punishing differentially according to age.

Explanations of female criminality that are evident in contemporary penal rhetoric can be traced to early-nineteenth-century beliefs (involving a contradiction between the role of women as 'guardians' of public morality and their supposedly greater moral susceptibility) about female vulnerability and purity (Heidenshon 1994). These typifications of femininity, long used as an argument for excluding women from public life, have all been transformed to justify stricter surveillance in prisons. They have not only shaped current practices in women's penal establishments, but are also the basis on which discourses and practices that discriminate against women have evolved, developed and remain prevalent. These ideas underlie the theories which reduce female crime to biology, expressed in terms of their failure to adapt themselves to their supposedly natural biological and socio-sexual destinies. As a result, criminal women are those who not only break the law but who have offended their gender role expectations and thus have been presented as 'other': 'other than real women', 'other than real criminals and other than real prisoners' (Carlen 2001: 266). At the same time explanation is sought for such deviance in a way which does not happen with male law-breakers. Paradoxically, it is found in the 'natural weaknesses' characteristic of females which, however, rather than excusing them, is often used to justify closer punitive surveillance. This can result in debates about certain women criminals like Myra Hindley, in which one side claims she is, in effect, 'not really a criminal' since she acted in accordance with a feminine susceptibility to being dominated, while the other side claims, in effect, that she is 'not really a woman', but has become unnatural in relation to her feminine nature.

Disciplining femininity in the female prison estate

The pre-scientific age of the sixteenth century punished those women who were regarded as deviant by virtue of their lack of economic or emotional dependency upon a male, and labelled them as 'doubly deviant' (Carlen and Worrall 1987; Galford 1984). By the nineteenth century women criminals fell under the scientific gaze of positivist criminology, which rendered women and women criminals to their 'essential natures'. The main proponents of this view were Lombroso and Ferrero (1895), who believed that women were mal-adjusted and less developed than men, as a result of the 'immobility of the female ovule [compared to the] activity of the male sperm' (cited in Carlen et al. 1985: 2). In addition women had, unlike men, the propensities to be 'cunning', 'manipulative', and 'deceitful' (terms commonly used to describe women's actions today), although criminal women in essence were non-womanly and masculine in nature. These views from the early nineteenth century are reiterated in the discourse of prison medical staff (PMS), judges and probation officers, and in the way prison officers and the prison regime attempt to infantilise and domesticise the women in their charge. These underlying misogynistic themes constitute women criminals as being both within and 'outwith'[4] femininity, criminality, adulthood and sanity (Carlen 1983).

During the nineteenth and twentieth centuries a plethora of texts were written on the aetiology of female criminality – for example, by Thomas (1923) and Pollack (1950 cited in Carlen et al. 1985) – reinforcing the psycho-biological position of Lombroso and Ferrero who attributed essentially different personality traits to women and men. They argued that, through their 'essentially' passive natures, women were less capable of committing crime than men. In comparison, then, aggressive behaviour was assumed to be an 'essentially' masculine characteristic. These typifications of the supposedly 'essential' natures of men and women permeate current practices in women's prisons. Hence, the theme of Thomas' solution in *Unadjusted Girls* (cited in Carlen et al. 1985) was that delinquent girls should be made to adjust to their conventional female roles. This view implies that women criminals can be cured or rehabilitated: in the past this meant using methods such as 'hobbling' and 'intense prayer', through to lobotomy, and in modern terms, it is seen in the over-use of psychotropic drugs. Even as late as 1968, Cowie and Slater's central tenet was that female delinquency was caused by a chromosome imbalance which makes criminal women, but in particular young women, act like men, and that this can only be rectified through medicine or through being placed in the charge of their fathers or husbands (cited in Carlen *et al.* 1985). A more recent example of this paternalism and patriarchal control is given by Carlen (1983), who was told by Scottish sheriffs and magistrates, 'that a woman living with her husband and children would be less likely to get into criminal trouble than would a woman leading a less conventional life style' (Carlen 1983:85). These ideas are a salient undercurrent feature in the discourses and practices in women's penal establishments. The idea that women are more likely to be 'mad than bad' is a ubiquitous theme in criminology (Carlen 1983:2) and certainly has had effects in penal practice; when women offend they are likely to be seen as being in need of care or protection and/or psychiatric help rather than deserving more overt penal sanctions. Giallombardo (1966:18) illustrates the dichotomy between men and women in her statement, 'male criminals are…feared as dangerous…women who commit criminal offences tend to be regarded as misguided creatures who need protection and help'.

A further consequence of the patriarchal and paternalistic conceptions underlying the responses to 'offending women' is seen in the type of work and training provided for the women in penal establishments from the eighteenth through to the twentieth century, predicated on assumptions about 'their natural skills of cooking, cleaning, laundry work' (Heidensohn 1994: 25) and motherhood. This enforced cult of domesticity (Carlen and Worrall 1987) continues as an ideological force associated with situating the female offender into dependency and into the home.

The history of the present – Prison *as* and *for* punishment

The above discussion illustrates how typifications of femininity influence the types of punishment delivered in prison. It has been argued that prison is not *as* but *for* punishment, not solely based on the deprivation of liberty but on what goes on behind the surface once in prison. It can be argued that discipline, individualisation and normalisation are pivotal to the institution, and that, while this is true for all prisoners in theory, it is to women that this project is applied with most zeal and thoroughness.

Moreover, by treating elders in an age-blind fashion or by explaining their crimes and behaviour in prison by reference to their ages, these discourses serve to normalise their behaviour in relation to stereotypes of old age. One can argue that this failure to understand the experiences of elder offenders, and in turn to dismiss the needs of elders, results in a form of elder abuse.

Women in later life recognise how the system inadvertently places female elders to the margins of prison life. Surrounded by fear, the abstract and intimate intrusions of the penal gaze, the women survive by removing themselves to the periphery of prison life. This enactment of self-withdrawal reflects the deeper crisis of the legitimacy of the penal system. The crisis lies in the lack of recognition that elders are in prison. Moreover, this lack of recognition indicates how the system fails to understand the differing ideological, physiological and psychological needs of women in later life. The achievable aim of institutionalised violence towards elders takes the form of being dismissed, degraded and denied, which further estranges the self from effective agency. The landscape of the prison painted by the elders illustrates how the induction into the prison world of strip-searches, loss of control, the new time order, block routine, etc., serves to sever the continuity of the life threads outside the prison gates.

It is the lack of differentiation according to need within the prison system that is experienced as further punishment. The internal workings of the prison machinery infantilise the women, regardless of age, disability, experience and academic qualifications. The process of homogenising the women creates tension amongst the women and between the women and the institution as each woman occupies a different temporal space. Furthermore, it calls into question the legitimacy of the penal system when the prison is not *as* but *for* punishment. The punishment varies from the expressed intention of the deprivation of liberty to the reality of the constant bombardment of the minutiae of punishment beyond the walls of freedom. Prison becomes a site of perpetual surveillance, subjecting women in later life to indefinite punishment without limits. In prison visibility becomes a trap: 'It is the fact of being constantly seen, of being able always to be seen, that maintains the disciplined individual in his subjection' (Foucault 1977a: 187). The paradox here is that elderly women are, in some respects, invisible and this is also a trap.

As outlined above, applying a Foucauldian lens demonstrates the conditions in which female prisons emerged, the role of power and the types of punishment in prison. The typifications of femininity that are operationalised in prison become techniques that structure the punishment, the educational facilities and define the 'appropriate' response to offending behaviour of older women in prison.

Women, old age and the criminal justice system

In order to understand and analyse women's imprisonment, in particular the experiences of what it is to be an older woman in the criminal justice system, it is crucial to understand the factors informing these experiences. This section examines how elders negotiate, internalise and relate to the abstract gauging of age to their subjective experience of the ageing process (Biggs 1997; Featherstone and Hepworth 1983, 1991), both incorporating and resisting the prison coding of chronological age. Furthermore, this chapter will examine how the concept of age is placed within a custodial setting and in turn becomes displaced under the disciplinary gaze. The displacement of ageing, experience and knowledge aids the process of the (de)fragmentation and the reinvention of the self under the penal gaze.

A number of themes or perspectives on ageing are identifiable in the voices of the women. This is by no means an exhaustive list but it certainly illustrates both the complexity and the diversity of the meanings given to age by the prison, by the younger women, by the 'free world' and by themselves.

It can be argued that to be in one's fifties on the outside, although there is certainly a stigma attached to the physical appearance and sexuality of older women, is certainly not to be 'old'. Indeed, there is some research which confirms the popular idea of 'life begins at 40' for many women; that is, when the majority have completed the onerous years of parenting, and now have more resources available. Thus, for women the middle to later years are often a very positive time, and this is reinforced by the fact that a woman is likely to have many friends of a similar age who form her reference group (Corston 1999; Evers 1983; Friedan 1993; Harrison 1983; Jerrome and Young 1983). However, to be 50 or above in prison is to be defined as part of a highly 'deviant' minority within the institution; there is no 'script' for being in this position, no established reference group, and the younger women who form the large majority have a power to define and label one from a youthful stand-point which is unmatched on the outside.

The tensions and contradictions created by ascribed age and subjective age are not so salient to elders on the outside, because there it would be 'normal' to be this age. It would be a 'less prominent signifier' – that is, age would not be a conscious issue in most contexts – whereas in prison it is nearly always being made conscious, both because of the elder's minority status and because of the peculiar gearing of provision to the younger group. For some elders being of a certain age brings with it a degree of respect, thus turning age into an asset. What the elders have revealed is that, in fact, one does not normally think about one's age much; that it is within the institutional context that age becomes significant, and it is this which gives rise to the feeling of a discrepancy between ascribed age and the subjective experience of self. The elders felt that they were being made to think in an artificial way about themselves in terms of age because they were so much at the mercy of how others see them (the other prisoners and the officials). The effect of 'the gaze' (being defined from an alien vantage point), loss of autonomy, and the effects of both on the sense of self, is important in understanding the struggle to retain the power of self-definition and the way this in itself results in new aspects of self being forged. Thus, for example, the elders' struggle is to preserve self-definition in the face of a 'gaze' that constructs them on the criterion of age, and in this struggle they also develop a new self-definition which involves a sub-verted version of age. Anita Arrowsmith[5], a first-time offender, describes how she created a new self-definition in order to survive in prison:

AA: The only way you could get out of the room was if you were on twenty minutes exercise out in the yard or in the gym. If you volunteered to go to gym which meant you stood the chance of getting searched. They called it 'Blacks' and 'Reds'. That's the drug squad.
I stood so close to the girls as we were lining up that I had to hold my pockets like this [she demonstrates this by clenching her pockets tight]. I heard that they'd [the girls] been passing drugs and things. I was told to watch that they [the girls] didn't put anything in your pockets.

AW: Oh, right.

AA: So I was *feared* for that. You would have to walk along the wall and they'd bring the dog to meet you. If you didn't go to the gym you were locked up. I mean being locked in a dorm and there's one toilet in the dorm for seven. You had one sink, for the seven of you. Um, it's quite embarrassing because the door is a half door. So you see the top of you and the bottom of you. It's quite embarrassing going. I used to wait.

If I was dying to go to the toilet, I'd wait till the door was unlocked and I used the outside toilet where the bathrooms were. I didn't take a bath. I didn't have a shower for three weeks. Because I was afraid at getting any germs, picking anything up. They weren't the cleanest, you know.

I go to the gym. I mean at my age, going to the gym. I've got three grandkids, and I felt so lonely. I just used to go to the gym. Just so I could get out of my room. [emphasis in original]

Anita Arrowsmith
Age: 53
Time spent in prison: 4 months

Moreover, the elders seem to view age as a process of declining abilities and, in some sense, of decline in intrinsically desirable human qualities: thus, they appear to look back and view themselves as being 'less' than they used to be. This model of ageing is dichotomous in that it utilises one dimension – the presence versus the absence of characteristics assumed to be intrinsically desirable. The extracts illustrate a resistance to/fear of the dominant conception of 'growing old', expressed in the reference to 'youth' (Biggs 1997; Wahidin 2002). This reference to the dichotomous model of ageing which contrasts young/then with old/now is an example of the processual nature of 'ageing' and the internalisation of ageist discourse by the women.

Understanding ageing

In the outside world the ageing process both for women and men is gendered, constructed as a time of systematic and forced withdrawal, of transition from productivity into retirement, of being placed into zones of non-identity (Phillipson 1982, 1993, 1997, 1998; Phillipson and Biggs 1998). For men this is constructed as a time of redundancy in relation to the stereotypical/traditional role of breadwinner, and the loss of an identity and status rooted mainly in the workplace. For some men, however, this period provides a relished opportunity to enjoy the prerogatives belonging to membership of a chronological age group from which others, i.e. younger members of society, are excluded. As we shall see from the extract below, this time becomes a period in which the woman's gendered identity and space are embedded in the growth and development of grandchildren. For Anita Arrowsmith, a mother and a grandmother, she goes through the worries and vicissitudes about the lives of her children and grandchildren, yet relating to them both on a different level as mother and grandmother:

AW: What does growing old mean to you?

AA: I think growing old is a nice part of life because your children have grown up. Although you still worry about them. And then when you've got grandchildren, you go through all the same things that you did with your own children. However, it is also *a time* for *you.* To enjoy more time with your partner instead of all your time being for other people. Spending time in the garden, cooking; I started to learn the piano. [emphasis in original]

Anita Arrowsmith

So, for many of the women, especially those in the early stages of their imprisonment, there was a sense that, until their imprisonment, they would have viewed, and had viewed, this period of later life as a time for new possibilities. As Alison Anwar states, '[to do things] that [I] haven't been able to do in the past'.

The identity of older women on both the outside and the inside is constructed around roles within the kinship and family networks; the women's understanding of ageing is largely based on the private sphere. The familial supports cushion the perceived negative effects of ageing, as some women make the transition from being carers to being cared for (Arber and Gilbert 1983). As we can see 'growing old' for Julie June (who was 54 at the time of imprisonment and was serving a life tariff) would normally mean:

JJ: Having your family around you and you sort of relate back to what you perceived as people growing old when I was at home. Um, family is very important to me, my dad's grandma and my mum's grandma lived with us until they died. Growing old would *mean making sure you looked after the older generation – that's always been very important to me.* [emphasis in original]

Julie June
Age: 54
Time spent in prison: 6 years.

For the majority of the women the meaning of age centres around their families and those with whom they are in contact. The role of the family allows some elders to 'grow old gracefully', as is the experience of Anita Arrowsmith. This period is viewed as less transitory and more settled than her younger days:

AA: Me and my husband we were just settling down to life. Just enjoying one another's company. Just being together and just relaxing.

Anita Arrowsmith

However, in the case of women in prison these roles will also become part of their resistance to an identity based on their age as interpreted by others: thus, as with every other aspect of self, the women's experience of their own age will involve that negative or oppositional element, the 'what I am not', the sense of the self as engaged in a resistance to an externally imposed identity. Of course, this will be part of the psychology of any person who is aware of being constrained by any externally imposed definitions/stereotypes. Nonetheless, there is a difference, as the following chapters will demonstrate, because for prisoners there are few spaces in their life when they can get away from the externally imposed identity: the significance of the ubiquitous prison gaze is evident.

The concept of age is relative (to situation, culture, etc.); the cut-off point for being an 'old' woman in prison is arguably very different (and much younger) than for being an 'old' woman on the outside. On the outside one has a multiplicity of roles: to one's children and grandchildren, one may have characteristics of being an elder; at work one's age may have little importance, or one may be posited as a 'mother-figure' to younger colleagues (which is not an elder status in the same sense; if anything, it rather infantilises the younger people). In prison, it may be that an 'elder' is anyone set apart by the fact of being 'not young' and hence culturally different, or by having needs/experience which the majority of the prison population are unlikely to share.

For Wan-Nita, her life on the outside 'has gone on a car boot sale':

WW: It's *gone*. It's all *gone*. It's *gone* on a car boot sale. [my emphasis]

AW: Does that includes all your financial…?

WW: Everything. Everything [she pauses] everything's gone.

She later goes on to say:

WW: Because I'm doing a life sentence, there's a difference to begin with, they [the non-lifers] know when they're getting out, and I don't! You know that's the *big difference*. I don't see that I should have any privileges or anything other than somebody else. I just want to be treated like a *human being* and I want to be treated with *respect*. I also don't want to be *continually punished* whilst I am in jail when I'm already punished for coming into jail. You know, it's all the little things that add to that makes it feel that you are being punished further. [emphasis in original]

AW: Like what?

WW: Like this volumetric control, trying to fit your life into two boxes. How can anyone doing a life sentence fit their life into two boxes? They [the prison officers] will take it. What doesn't fit in the boxes has to go. Now, my life on the outside has gone – *has gone on a car boot sale.* Here we are again, seven years down the line, and everything has to fit into two boxes.

AW: Will they keep it in the store for you?

WW: They [the prison officers] will send it to some storage place somewhere. I don't know where. If I can't have it with me I don't want it at all.

Wan-Nita Williams
Age: 52
Time spent in prison: 7 years.

It is the lack of support within the prison and the lack of support waiting on the outside that for Wan-Nita Williams, means that 'growing old means being alone really. I'm afraid to be alone, I don't want to be old and alone'.

The fear of the unknown

The body, and the passing of time, are salient in understanding the ageing process giving insight into the fears and anxieties that fuel elders' perception of their 'self' when released with a criminal conviction into an ageist society (to be discussed later). Margot Metcalf fears the process of ageing, because for her it signifies losing the right to claim a role which carries the accolade of being wise. She states:

MM: I don't look forward to it. Maybe if we can just start to…in our society to respect wisdom – the wisdom of age. Um, but society doesn't.

Margot Metcalf
Age: 54
Time spent in prison: 9 years

The fear which furthers the women's sense of isolation and loneliness is the fear of becoming a burden to others and becoming dependent in a society which negates the experiences of elders. Petra Puddepha argues:

PP: *I don't mind* the idea of *retiring. I do mind* the idea of being um a *burden,* a *drain –*
a *drain* on the resources of the state. [emphasis in original]

Petra Puddepha
Age: 55
Time spent in prison: 1 year

It is the fear of senescence, the loss of control both psychologically and physiologically, the bodily betrayals of age, that serves to fuel the women's feelings
of terror of what age may bring (Featherstone 1982; Featherstone and
Wernick 1995). As the ageing body begins to fail, it becomes a receptacle that
no longer represents the inner self. For Kate the fear is grounded in:

KK: Being helpless, I think. Being unable particularly like Alzheimer's or Parkin-
son's disease. I mean those diseases trap the person inside a body that isn't
functioning properly and that's frightening.

Growing old, being put to pasture – I'm terrified. Alzheimer's, my God, it
blows your mind when you think your mind completely goes and you're back
in your childhood aren't you?

Kate King
Age: 53
Time spent in prison: 13 years

These comments indicate the fear of losing control, of being redundant in a
society which celebrates the youthful body. It is the frail body, the lack of
bodily control, regression and the fear of possible dependency on others
which leads to the fear of growing old. The common thread running through
the extracts is the connection between the woman's traditional caring role and
the particular fear of the diseases which many women feel.

The ageing process is thus multi-faceted. It is experienced on various
levels ranging from a period of time which enables self-reflection, time for
oneself, to a period when the inner self is betrayed by the body's loss of functions. Marcia Morris suffers from water retention and this is exacerbated by
the prison regime. The lack of medication for this condition makes her job,
which requires her to stand, very painful indeed:

MM: It's my blood pressure and it's my heart. My body keeps the water inside.
Sometimes, like now it's not swelling. But that's because it's the morning. But
if you come and see me later this evening, then you will see the swelling in my
legs. It's very painful.

Marcia Morris
Age: 58
Time spent in prison: 2 years

This disconnection of the sense of self from the experience of the body as the body begins to 'betray' the self threatens a loss of self-image as a competent, rational adult, a loss of agency which is a threat to the very survival of the self. It is this fear of the betrayals of the physical body, being put out to pasture, growing old alone or becoming dependent on others which fuels the need to arrest the ageing process.

Through the women's stories one can observe the role of governance and regulation, employed by the women to inscribe both informal and formal social control on their bodies, which paradoxically aids their resistance to the dominant conception of 'growing old' by the reference to 'youth'. As Henrietta Hall argues, 'I don't want to grow old. I want to stay young if I can.'

As with many elders in the study one of her major fears was of becoming dependent:

HH: When you are old you sort of seem a responsibility on society. As you get older and as soon as you start to lack independence, you've got to rely on somebody else.

Henrietta Hall
Age: 52
Time spent in prison: 7 years

Prison has accelerated the ageing process in terms of physiology and for many elders they face the prospect of being placed as a lone female in yet another institution, the residential home.

Suffering from several age-related illnesses through the lack of adequate medical and nutritional care whilst in prison, Henrietta will leave prison only to fall under the medical and welfarist gaze. She says of her mother:

HH: They had to put her in a residential home. *She hated it.* Because her freedom had been taken away from her. Her independence had been taken away from her. I could end up in a wheelchair. That's why I don't want to grow old – that's when your independence goes. [emphasis in original]

Henrietta Hall

The sense of loss suffusing in such accounts relates to the notion of prison not *as* punishment but *for* punishment. It is through the loss of youth, of health and hence of hopes that the years spent in this closed prosthetic environment bring punishment far exceeding the 'mere' abstract loss of freedom. As time passes, the visible signs of imprisonment become inscribed upon the body (Falk 1985; Frank 1990, 1991; Shilling 1993).

In terms of the tension between the conception of later life as a period when more time and new opportunities become available, and the construction of ageing as a process of decline bringing profound experiences of loss, the effect of imprisonment frequently reinforces the latter by throwing into relief the denial of the former. The ageing process is interpreted by the women as a comparison between the past, before prison and the now, whereupon the loss of both, the actual past and the once anticipated future predominates, and the new future is comparatively uncertain. The movement out of prison will bring new freedoms rather than bringing the freedoms expected then, before imprisonment; the loss of liberty has generated other losses, but also other challenges which have to be met on the outside: for example, learning to drive a mobility car. Molly Mossdale's understanding of age is one of:

MM: Slowing down, not being able to do as much. As far as I am concerned being disabled. I have rheumatoid arthritis, which has meant that when I go out and all the things I have dreamed of doing whilst all these years inside, I just can't do now. For example, being mobile, walking rather than using crutches or the wheelchair. I loved sports. I really loved them, and now it's an impossibility. I was independent as much as possible but I am not now.

I think young, but I know I am much older than I think. I am still thinking like when I first came into prison and what I could do then. I know I can't do that now, but I am going to try. And whilst I am eating my own food; choosing my own food, I could lose weight. I like to think young. I am going to try and enjoy myself and see as many places as possible and make up for lost time.

Molly Mossdale
Age: 53
Time spent in prison: 20 years

Although excited at the prospect of leaving prison, she is acutely aware of the psychological effects prison and the process of institutionalisation have had on her. Once a teacher who commanded respect, she finds that:

MM: I used to be confident, but I am not confident at all now. I am always stepping back waiting for other people to take the initiative. I think that will stay with me for the rest of my life now. I am always apologising for things before I do anything, just in case it's wrong. I am always on the defensive. I never used to be like that. I can't get over that now, it has been too long.

When I asked her what she didn't like about prison, she stated:

MM: Taking away our ability to think for ourselves. Taking away any feelings that you can be responsible for your own destiny, that you can have self-respect. Self-respect has just gone through the window.

Molly Mossdale

For other women, leaving prison brings a new label and heralds another externally imposed transition to being defined by others and given pensionable status:

AW: How do you see your future when you leave prison?

KK: I always try to be realistic about everything. I don't like living in cloud cuckoo land. I think I'll be fifty-seven or fifty-eight. Two years off my pension. I think employment is out of the question, not only because of my age, but also the stigma of having a life sentence. Lots of factors are against me, but I couldn't sit on my backside and do nothing. So if I'm not studying, I'll do voluntary work. I could never vegetate. I would do something.

Kate King

The interpretation of ageing for this elder on this journey through the life course is also informed by watching others succumb to age-related illnesses, thus feeding the fear of what old age may bring. For some, as we have seen, it is arresting the onset of the visible ageing process that places physical ageing at a distance, the women reinventing the self through wearing objects which signify youth (Featherstone 1991; Featherstone and Hepworth 1991; Ginn and Arber 1996; Hepworth 1991; Hepworth and Featherstone 1982). For Kate King she wears brand-named shoes from the 'Caterpillar' range. But at the same time women in prison fear the possible onset of decrepitude and dependency. Such fears are reinforced by the increased frequency of deaths of significant others, one of the hallmarks of advancing age and the passage of time, and a forcible reminder of one's own mortality:

CC: Another thing about our age is that our favourite uncles die off [she laughs]. It's true, yeah people get thinner on the ground as you walk forward in age. It is one of the depressing facts.

Cath Carter
Age: 55
Time spent in prison: 4 months.

As Molly Mossdale states, 'it is harder for the older person to fit after [being] in prison for so long.' For many, and including Molly, all they want to do is to 'get lost on the outside', 'to enjoy life', and 'make up for lost time'. But Molly is one of the fortunate ones who have the economic security to be able to 'see as many places as possible'. Ultimately, the ageing process for all women both on the outside and within the walls should be one which allows older women to have the means of support which will enable them, as Yvette Young puts it:

YY: To grow old gracefully [She laughs] and to live a good life.

Yvette Young
Age: 53
Time spent in prison: 1 year

This discussion certainly illustrates the complexity and the diversity of the meanings contained within the concept of age based on the abstract chronological markers as one travels through the life course. On a general level, it demonstrates how meanings of the ageing process confine and define elders in the social hybrid of a residential community constructed by the penal machine.

The analysis of the meaning of age draws out how women in later life come to know and give meaning to the contradictory and complex nature of chronological age and how the process of ageing becomes yet another defining feature of their lives, 'then' contrasted with 'now' and their lives on the outside. The threads of the above discussion illustrate the diversity of how and why women in later life experience the ageing process.

From the life-course perspective, Erickson's (1983) stages of life no longer provide an adequate description of the progression through life, failing to reflect the blurring of boundaries in contemporary society. The blurring of age-norms, norms of 'femininity' and conceptions of what is 'appropriate' and 'socially acceptable' for different phases of life, provides alternatives to the stereotypical image of what it is to be old. The relaxation of chronological age boundaries replaces the rigidity of the traditional life-course boundaries with their predetermined 'rites of passage', with the prospect of arresting the ageing process (Featherstone 1991; Phillipson 1998). In contemporary society women in later life no longer conform to images like this. As Veronica Vicar says:

VV: Things have changed so much. When I was young a woman's life at forty, I mean she was absolutely finished. You know she had a sort of a funny little hairstyle and grey hair and just sat in front of the fire washing and ironing. But that's all changed now.

Veronica Vicar
Age: 52
Time spent in prison: 8 months

Lifestyles for women in later life are seen as more fluid; women of 40 are having children and taking part in the opportunities made available in the move towards life-long learning. These changes make it less appropriate to treat work and education as indicators of age as was done in the past (Bernard and Meade 1993). It is argued by Neugarten (1996) that the consumer images of later life are becoming more and more 'age-irrelevant'.

Age under the penal gaze becomes fragmented, composed of different things dependent on time, structure and place and thus has particular consequences and effects.

TT: I think they [the criminal justice system] regard *men as criminals* whereas as women, if they do things wrong are *sort of treated as sick people, not criminals, you know*? A woman is not criminally minded – so you know these *silly* courses, you know like sewing and needlework. I mean I'd rather be out there doing something constructive you know, woodwork or something, something like that [laughs]. Why do they give *women, women's jobs*? They've never thought that maybe we would probably like to learn something else. But all we have here are sewing rooms and the *laundry*. [emphasis in original]

Tokwan Thomas
Age: 51
Time spent in prison: 4 years

Age in prison is employed as a form of seniority demanded by the officials' 'expectations'. Elders in prison are exploited by the prison system which posits them as carers (maternal figures), yet they are invisible as individuals because they are perceived as lacking feminine markers (of sexuality and fertility-reproductive capabilities). It is within the space created between the expectations of the disciplinary machine, the woman's understanding of age and how younger women construct elders, that other techniques of control and punishment are formed. This space opens up a room for women in later life, as Gertie Grangley argues, potentially to be victimised and:

GG: To [be made fun] of behind your back and [to be] call[ed] names. To me – for an older woman [being] in prison is lonely. It's a lonely time for an older woman because they don't take the needs of older women seriously, you know? You can start a conversation and they [the prison officers] and the younger women ignore you or walk away.

Gertie Grangley
Age: 59
Time spent in prison: 1year and 3 months.

The extract below demonstrates the effects of punishment on the body showing how Alison has become alienated from her body:

AA: Inside I don't feel old. But my body feels old. Healthwise – I have no energy and my bones ache all the time. When I was at home on a morning I'd be as bright as a button. I'd be looking forward to the day. But here, it's such an *effort.* You seem to be *dragging* your body around all the time. You are *conscious* of *your body.* You know, it feels heavy all the time. *Your heart is heavy all the time.* Your feelings are all – there is no light heartiness. [my emphasis]

Alison Anwar
Age: 51
Time spent in prison: 2 years

It is her body which feels old. It is her body which she is conscious of, dragging the body with her rather than it being part of her. She describes how internally/subjectively she is reminded of a certain time before prison, distinguishing between the young/old; then/now; freedom/deprivation of liberty; agility and heaviness and melancholia. The loss of freedom, loss of time spent in prison becomes couched in terms of the performance of the body then (before prison) and now. For Molly Mossdale it has meant:

AW: In terms of health would you say…

MM: *Deteriorated badly.* There is nothing else I can say. The sheer boredom in prison. I came in to prison at nine stone, which is one stone overweight than I should have been. I was a healthy person; I was active, I played a lot of games, badminton and tennis. When I came to Penjara I went from nine stones up to sixteen stone. That was sheer comfort eating. I have rheumatoid arthritis, which has meant that when I have gone out and all the things I have dreamed of doing whilst all these years inside, I just can't do now. [emphasis in original]

Molly Mossdale

For others the techniques of power employed by the carceral realm become a tool to negotiate, resist, modify and in a sense arrest the effects of the system, the sentence, and the environment in its process of metamorphosing the body under the prison's gaze. Wan-Noor Winter from Holland, who at 51 found herself in a British jail, says:

WW: And when they say don't let them grind you down it's true.

Wan-Noor Winter
Age: 51
Time spent in prison: 6 years

Expectations

Women in prison are constructed in relation to masculine standards of normality. If we take away these standards of normality which in turn denote otherness, what is normality and what standards are offenders measured against? Women in later life are homogenised under the punitive gaze, but the contradiction lies in the fact that, on the one hand, they are *not* treated as objects of knowledge, but on the other they are treated as a group that brings certain qualities to the prison environment. Elders in prison find themselves placed in a nexus of prison expectations on them to nurture, control and guide the younger women. It is interesting to note that it is common practice to separate older men from younger men but, as yet, there are no facilities to separate older women from younger women, and this difference appears to be based on socially constructed roles of femininity and masculinity. The essentialising discourse of femininity locates the elders as 'carers', 'nurturers' and teachers of morality. The separating of older men from younger men is based on discourses which serve to construct a masculinity which excludes the above (carers, 'nurturers' and teachers of morality), but with one distinction, that older men are seen as more likely to corrupt younger men.

The gendered body in prison is a discursive site in which power is produced, acted upon, engaged with and received. These aspects of power allow spaces for resistance to emerge, enabling power to be positive and at the same time negative (Bosworth 1999; Foucault 1982a; 1982b). The extract below shows how, through adversity, Myra Hindley was able to enlist the help of others given the lack of provision for those elders who are immobile or disabled. Julie June recollects how women in general with age-related illness are not catered for in the prison environment by giving this particular example:

JJ: Like when Myra was here, I think she could have perhaps done a little more than she perhaps did. I was on the yard when she broke her hip about 6 years ago, she fell on —. She was in hospital for a few weeks and then she came back here and was in her cell. Really she should have been on a prison hospital wing. But there are no facilities for that, here at Penjara. I think that's really bad to say it is a long-term wing. I was saying about Myra, when eventually Myra came back to the wing she was put on the 'two's'[6] 'cause we have no cells on the flat[7] here. It wasn't ideal, people were having to carry her flask and people were getting fed up of carrying her things up for her.

I mean eventually she got stronger and I think perhaps she could have done a little bit more that she did. But it was with difficulty. She had crutches to begin with, then we got her onto a stick. Um, but it wasn't ideal. She should have had a cell on the flat. Um, this is the problem with anybody who is *infirm and in prison*, I suppose. God I hope it never – listen to me [laughs]. [emphasis in original]

Julie June

The second oldest elder in the study, at 73 years old, benefited from ageist stereotypes, as younger women would complete her prison chores:

RR: She would take the washing, fetch it, bring it back and iron it. She didn't let me pick anything up.

Rebecca Rose
Age: 73
Time spent in prison: 7 months

This is a good example of how normative femininity in prison is centred on the ageing body and its socially constructed gendered duties and obligations. In terms of image and the body in the institution, one can argue that the two are in a state of flux, dependent upon the constructs of a particular locale, time, space, etc. One cannot argue that the performance of the body is solely to receive punishment.

In the extracts below the women are posited into roles that are defined by state mechanisms of control. The essentialising of their identity as women and as elders, serves to further the pain of imprisonment. Wan-Nita Williams describes the additional responsibilities placed on elders in prison:

WW: It's hard being an older woman in prison because so much is *expected* of you. The prison expects so much, you're supposed to think differently to the younger ones.

Wan-Nita Williams

Margot Metcalf, who has served nine years of a 12-year sentence, elaborates on how the pains of imprisonment are multiplied and generally go beyond the deprivation of liberty.

MM: I'm sick to death, because you're over fifty, they *expect* you to put up with whatever these young ones want to dish out. At the end of the day we're all in prison and we all want to go home! [emphasis in original]

It is the expectation versus the realities that place older women in a position of cumulated jeopardy.

MM: Expecting us to be able to put up with all the shit that we have to live with around us, to live in the drug situation and expecting better of us because we're older. We have to put up with it. They just *expect* so much from us you know, they expect – they'll put a smack head or a noisy one on this house, hoping that the older ones on this house will calm them down. *We're here to do our own sentence not to do somebody else's and that shouldn't be expected from you.* [emphasis in original]

Margot Metcalf

Many of the women found that the 'expectations' of the prison system informed the way officers and younger women in prison posit and construct women in later life. Molly Mossdale describes the devastating effects this has on her self-esteem:

MM: As an older woman you are expected to provide [for] the youngsters. They'll come to you, and say, 'You don't smoke – can you get us so and so?' You don't do so and so, and you get private cash – you can get so and so. Then they say, 'Grandma can you do this? Grandma can you do that?' They expect far more of you because they are youngsters. It is this sort of attitude that makes you feel as if you're on the heap already!

Molly Mossdale

The expectations of the younger women posit women in later life as providers/nurturers as the above clearly states, reinforcing feelings of isolation, alienation and resentfulness at the construction of otherness. In the extract below, the subjective age is 'middle aged'; the younger population furthers the feeling of dissonance between the internal and socially constructed notions of age. Edith Ellis feels older than she would on the outside because the age polarity of old/young becomes magnified in prison.

EE: I feel older than most, especially in here I think. There's more difference I think when you're put in jail, nearly all of them here call us Mam.

Edith Ellis
Age: 54
Time spent in prison: 4 months

After hearing that a younger woman wasn't able to speak to her sick daughter, Rosie Robottom gave the woman her own phone-card. Rosie later found that this act of kindness opened the flood-gates for others to ask:

RR: Some treat you like a piece of shit – they'd come and borrow, borrow, borrow all the time.

> Rosie Robottom
> Age: 56
> Time spent in prison: 8 months

Cath Carter found herself in a similar position when she gave some sugar to someone, which set off a chain reaction:

CC: If you are too nice, you will be walked on. It is misinterpreted here, you are seen as either a do gooder or a fucking know it all. The mentality here is, why would you give anything away for nothing? What's in it for her – that sort of thing. So this is a very cynical and sceptical place and you know – I wasn't streetwise. You are seen as *daft*. If you give your things away. I couldn't walk into the house for a while because I gave some sugar to someone. As soon as I'd open the door – 'Got any sugar, got sugar, got sugar' – Bang, bang, bang. They would pull the curtain away from the window on the door, which they are not supposed to do.

> Cath Carter

The expectations of the prison and those of the younger women serve as a series of attacks on the identity of women in later life, increasing the sense of loneliness, isolation and also of infantilisation. Although elders are looked upon as providers, the visible signs of ageing can be used to reinforce the feelings of rolelessness, powerlessness and embarrassment in a closed but replica society which places value on the youthful body. The above serves to push elders to the periphery of prison life, avoiding the centre stage where women in later life become targets to be victimised, harassed and intimidated by the constant demands made on limited resources.

Resistance to ageist discourse

The above discussion illustrates how age becomes a visible marker upon bodies which have been constructed as beyond, but not lacking, identifiable codes of femininity. Despite the paradox, this is affected in part by expectations upon them to assume responsibility for others, yet at the same time they are excluded from the prerogatives, rights and responsibilities of adulthood by the prison structure. These expectations act as further punishment: as Margot Metcalf states, 'We're here to do our own sentence not to do somebody else's.' Women in the study actively engage in constructing their identity in relation to the effects of imprisonment. It is the construction of the *other* or a fear of what not to become, that preserves and motivates elders to resist the institutionalisation of the body under the prison gaze, thus maintaining a positive self-image by contrasting their body to that of one of the many perverse consequences of the prison, such as the 'slouch and the shuffle'.

In response to ageist remarks made against elders in prison, women with self-esteem can and do retort by placing the body, the youthful body as a means of reasserting their identity. After months of being harassed because of her age, Cath Carter retorted:

CC: I think I have enough going for me to take it in my stride [She laughs]. I feel if I want to be bitchy I can turn round and say, 'If you look as good as I do when you are in your sixth decade you will be all right'. It is easy to be pretty when you are young.

Cath Carter

The role of the body, the way it looks rather than the way it feels, is important in how women in later life resist the positing and institutional inscription written on the body. This was clearly articulated when Wan-Nita Williams stated:

WW: I'm going to get a job in a gym, so that when I go out of jail I'll be quite fit. I want to be fit and that's what I focus on whilst in prison. I don't want to be fat and old when I get out.

Wan-Nita Williams

In a similar vein Kate King equates activity, fitness, the 'feel good factor of age' with youthfulness:

KK: I'm fifty-two this year, fifty-two or fifty-three – fifty-three this year. I'm very young and very active and very fit. I try to keep as young as I can.

Kate King

The above are examples of how the meaning of age is interpreted by the prison system, the younger women and the women themselves. The women actively resist the positing of their essential self by the penal authorities on the basis of age. However, for some the interpretation of growing old implies vulnerability. Some women collude with and utilise this construction of age in order to survive in prison. For Yvette Young, as a first-time offender, HMP Holloway was:

YY: [my] worst nightmare. I started to cry and this girl came up to me and she asked me what I had done. Another girl came in and because I had cigarettes, she began asking for a light, and then for my cigs. But she was asking for cigarettes from everybody. A big girl says don't get hassling her, she's my auntie.

AW: Did it bother you being called auntie?

YY: No. You could say it acted like a shield.

Yvette Young

Here age is elevated and stereotypical discourse creates a protective force when age is interpreted in terms of vulnerability. This also illustrates the effect of the meanings ascribed to age in serving the interest of the offender, who is consequently colluding with patriarchal and ageist discourse. The intersection of class and the role of age as a signifier of a claim to respect is important in conditioning understandings and interpretations of the ageing process and the performance of the body in the carceral realm. Cath Carter remarks on the paradox of age in prison:

CC: If I ever swear, I'm often told off by some of the younger girls – you know, that they don't expect that sort of language from me. So they put me in that position of their mother – [laughs]. The girls say, 'It doesn't sort of sound nice coming out of your mouth that sort of thing'. And so that makes you smile. I've had people in their twenties come up to me and say, 'It's disgusting the way they [the prison officers] spoke to you. They [the prison officers] have no business of speaking to you like that. You are my mother's age', and all that sort of thing.

Cath Carter

Although the manufacture of the aged identity in prison is one which regulates elders' agency as they are expected 'to know better' in relation to the younger women. They are at the same time denied adult responsibility and respect. Jane Jobson illustrates how seniority becomes displaced by the penal regime:

JJ: All the same I'm old enough to be their mother. To be spoken to, like they [the prison officers] speak to you is really degrading. I've never been spoken to like it.

Jane Jobson
Age: 66
Time spent in prison: 6 months

The term 'prism' in Foucauldian theory describes how, as one enters the carceral realm, age becomes a defining variable. As elders in later life enter the carceral prism they enter a new time order, and the outside meaning of chronological age becomes refracted, their conceptual/experiential knowledge of their self distorted, modified, separated and then reconstructed under the penal gaze. It is by examining how the meaning of age becomes refracted that age can be understood as a construction, socially produced by the structure, the younger women and the women themselves. This idea of refraction allows age to be viewed as a trajectory, not permanent but transitory. Age under the penal gaze becomes fragmented, composed of different things dependent on time, structure and place and thus has particular consequences and effects, just as a single source of light enters a prism and in turn the light separates to form transgressive spaces and transgressive aspects of itself (in terms of different colours).

The interrogation of the meaning of age as constructed by the carceral prism is imperative in understanding how women in later life are defined, confined and constituted by this version of femininity, which in turn provides what it means to be an elder female in prison. For others, their lives before prison govern and inform their performing role in prison, positing younger women in prison under a benevolent gaze. Bea Breton, a grandmother of 62, found herself in trouble for the first time. The quote below illustrates that, although placed within the walls, a mutually benefiting relationship can and does emerge across generations:

BB: I'm always looking at these girls and thinking how young they are and I think about my grandson straight away – comparing them. If there is any way that I could help them I will. The two young girls come on our house and I said, 'Don't do that, don't go mixing with those women and if there is anything you want come and ask me. And if I can help you, I will.'

AW: So you look after them?

BB: Yes, yes. I think I do. But they say they look after me now. [Laughs]

Bea Breton
Age: 62
Time spent in prison: 2 years 4 months

Although prison homogenises women in terms of their criminal label, it is the women who recognise the differing needs of women at various stages in the life course. Anita Arrowsmith comments that:

AA: In Holloway, if they saw you walking up a landing with say a mop and bucket, a youngster will come along and take it off you and say, 'Let's take this down to your room for you', or something like that.

Anita Arrowsmith

The experiences and the tacit knowledge of life before prison, the life threads of familial responsibilities, motherhood, becoming a grandparent, the role as a carer inseminate life in prison. Anna argues:

AA: Well really, I like to do it anyway because these kids in here are the same age as my own children. That could be one of my children, you know, in prison. I'd like to think that, I mean God forbid, but you know, say one of my kids went to prison. I'd like to think they'd got somebody they could talk to and you know somebody who could help them.

Anna Arnold
Age: 50
Time spent in prison: 4 years 6 months

Conclusion

This section adds to an understanding of the relationship between ageing, the self, and the external and internal definitions placed upon the ageing female body in prison. Failed hopes and dreams on release become imminent reminders of lost youth, lost time which is time served and lived through but not in any real sense lived. Under the carceral gaze youth is experienced as an age status, a state of continuing strength which is reinforced by contrasting the body then to the frailties of the body now (Bourdieu 1978; Featherstone 1982).

In prison 'age' is used to discipline and further punish the women in the study, by excluding them from certain activities. This is because they are 'deemed to have had their life and should have known better', as one officer claimed. Lack of provision for elders reinforces their sense of dislocation, loneliness and alienation. It is a reminder of the lost dreams, lost life, lost time and general dis-identification with the outside world. It is by identifying how age and discourses of femininity are used by the prison officers, the elders and the younger women, that we come to understand how elders in prison constitute and make sense of their experiences.

This book will focus on the latter half of the prison mission statement: 'to look after them with humanity and help them lead law-abiding and useful lives in custody and after release'. This statement is germane to both the female and male prison estate. On the surface level, it encompasses the diverse range of offenders, offences and life years that are found in any prison (excluding young offenders institutions). However, as the chapters unfold and the reflexive accounts of the women illustrate that when applied to older women in the criminal justice system, this is more rhetoric than practice or policy. The voices of the elders will evocatively share with you, the reader, how they, as older women in the criminal justice system landscape the topography of prison as they make the journey from 'court to prison' to being a 'forgotten but significant minority' in prison.

Wan-Nita Williams explains:

AW: What does growing old mean to you?

WW: Oh, old and lonely, rolling rollies like a little… Growing old means being *alone really*. I'm afraid to be *alone*. I don't want to be old and *alone*. [emphasis in original]

Wan-Nita Williams

To prevent the latter from happening and to rectify the hiatus between policy and practice:

It is essential that every woman prisoner, of whatever age, should be faced with what I have called a full, purposeful and active day. This means that she should have a programme designed not only to challenge her offending behaviour, but to give her social and economic tools with which to face the future. (HMIP England and Wales 2001:5)

Notes

1   A phrase from Foucault (a biological metaphor, in fact, used to denote a kind of power which reaches into every part of the 'body' of society. Capillaries (literally) are a multitude of small intersecting fibrous channels (the word comes from 'hairs') through which blood circulates, and this idea is meant to shift our attention away from large-scale centralised power of the state towards the less visible operation of decentralised networks. Foucault says this is the most important kind of power characteristic of modern societies, which he illustrates by, among other things, the discourses and practical knowledge of various professions and academic disciplines, etc.

2   'This is not a history of ideas: its domain of investigation is that of practices and techniques, of thought as it seeks to make itself more technical. The genealogy works towards an account of the ways in which 'the self' emerges, not as an outcome of enlightenment…but out of a number of contingent and altogether less refined and dignified practices and processes' (Rose 1996: 159).

3   'The analysis of discourse involves the deconstruction of coherence to reveal the underlying paradox and expose the absence of that which has been represented as being present' (see Worrall 1990:8).

4   Outwith is a Scottish word. Its meaning as given in *The Concise Oxford Dictionary* is 'outside', but its structure conveys the more subtle meaning of 'beyond (out) but not lacking (with), which conveys the 'contradictory states of consciousness engendered by the competing definitions of the woman' (see Carlen 1983:17).

5   Name and places have been changed to ensure anonymity.

6   'Two's' is a term used to denote the second landing.

7   'Flats' is a term used to denote the ground floor.

Chapter 2

From Court to Prison:
Women on the Edge of Time

This chapter will chart the elders' transition from wider society to court and then to their final destination, prison. It is by tracing the experiences of elders from court to prison that one begins to see the types of punishment in operation and how elders adjust to the new order of punishment and discipline. It is from these initial moments that their label of 'offending woman' begins to override their life experiences. I will discuss the way prison penalises women by denying them recognition of the roles and responsibilities which they have been used to occupying. It is through exclusion, fear and the isolation that for elders prison becomes characterised by its invisibility, its domesticity and its infantilisation. Until this changes, older women prisoners will still be denied their existence and while prisons exist, 'it is unlikely that there will be any imprisonment so enduring as the imprisonment which is denied' (Carlen 1983:218).

Initial reception: from court to prison

Throughout the literature it has been documented that women's prisons, children's homes and other residential communities are no less than men's prisons, places of violence, where violence becomes a common currency that has to be learned, feared and used as part and parcel of resistance to a total institution, as a means which one has to use in order to survive. Learning the techniques of survival begins with the initial reception from court to prison.

The women found the mode of transport from court to prison humiliating and degrading, fuelling their fears of what prison might be like even before they arrived at the prison gates. Their initiation into mechanisms of disciplinary control was the 'sweatbox' or 'meat van'. One officer as he showed me round the vehicle described it euphemistically as a 'cellular vehicle'. The van consists of tiny sectioned-off cells on each side, each with its own window which enables the women to see out but does not allow outsiders to see in. Like many others Lorna Langley found herself under the juridical stare for the first time and described the transfer from court to prison as:

LL: Terrible, it was terrible from the start because you go in a sweatbox which I don't suppose you know what it is. It only consists of this much space (she draws the dimensions out) you go in from court to this sweatbox. You have handcuffs on here (she points to where they go) and then they make sure you sit down. They remove the handcuffs. [Pause] It was a horrible experience.

Lorna Langley
Age: 73
Time spent in prison: 2 years

Alison Anwar describes the process:

AA: I was terrified. I was really frightened. Well, they took me back down to the cells first of all. I was ill. Then the Group 4 van came for me, I was as *skinny* as anything. My spine was *sore with* all the rubbing you know along the metal. My bones in my bottom were sore from the metal seat. They won't stop for you to go to the toilet.

Alison Anwar

The extracts poignantly describe the conditions as claustrophobic, inhumane, and being treated purely like cattle, going to and from court. These tiny compartments were far worse than the mini-buses and taxis that were previously in service. They all wanted to know why they had to be handcuffed from reception to the waiting van as this all took place in the security of the prison and seemed totally unnecessary. The lack of awareness of elders' needs, the unnecessary use of restraints in the light of their medical conditions and ability to abscond, raises a series of questions of 'rights', 'risk' and 'need'. The women complained about being put in handcuffs when they went to and from court or to hospital.[1] They found it very degrading and felt it showed no respect for their maturity. They felt that the doctors should recommend alternative forms of transport on the basis of their health needs, and question whether it was necessary to use such restraints. Elders felt degraded and infantilised by the process of being 'herded and treated in the same way as a fifteen-year-old' (Alison Anwar).

AA: It's a big Group 4 wagon. They lock you in and they don't let go of your handcuffs. You're sitting in there and they take your handcuffs as you are sitting down. You are sitting on very hard seats – steel seats and you are cramped out all the way to London to Durham.

You are just sitting there in this sweatbox with a steel grid in front of you and a window on the side. That's how you have to sit for three or four hours maybe five hours. It all depends on how much traffic is in London at the time.

Alison Anwar

Many of the women's narratives reveal that not only were seat belts not provided but that they travelled, for example, from Holloway to Durham, a six-hour journey, without stopping. The lack of specialist care around 'old' women's bodies can cause women who have a strained/stressed bladder, who are menopausal or menstruating a great deal of distress and discomfort. One elder found herself in an embarrassing situation due to the discontinuation of her incontinence tablets. The women found the mode of transport to and from court, as already discussed, to be inhumane, inappropriate and placed them under increased levels of duress. All in all, the cumulative effects led to the elders being very frightened. Julie further states:

JJ: You get a set of handcuffs on and then you have another set cuffed to an officer. So you are double cuffed. They are *the big manacles. They are the big male cuffs. They have to have shoulders put in them to fit our wrists because our wrists are a lot thinner.* [emphasis in original]

AW: Isn't double-cuffing a recent...

JJ: Um, well it's within the last eighteen months to two years. It's new legislation, isn't it? And um, I just think *it's inhumane*. The skin from both my wrists had come off completely by the time I got to court. I was in these double cuffs all the way to London. Where am I going to run to? [emphasis in original]

Julie June

The above demonstrates the contradiction between the 'official' version of punishment in modern society which holds that the punishment consists of 'deprivation of liberty', and that physical punishment is degrading and inhumane, and the reality which is that 'corporal punishment' (suffering inflicted on the body) is a regular (perhaps inescapable) aspect of punishment. Of course, this physical punishment would be made less inhumane if practices such as unnecessary handcuffing or the deprivation and discontinuation of prescribed drugs were abolished (thus reducing the role the very arbitrariness and pettiness of such practices plays in underscoring the rights of the carceral regime over the prisoner). However, the essential point is that the reason why the removal of liberty constitutes punishment, is that it takes away one's ability to act to prevent pain/suffering to oneself or to improve one's health and well-being (i.e. in other words, all such punishment is corporal punishment). This mechanism of depriving a person of her liberty is a good example of 'power over' in the traditional sense, which Foucault critiques. The idea of depriving a person of liberty means denying, or having the right/ability to deny, someone the means to act in their own interest when they perceive the need to do so.

These practices illustrate the tensions between rights and risks, between the individual needs of the women and the needs of the prison regime, which remain, as we shall see later, in contradiction to each other. Moreover, this contradiction is indicative of the nature of this exercise of power to act arbitrarily, far beyond any operational justification. Unless the prison service recognises the elder female offender, mistreatment and neglect will be an inherent and a pervasive facet of prison life.

Perhaps more than any other segment of the prison population, except the very young, offenders in later life challenge the boundaries and assumptions that necessitate traditional methods of crime control. The problems that women in later life experience in the prison system arise from a system that is geared for the able-bodied young male:

OO: You're locked in this box and you've got a sandwich, an apple, or an orange and if you need a drink of water, they pass it through the top of the door for you which actually for an older women – I mean the younger ones might not have found it so bad but I found it *horrendous*.

Olivia Ozga
Age: 57
Time spent in prison: 2 years

This extract demonstrates a recurring theme throughout: the appeal to age to rationalise feelings and behaviours. This appeal to ageing is an example of the importance of the construction of age to how elders give meaning to their imprisonment (i.e. feelings are structured by the age construct). Moreover, the above highlights the lack of information women are given about their rights in relation to need, and that the way they are treated is dependent upon the drivers and officers-in-charge. In *Invisible Women* Angela Devlin writes of the general disgust members of the prison service have about the use of sweat-boxes. A female governor said, 'I believe EC regulations cover conditions for livestock transportation, but contain nothing about the transport of these women' (1998:20).

The prison landscape

> Prison hardens and deadens; it concentrates: intensifies the feeling of alien-ation; it strengthens resistance. (Nietzsche 1996: 62)

The geography of state-sanctioned exclusion creates a space for a world to emerge, which requires a new survival code. Prison is not a panacea for soci-ety's ills; on the contrary, it exacerbates the violence, prejudice and discrimi-nation in society at large. The medical gaze and juridical stare intrudes into the interstices of the body. Private lives become a commodity of the penal system, which others deal with, within a public space. This has been documented at length through the voices of the women and in ex-prisoners' accounts (e.g. Arrowsmith 1970, 1983; Carpenter 1905; Dostoyevsky 1949; Kelly 1967). Serge states that prison processes bodies to 'create houses for the dead: Within these walls we are a few thousand living dead' (1977:31). The severance from the world outside compounds and reminds the women of their estrangement and dislocation from the outside:

WW: Prison is like living in a make believe world, this is so unreal you know, it's unnatural.

AW.   Why is it unreal and how is it unnatural?

WW: It's just an unreal world that you live in, everything is false.

Wan-Noor Winter

This comment recognises that the panoptic machine creates an isolated, governed, yet unreal world. The gaze, the watchful eye, is a pervasive inherent feature of prison life supported by the prison staff and the prisoners. If every-thing in prison feels false, the women, as we shall see later, argue that knowing what is 'real' enables techniques of resistance. The architecture of certain prisons 'inhibits the good'; women's prisons are placed in remote and inaccesible places, making visits by elderly parents, children, grandchildren harder, partly because of their own mobility problems and the consequent high cost of travel. This intensifies the sense of dislocation, creating greater difficulty for the elders in retaining what is felt as their 'true' identity. Ellen Evergreen believes that by going to prison she contributed to her mother's death.

EE: Well I think about my mammy, she had two strokes because of the travelling over from Ireland to visit to me was too much for her.

I miss my mammy. I miss my girls. I miss my mammy the most because I *blame* myself. She died because she had the stress of me being in jail. She had to visit me and she was *old* and *sick*. I harbour resentment towards the prison, the Home Office for not letting me see her. Just once, they could have let me see her. I just wanted to see her to say good-bye. [emphasis in original]

Ellen Evergreen
Age: 50
Time spent in prison: 11 years

Orla O'Reilly argues that the facilities for visitors at Penjara are not conducive to creating a relaxed and informal atmosphere. At one time the women were able to bring their own food to visits but that has been taken away from them. Moreover, there is the overriding presence of control and surveillance; 'the visits room is only very small. There are only five tables. We now got five cameras plus two officers':

OO: As you go off the wing through that first door, the visit room is just there [she points in the direction of the visit room]. Just have a peek in as you go pass. Um, it's a very small visit area and we used to take a tray through with a few sandwiches and a packet of biscuits and you'll take your flask through and provide the coffee. Well, all that got stopped, and now we've got vending machines, which makes it very *clinical*. They are not always filled up for visitors who have travelled – my visitors take about two and a half hours to get here, some take longer. They travel all this way and the drinks machine is empty. The visits room is only very small. There are only five tables. We now got five cameras plus two officers. And there are no facilities for the children.

Orla O'Reilly
Age: 54
Time spent in prison: 14 years

Severance from the outside world

Physical removal from society into this geography of exclusion and inclusion is further compounded by the actual location. One particular prison has become known as 'the living tomb', 'the concrete coffin', 'the 'submarine' and for others 'hell above ground'. Women in general find the sensory deprivation and cocooned nature of Penjara pushes them into finding techniques to keep hold of their sense of their selves, their life before prison. As their world outside recedes, and prison life becomes more real, holding onto the past becomes an imperative part of their survival:

AW: Do you feel that the longer you're in here the more distant you become with what's going on the outside?

AA: Oh, yes. You start to forget and that's frightening actually. You forget what it's like to look through your window at home. You see this place is very *oppressive. You never get off the wing. You don't get to see the sun, or the moon, or feel the rain on you.* [emphasis in original]

Alison Anwar

The sense of exclusion from the outside world and the claustrophobic nature of Penjara is internalised on many levels. This is a good example of the different ways in which the geography of place contributes to the sense of exclusion and severance. Anita's view from her cell overlooks no trees or gardens but 'row upon row of barbed wire'.

For one woman the severance from the outside world was magnified by the sensory deprivation of existing, not living, in a prison which has been likened by the elders to living in a 'concrete tomb'. Molly Mossdale says prison has left her:

MM: Traumatised by the sensory deprivation. We were in this old castle, the windows are way up at the top. So you never saw out unless you were on the top floor, you never saw a whole sparrow. You had five different nettings outside your own room. You never saw a whole tree or a whole sky, you didn't see a whole anything, it was like a patchwork quilt. It shut you off completely from the outside world. All you could hear were the pigeons because they were being fed but apart from that, you didn't see any birds at all.

You had a concrete yard about three times the size of this room about 9' by 12' roughly, we just went round and round. You are in a prison, which is within a prison. You never saw anything. All you could see was the top of the cathedral.

Molly Mossdale

AA: Just to get off this wing, you go through one gate and then you go through another gate and if you look over towards the other way, they have actually put a fence up just over the other side. The view from my cell is just row upon row upon row of barbed wire.

Penjara is a unique unit. There isn't another women's prison like it. *We are contained. It's claustrophobic. We come through a door for a meeting. We come through a door for gym. Another door to go to the workshop another door to visits. Another door —*

the doctor's on the wing on the men's side. The chapel's on the wing. The only time at all that you get off this wing is when you go for an hour's exercise on the exercise yard. That's all you get. [emphasis in original]

Alison Anwar

The indignities of being strip-searched is a constant reminder that they are the property of HM Prison Service, a reminder reinforced by the severance from the outside world, the policing, and regulation of their bodies:

AA: If you go to the workshop you are searched. When you come back you are searched. When you go back again in the afternoon you are searched. *Searched all the time.* [emphasis in original]

Alison Anwar

This multi-faceted assault on the body causes some women in later life to retreat from the prying gaze because as Alison states:

AA: There is no looking forward to those feelings. There are no feelings of just being able to be on your own. You are being *watched all the time.* [emphasis in original]

Alison Anwar

JJ: I couldn't sit, because there was no handle, and it stood out as a faceless door. *There was no way out.* It was a way of telling *you that you were locked in. Maybe this tells me something, that I've been in prison far too long,* long enough. I sometimes think, oh I'll be glad to be locked in tonight to get away, to be on my own. Whereas I never used to be able to cope with that time in my cell. Now I look forward to my *solitude.* [my emphasis]

Julie June

The above demonstrates how no one goes unscathed. Julie retreats into solitude, but sees this as a sign of the damage done to her by being in prison. The close and claustrophobic conditions of the first stage of the lifer's progression in the system compound the feelings of dislocation from the progression of time on the outside, of severance with the familiar, to an environment which is transitory in population and permeated by violence. These variables increase the effects of dislocation, losing the mirrors which support the habitual sense of self. This fear is exacerbated by not knowing what lies ahead, the denial of autonomy and in Julie's case not knowing when she will be released.

The women objected to the way their lives before imprisonment were excluded once they entered the prison gates. The process of homogenising the women creates tension between the women themselves as each woman occupies a different temporal space depending on what age they entered the system, how long they have been in prison and how long they have to serve. Furthermore, it calls into question the legitimacy of the system of sanctions used to regulate prisoners' behaviour.

Julie June argues that:

JJ: The *trouble* in prison and especially in Penjara is that if somebody does something *wrong that person is not punished*, the privilege of whatever is taken away. We used to be able to go to the shower in dressing gowns. But somebody started going with a towel wrapped round them or a little bit of a night-shirt showing half their bodies. The officers rather than pick that person out and say, '*You* are either on report or you don't do that again', they withdrew the privilege. I just mentioned that at the council meeting. I said, 'It's wrong that we are *all punished* for a few things that one or two do *wrong*!!. [emphasis in original]

Julie June

The incident could be rectified by correcting the misdemeanour rather than punishing the 44 women in Penjara. The prison machine is seen here as stripping the women of agency by severing connections between personal actions and their consequences. A central effect of imprisonment itself, this erosion of agency is compounded daily by the minutiae of the numerous petty punishments by means of which authority is established and enacted:

WW: You're already in prison, you shouldn't be punished again. The other day here on the house, we all had to line up against the wall like two-year-olds because these girls broke into the NACRO [National Association for the Care and Resettlement of Offenders] office. *I'm too old* to be having to do that, stand like a two-year-old in the hall. [emphasis in original]

Wan-Nita Williams

The above statement demonstrates that the age-related 'excess' of punishment is a product of Wan-Nita's own construction of the meaning of and her internalisation of her age. This is a good example of an assault on selfhood, but by a breach of the usual cultural practice of confining such treatment to the young. The modalities of punishment are a constant reminder that their bodies and possessions belong to the prison service:

ZZ: If anything on the house happens with them, *you are in trouble as well*, because you get your room turned over and everything is the same. *Strip searched*, as these druggies. That's why you should have a *house, a house for older women to go to*. A separate house. They [the prison officers] are still mixing the likes of us with all these druggies and young offenders, so if anything happens with them on the house, you are likely to get strip-searched yourself and your room turned over. A full strip search. [emphasis in original]

Zadie Zing
Age: 52
Time spent in prison: 3 months

The insidious gaze pervades all aspects of life from the intimate intrusions upon the body to the written thoughts of prisoners becoming the property of HM Prison. Letters and phone calls are important to all prisoners since they afford some contact with the outside world, but this is made difficult by the prison regime:

AA: The officers read the letters. They spend all morning sat up there in Censors,[2] reading people's mail. It's got me so I can't put down my feelings on paper. They read the mail before it is sent out and when it comes in. It's really restricting me with my letters. I don't want these people [the prison officers] to read my innermost feelings. You are cut off from the outside world. It is a terrible invasion of your privacy. I can accept them having to take it out and shake it. But to sit down and read them.

Alison Anwar

Throughout this section the elders in the study show the processes by which they develop defensive strategies to gain control and give meaning to the situation they find themselves in:

JJ: You have *to work hard* at *not becoming institutionalised.* Because you see people *being* institutionalised. I mean sometimes you go for a shower at the same time every day because you know you've only got so much time left. And sometimes I'll say to myself, 'I'm not going for a shower tonight'. And I think you fill your flask at a certain time because it is ten minutes before lock in. And I think, oh, no and you know, it's a battle. It's a battle/a struggle to keep your own, um [pause] to feel that you *are* still your own person. [emphasis in original]

Julie June

It is the fear of capitulating to the routinisation of prison life that aids the preservation of the outside self:

MM: Now you go in the telly room and turn round and say, 'I don't want to watch this tonight, do you mind if I watch the other side?', murder breaks out. So fancy letting yourself get in that state. So what I will do, I will stop my routine, I'll think hang on, like say for instance I'll go through a stage, I'll watch a lot of telly, then all of a sudden I'll stop doing that and then I'll spend more time in my room.

Margot Metcalf

The women found the landscape of exclusion, the architecture, the constant surveillance, the terse atmosphere alien to the self and it was experienced as further techniques of state-legitimated pain. This is illustrated below. For this woman and others, prison is a surreal world, where a different time order operates, where in order to survive they become 'suspended' in time:

TT: I think you just go in a sort of an area where you don't know quite – you're neither up there or down there or in the middle. *You're just suspended*, you just can't comprehend what's going on. [emphasis in original]

Tricha Tate
Age: 62
Time spent in prison: 6 months

Anna explains that for her, life in prison from the initial sentencing to incarceration can only be described as a dream, a period where you become suspended from the free world:

AA: To be honest I thought I was in a *nightmare* and when he [the judge] said 'Four and a half', I thought he meant months not years. I never even cried, you know, then they took me down and I heard my kids crying and screaming and it just hit me then; I just couldn't believe it. I thought well, I'm in a *nightmare*. I'm dreaming, somebody's going to wake me up, and say, 'No Anna, no, you didn't get four and a half years'.

Anna Arnold

The women's narratives show how, as elders, they are unaccustomed to the brusqueness of prison life from fellow women and members of staff. The process of the body reinventing itself under the disciplinary gaze increased the pains of punishment (Foucault 1977b). The elders in the study felt dis-identified, role dispossessed, disorientated and frightened by the cacophony of prison life:

YY: It is a shock when you first come into prison, you know, all these doors slamming on you, and there's officers telling you what you can and what you can't do.

Yvette Young

The pains of prison can be lessened if the prison system takes into account the differing needs and profiles of women in their 'care', explaining the nature of their induction into this 'unreal world':

YY: Cor [chuckles]. God another world – terrible. Absolutely terrible. Well it's disgusting that's all I can say about it. It's disgusting. You walk in and as soon as you walk in one of the officers said 'fresh'. You walk in and you are searched. And you don't know what you are doing. [emphasis in original]

Yvette Young

It is the not knowing, the unfamiliarity of the environment, which posits women in later life in a vulnerable position in relation to the younger women. As the gates shut and the outside world recedes, the prison begins the process of constructing the female older offender:

YY: You walk in this dirty, filthy place. You walk into a big room and you are just sitting there and all of a sudden you hear 'next'. You don't know what you've gotta do. Because you've never done it before. They class you as a *criminal. You are all the same. You've done wrong. No matter what age or what colour. You've done wrong! You're the criminal! And they* [the prison officers] *don't believe anything you say because you are a criminal. Why should they believe yer? So when I was being stripped searched and that as I said this one officer went 'fresh'.* I knew what she meant. This person hasn't been in prison before. [emphasis in original]

Yvette Young

The frustration of being denied a voice and denied rights over their bodies, and the lack of educational, recreational and adequate medical facilities available to elders, places women in later life on the edge of the penal machinery. The institutionalised violence elders face takes the form of being dismissed, degraded and denied, which further estranges the self from effective agency.

Over time the prison structure has changed cosmetically with the implementation of technology and better sanitation. It was only in 1983 that all the 16 women's prisons had full sanitation. Ellen Evergreen who, at the time of the interview, had served 11 years, recounts her first recollection of prison:

AW: What was your initial reaction to your first night in prison?

EE: Horrific. My word what a sight. The first thing I saw was Jane walking towards me with a great big potty. It was full and splashing all over the place. That was my first memory of prison. *Horrible.* [emphasis in original]

Ellen Evergreen

Cath Carter, an educated woman, a teacher by profession, found that the instability of prison life, the incomprehensible nature of the punishing regime, and the prison argot, led to a misidentification, which protected her from being used by the other women to smuggle in drugs. Her lack of knowledge of the prison world and her obvious confusion rendered her in the eyes of others a 'useless alcoholic'.

CC: The first question I was asked in Holloway, did I have visitors who would bring stuff in. I said, 'What stuff?' At which point they sort of [she sucked her teeth] and muttered, must be an alcoholic, a useless alcoholic and walked off. [We both laugh]

Cath Carter

For many of the women the clanging of the gates behind them, the harsh discordant sound of women and officers shouting, swearing and jostling was enough for them to believe they had entered 'hell above ground'. The extract below is indicative of a world of meanings and processes that are unfamiliar:

KK: When I first went into Risely it was a terrible culture shock. It was *horrendous*. I couldn't believe the things [pause] I saw, you know. When I went in there and they said take your clothes off, and put that gown on. Well I left my bra and pants on, and a screw came and screamed at me, '*All your clothes and knickers', you know*? After a while, you get used to it. If it's possible to get used to it. It is just so degrading. I'd never been so scared in my life. There were women sitting in blue gowns, effing and blinding. I wasn't used to people swearing, and I'd never been so scared. Some funny things happened. This nurse washed my hair in case I'd got nits. I said to her, 'Could you use conditioner?'

Now when I look back I think, what must they have thought. [emphasis in original]

Kate King

The initial reception into the prison world of locks, bolts, bars, handcuffs, strip-searches and an unstable transitory population was a frightening experience for the women as they enter into a world where different rules apply. The re-coding of their lives before to their lives now, the bizarre disjunction, has become a constant reminder of what has been lost and their continued punishment:

JJ: I was taken to Risley. That was my first experience of prison.

AW: And how did you find that?

JJ: Horrendous. I mean at the time I didn't know the in's and out of prison.

AW: Did anyone explain to you what Risley would be like?

JJ: No. It was on the hospital and one of the very first experiences I had which traumatised me terribly, was a male officer who um – a female officer explained that I could use the phone between a certain hour. It was like a telephone box type thing at Risley. I remember going to this particular officer and I said about using the phone. And he went you are not allowed to use the phone unless someone else told you, you could. He said, '*You what's your name?*

> *I said June. He thought I was saying my first name. He said what's your name? I said, 'June, Julie June'. He said, 'You – use your number'.* He was so nasty with me. Nobody sat down and chatted to me. This officer then said, 'You are ORO 252, *a number. Never forget that! You are no longer a name.'* I can remember thinking '*Oh golly*, what's happening?!' [emphasis in original]

> Julie June

The landscape of the prison painted by the women shows how the induction into the prison world of strip-searches, loss of control over time and prison routine serves to sever the continuity of 'knowing' and maintaining their past life experience outside the prison gates. This process enables the creation of the 'docile body' (Rabinow 1986:180) to be contained in the house of the dead. This idea of prison as a house of the dead has been described by several writers (Dickens 1985; Levi 1996, 1998; Serge 1963, 1977; Wildeblood 1955), and is reflected in a recurring theme within the transcripts of how the institution processes the women by dissociating power and agency from the body. Carpenter's assessment of prisons adequately portrays prisons today. He states that,

> Prisons are outwardly clean and decent and orderly: but inwardly what are they but withered sepulchres full of dead men's bones. (1905:120)

The prison environment and techniques of discipline attempt to efface what is known and familiar. The prison becomes a structure which contains the living dead.

The unnatural world of the prison compounded the women's sense of severance from the outside world. The hegemonic discourse of the carceral system placed all women regardless of age, health needs, ability or offence under the same pervasive carceral gaze (Howson 1998). The women, processed and introduced to what will become routine strip-searches, move from reception to their dormitories. The women bitterly resented that they were not sharing with women of a similar age. The lack of information available heightened their fear, anxiety, sense of loss and disorientation. Anita Arrowsmith's first night in prison would have been less frightening and less traumatic if she had been given a cell with women of either a similar age or a similar offence. She states that:

AA: For a woman at my age and having no previous convictions. I didn't know what I was facing, putting me in a dorm with seven youngsters. Anyway, I didn't go to bed that night. I just stood in a corner and cried *all* night.

> Anita Arrowsmith

The inmate culture of noise, drugs, sexual relationships being conducted in the dorms and the exuberance of youth made Anita's first night in prison unbearable.

AA: I don't smoke and I was put in a room with smokers. Every time I opened a window, they would close it. 'Cos they were cold. They were bashing on the doors for lights [prison slang for an officer to 'light up' women's cigarettes]. Do you know what I mean? It's like – if somebody had a heart-attack or a stroke they'd be dead before the officers come. And if it was a real emergency, you'd be dead. Nobody would have come.

Anita Arrowsmith

Forced to live under the intrusive gaze, private lives become public property. The lack of privacy, the exposure of their bodies to the purloined gaze of the younger women, and the constantly invasive and overwhelming social environment which is a pervasive feature of the total institution all served to heighten their fear and embarrassment:

AA: It was pretty awful really. I was one of seven people and they were all on drugs except me. They would be smoking drugs and all the windows would be closed and you will be locked in there with them. The next morning they'd all be throwing up. There were prostitutes and lesbians. It was awful, with only one sink and one toilet to share with seven.

Anita Arrowsmith

The stark reality of prison was brought home by the experience of being locked in with women whose behaviour and persona was unlike anything they were familiar with on the outside:

TT: I learnt more in a week about drugs and lesbians and that, you know, than in my whole sixty years of life and bringing up five children.

Tricha Tate

Another elder, Julie June, found her first night behind bars intimidating:

JJ: I was put in this *dorm* and they [the other women] told me to have this bunk. And then this really butch girl with a shaven head – came to me and said, 'Anything you need?' I went, 'No, I don't want anything thank-you'. One of the other girls explained that she was a lesbian and that she was offering her services [laughs]. That night, I didn't dare go to sleep. I thought, '*Oh please take me home*'. She had cuts here [she points to her arms], a tattoo across her neck and all her fingers were tattooed and she had her head shaven. I'd never seen any one like that before and I was absolutely horrified. [emphasis in original]

Julie June

Elders in prison have concerns about how they are marginalised within a space which aims to enable women across the life course to lead useful lives in custody and after release. Their experiences of institutional abuse, infantilisation and the denial of their rights go largely unrecognised. The social structures and processes that deny agency, coupled with the demands of the institution, create a state of institutional dependency and have profound and long-lasting effects on the individual.

Conclusion

This chapter shows how the discursive practices and physical techniques of punishment occur even before the elders are incarcerated, beginning with their journey to court and then to prison, continuing on reception and then through to the daily regime of prison life. The daily indignities incurred by the elders demonstrate that the punishment goes beyond the deprivation of liberty. The pains of imprisonment are magnified for elders by the inflexibility of the structure and the nature of a system that places elders on the periphery of prison life. Bringing elders from the margins of policy to the forefront will help alleviate the pains of imprisonment they face as a result of age discrimination. The next chapter questions the statement of purpose, which claims that it is 'our duty to look after them with humanity', implying that the prison estate is responsible for the care of its prisoners.

Notes

1   Section 5.21: 'Prior to the Woodcock inquiry women prisoners were handcuffed only in exceptional cases, where there was an unusual risk of escape or violent behaviour during escort. Since then the increased focus on security and the application of policies arising from incidents at high security prisons for men to all prisoners, including women, has placed unwarranted restrictions on women under escort. The vast majority of women are not an escape risk, nor do they pose serious danger to the public.'

The Woodcock Report was conducted by Sir John Woodcock following escapes from a male prison, HMP Whitemoor in 1994.

Section 5.22: 'We have heard of women refusing hospital treatment for serious conditions because they did not want to be cuffed in public' (HMCIP 1997:45).

2   'Censors': a place where prison officers read incoming and outgoing letters. The women reported that they have heard officers repeat contents of their letters and some women were told to re-write and omit 'lewd' descriptions.

Chapter 3

Prison Life: Now You See Me Now You Don't

I wonder who I really am,
I think I've lost me, can't you see, I just can't find the real me.
Has she gone into my dreams, can she hear my silent screams?
Who is there to understand or reach out and take my hand and tell me that
they really care?

(During the interview Wan-Nita Williams
read out this poem she had written)

The previous chapter follows the women's journey from their initial reception to court and then to prison, demonstrating the types of deprivations the elders experiences from the over-use of restraints (i.e. being double-handcuffed) to having their medication withdrawn. To divert the penal gaze from themselves, the elders, fearful and bewildered, fail to assert their rights. This chapter will show how women in later life recognise how the system pushes elders to the margins of prison life. The overall theme of this chapter is to demonstrate how, from the woman's perspective, the prison regime, the perceptions of and responses of the staff (and the way they are dealt with by the system) results in an assault on their identity. These disciplinary assaults are always mediated by particular forms of resistance/accommodations on the part of the women. To preserve their sense of self, the women condition and constitute the meaning of their imprisonment as women who are in later life and in prison. Rather like Lewis Carroll's heroine in *Alice in Wonderland* (1971), the women enter an inexplicable new world with different rules. This realm was entered in part through changes in the way that they were defined by the penal jigsaw, their reflexive selves and by the younger women. To understand the experiences of 'old' women in the criminal justice system, one must examine the discourses that give meaning to, inform and cloak their experiences of imprisonment. The process of the carceral world inscribes new meanings upon the gendered and embodied identity.

It is the interplay between all these aspects which defines the overall prison experience (Hockey 1983, 1989). These distinctions are important because much of the material is analysed in terms of the way women partly take up and use hegemonic discourse. It is through disciplining the body via the architecture, regime, space, time, and the constant intrusion and violation of the juridical/penal gaze[1] upon the body that the 'sartorial' mask is formed. Through the voices of women in later life one can trace their carceral experience.

This chapter examines how women in later life begin to 'live life in the shadows' of prison life via the regulatory impact of the penal 'jigsaw' upon their self-identities. As elders in prison are rendered invisible by the operational needs of the prison estate and through the lack of adequate provision, the lack of differentiation between women results in elders withdrawing to the shadows of prison life. As they enter into the mechanics of the prison world, elders are denied aspects of their identity on the basis of ageist and gendered assumptions but yet remain within the regime of gendered subjectification. Moreover, it is evident in all the scripts that elders are aggrieved that once in prison, their offence-free life outside and their maturity counts for nothing: they are still treated the same, regardless of their behaviour inside:

AA: You get put in prison and you automatically become a liar; *they think*, you're a *liar*, you are a *thief*, you are a *drug smuggler*. They don't make allowances for *normal people*. [emphasis in original]

Alison Anwar

The interconnecting modalities of penal power and the accumulation of assaults on their identity are insidiously less visible than the eighteenth-century mechanisms of disciplining, regulating and punishing women who not only break the law but who have offended their gender role. Their life threads as they age in prison become finer, in the process of becoming inculcated and enculturated into the carceral realm in which they find themselves.

Assaults on the self

The tense atmosphere of violence, overcrowding and fear seeps into every part of prison life, increasing the pains of imprisonment. The state delivery of legitimised pain operates on many levels and the pains of imprisonment are multiplied by the lack of appropriate facilities and acknowledgement of differing needs, pushing women into yet further exclusion. In other words, pain becomes invisible within discourses which are legitimised by imprisonment, i.e. rehabilitation, punishment/deterrence via some abstract 'loss of liberty', which is supposed to be essentially bad and yet at the same time somehow not materially painful. The reality of the physical and mental pain suffered by prisoners is actually the 'flaw' or 'contradiction' in the carceral ideology, hence it is often played down.

The internal geography of the prison landscape homogenises all women regardless of need or age to a reducible object, the prison number, a common denominator. The carceral laboratory, the prison, processes the body within a system with the

VV: *other type of fodder* [in mind]. *They know* it is a *steady stream all the time. Isn't it? So everything is geared to them, the* [younger women]. [emphasis in original]

Veronica Vicar

Another elder, Julie June explains how on her first day she was told that she was now a prison number:

JJ: This officer than said you are ORO 272 [changed to ensure anonymity], *a number. Never forget that! You are no longer a name.* [emphasis in original]

Julie June

The elders found that their age and their femininity are constructed very differently from those of the younger woman. The prison fails to address, but at the same time inadvertently rewrites and ambushes, the women's sense of self with the prison's mould.

Surrounded by fear, the abstract and intimate intrusions of the penal gaze, the women survive by removing themselves to the periphery of prison life. This enactment of self-withdrawal reflects the wider lack of recognition that elders are in prison. Moreover, this lack of recognition entails a failure to understand the differing ideological, physiological and psychological needs of women in later life. Alison Anwar states:

AA: They prefer people who swear and shout and who are common, and who go around in gangs and sit around in each other's cells. They [the prison officers] have no idea how to deal with somebody like me who is quiet and doesn't swear, and keeps herself to herself. This doesn't mean I'm not a friendly person. It's like they [the prison officers] did a report the week before. Your personal officer[2] writes down what kind of person, they put things down like 'She's buried her head in the sand'. 'She doesn't socialise.' I am on the phone every day to my family.

Alison Anwar

The above extract reflects the lack of fit between the framework within which the women are viewed and that within which they view themselves. Under a penal construction Alison is seeing a self whom she cannot recognise. To survive this new but closed world she has entered, remaining in touch with her previous life outside is vital. Indignant at the remarks made in her report, Alison finds their lack of comprehension at why she doesn't socialise unbelievable:

AA: And then they say you don't socialise. I don't particularly want to socialise with people like that. To be locked up with people like that. As soon as you get up on a morning you have to be with them. You can't get away from them. The only time you are away from them is when you are locked in. Plus the environment. It's something really you can't explain. For another person to know just how bad it is that person would have to experience it. I don't just mean come in and spend a couple of weeks here knowing at the end of two weeks you were going home again. You would have to have that *fear* in your mind, that was it for the next fifteen or twenty years. Can you try and imagine how that would make you feel?

Alison Anwar

Alison describes the constant psychological attack on her personal identity brought on by not knowing when, or if, she will be released. Others such as Molly found the sensory severance and the environment of Penjara impacting on her sense of personal identity, transforming her from a rather active and body-conscious young woman to one who became lethargic and overweight in the first two years of imprisonment. At the same time, the effects of the regime stripped her of her sense of self:

MM: When I came to Penjara, I went from nine stones up to sixteen stone. That was due to sheer comfort eating.

She continues that the prison is:

MM: Taking away our ability to think for ourselves. Taking away any feelings that you can be responsible for your own destiny, that you can have self-respect. Self-respect has just gone out of the window.

Molly Mossdale

In contrast to the above, it is this process of the effacement of identity and personal autonomy by the prison regime which makes prison a 'hazard rather than a deterrent'(Molly Mossdale).

Kate's coping mechanism was to control her body weight:

KK: I started putting my finger down my throat and that kind of thing.

I'm still very, very conscious about my weight so I suppose yes, it's not left me. It's common in here. You have so much time in here on your hands that I suppose eating does comfort you and when you're missing people and the longing that you feel to see them. I mean you have to supplement that longing with something, don't you? So I think that eating disorders are created by the problems we have. You see, the only thing we have control over in here is our bodies.

Kate King

Women in later life find that, once in prison, personal space and physical space have to be reconfigured in light of the pressures of living side by side with other women and the restricted space within prison. The environment places all women regardless of age, ability, mobility and ethnicity in a social structure which attempts to cultivate clones, thus discriminating against and further excluding women in later life:

MM: I think too many of the officers have no respect for older people. We are all lumped together as criminals. They don't realise that we have got separate needs. They don't realise that we are getting older and their day will come as well. We can't do the things at the speed that everybody else does.

Molly Mossdale

This comment is representative of how women of this age feel. This jail-craft of gates, bolts and locks and the re-moulding of the body places all women under a universal stare. The lack of recognition of difference leads women in later life to place themselves behind the scenes in order to survive. Veronica Vicar argues that:

VV: The prison officers only know how to deal with the sort of young ruffian element. You know it's like quiet polite older women and girls – it amazes me, they tend to find them quite threatening [she laughs]. Just because, they don't know how to box with them. They have only been trained to deal with the younger women. I don't know what the training consists of but you know if you're sort of a drug taking ruffian they seem much more at ease with. And then of course, you are older than the majority of officers. They [the officers] don't know what to do with us.

Veronica Vicar

The noise, and the generational differences in language and modes of femininity, place women in later life in an isolated, confined, lonely and vulnerable space. Withdrawing from the night-time activities is also a mode of resistance to the possible assaults on self. Alison echoes these sentiments:

AA: All this shouting and then you've got all the different music from all the other cells. It's a wonder, it doesn't send you insane. I mean there are times when you do feel like a really boring, *miserable* old person because you're not walking about like this [she clicks her fingers]. But having said that I'm not going to change because of that. Why should I change? [emphasis in original]

Alison Anwar

It is important to recognise how Alison uses 'I' in the last sentence. Here the attitude expressed in this statement reflects a sense of identity, which is partly defined by her own determination to resist the pressure to change. The experiences so far have shown how they progress from the centre to the periphery in order to do their time quietly, to retain a sense of self in a system in which the consequence is to construct a prison identity.

Even authority figures are left waiting as the younger women push past. It is the differing socialisation patterns of femininity and expectations of women growing up in the 1940s and 1950s which juxtaposes its habitual itinerant to how elders manage their identity in prison. Rather than learning to survive by becoming like some of the younger women, older women are resigned to the fact that they are the last ones in the queues, the last ones in the dining hall and the least likely to get what they want.

MM: The young ones never want to queue but they all want to push.

Margot Metcalf

PP: Queues are another matter. There are some people who habitually sort of jump the queue. But I think, you have to make a decision, is it really that important that it is worth making a stand about it. Um – it is probably not going to achieve anything at the end of the day. Or is it better to just let it go and resign yourself to always being the last one in the queue.

Come to think about it, it's the older women get pushed to the end of the queue. I think possibly we tend to be a little more courteous and we stand back. Um rather than pushing in. I mean quite often, I have stood at a door to allow an officer to walk through and then ended up with about fifteen others going through, pushing past the officer as well.

Petra Puddepha

Elders avoid certain times such as association because, as Yvette and Gertie argue:

YY: You can't watch what you like on the television because of the youngsters. They'll all start giggling and you can't watch it anyway. It's so degrading.

Yvette Young

For Gertie, like many others in the study, it is the degree of noise and intimidation that prevents her from participating and exercising her right to watch television:

GG: The noise does my head in. And when you go in there they have the television on too loud. They can't have it at a normal tone. They have to have it on full belt. I just walk up and get out. Older women are easy targets for the younger women. They ask you things. I'll be hearing those voices in my sleep saying, 'Have you got this?' 'Have you got that? 'Have you got the other?' They are always asking for things and I think that's because I am older. If I have a brew, they'll ask if there's any going. It does my head in because every time you do anything, it is *'Save* me some of this', *'Save* me some of that'. It does my head in. I'd rather be bored rather than sit there and listen to them.

Gertie Grangley

And Cath Carter argues that:

CC: You don't have minority rights. I mean – I have not seen one programme on television I want to see. I don't even try. The majority want to watch *Coronation Street* followed by another one, *EastEnders,* followed by *Brookside* etc.

Cath Carter

Some experience overt displays of love between the younger women and the lack of modesty as 'unnecessary':

MM: You've got to realise that a lot of these young ones – there's a lot of trouble and most of the trouble is caused by drugs, smokes and lesbianism. What I mean to say, who the blinking heck is that sitting in the common room? They've got their arms round each other kissing, I mean who wants to see that? It's unnecessary. I mean, I've got nothing against these girls, I get on all right with them. But you know if I could choose, I would move on a different house with older people because there are two main things with the young ones, lesbianism and drugs.

Margot Metcalf

The competition for space in prison, such as owning a seat in the television room or the time spent queuing to use the phones, creates the space and time for women in later life to be further victimised by other women:

PP: I think there's a lot of intimidation. Verbal intimidation. Particularly over the telephones. You can imagine it is a *life-line to every girl* in this place and a lot of them stretch it. They'll go over their ten minutes and if you tell them, you'll get a load of verbal abuse. There is a lot of intimidation here.

Petra Puddepha

Veronica Vicar withdraws from the association room:

VV: I sort of think, oh well, I won't just watch the television. You know you don't want any trouble – you could have confrontations twenty times a day.

Veronica Vicar

The fear of reprisals and derision from the other women prevents many of the elders from using what facilities there are. Their age and capacity to be intimidated becomes a source of amusement for others; Molly Mossdale became the butt of one of the younger women's jokes, when:

MM: They [the younger girls] hid my sticks, because they thought I was joking about my disability and then they realised that I wasn't messing about. They don't do it now – they realise you are not faking because you literally can't move. They will suddenly realise because the officer will come and say, 'You were late for check[3], what happened?' I've lost my sticks, somebody was playing around.

Molly Mossdale

Rebecca Rose, aged 73, found herself at the receiving end of a practical joke which resulted in her being admitted to the hospital:

RR: One night she hid behind the door and I just came out of the shower. She jumped, and I nearly jumped out of my skin and I screamed, you know? It really frightened me, but it was only a joke. I couldn't breathe, the doctors had to come out.

Rebecca Rose

Life in the shadows

The prison landscape cultivates and structures the meaning of imprisonment for elders in a way which is strikingly different from the meaning for younger women. Elders in prison find the regime, the noise, language and the denial of femininity alien in ways which are generation specific and, furthermore, act as a variant of penal punishment. The lack of acknowledgement and sensitivity to the needs of elders in prison places elders, as we have seen, on the outer margins of prison life. The process of being denied and rendered invisible by the penal jigsaw is a complex one of re-coding the body which can be seen as a project orchestrated by the prison to cultivate and shape the women's identities.

Women in later life, especially if they are first-time offenders, escape to their dorms or single cells, disengaging from the activities because of the pervasive air of violence and intimidated by the 'hardened young habitual criminal'. Moreover, there are some women who would prey upon their naiveté about the prison culture and try and get the older women to hold drugs for them, pass on messages and play other subordinate roles within the prison hierarchy. A letter received from Sheila Bowler, who in 1998, after five years in jail, was acquited of the crime of murdering an aged aunt, states that:

SB: I have known elderly women to be very intimidated by the 'hardened' young habitual criminal who regards prison as their second home, and they try to get prisoners older than themselves to hold drugs in their room thinking that they are not so likely to have a 'spin' [an unexpected search of a prisoner's cell] as the young offender with a long history of drug abuse.

She further states:

SB: There is a danger of coming across a mature woman who is a habitual criminal, perhaps having indulged in fraud over a number of years and who befriends an unsuspecting older woman, conning her into giving all sorts of favours. The staff although aware of the situation will do nothing to stop it except perhaps have the offending person 'shipped'[4] to another prison.

In order to do their time quietly, and to avoid situations such as these, women in later life remove themselves from potentially volatile situations:

OO: It is egg-shell time all the time I think and that's how I view prison anyway. A continuous walking on egg-shells. It's hard. It's mind blowing sometimes and I just like retreating to my room. It's safer there.

I never come out in the evenings apart from to make a cup a tea or have my shower. I come out at quarter to eight to go for the last check [see note[3]] and I

am in my room. I can't remember the last time I spent the evening watching
television here.

Olivia Ozga

These acts of withdrawal from prison life becomes misconstrued by the other
women as 'snobbishness', and by the officers as 'not dealing with their new
surroundings'. They are punished by the label that others place on them, and
when reports state that they have buried their heads in the sand, as in Olivia
Ozga's case. Their conduct and quiet disposition allow officers to render their
needs and requests secondary to those of other women. As Veronica Vicar
states:

VV: Those who cry the loudest get the most attention. So you see, older women
don't do that. And we don't get the help that we are entitled to. But you know
a young girl, that is pecking at them 24–7, will get what she wants. But that's
prison.

Veronica Vicar

Other elders, unwilling to play the game or battle with the carceral machine,
survive the onslaughts on their identity by withdrawing completely from
officers and from the other women. It is a fear of not knowing the rules and
nuances of the game that places them on the fringes of prison life, unwilling to
subject themselves to further indignities. This makes their time in prison one
of extreme loneliness, but at the same time, it shows their resilience and forti-
tude in an unnatural environment:

AA: I don't like to complain in case I get into trouble. Therefore you are lowering
yourself all the time. In other words you are like begging. You are frightened
to ask because you are seen to be playing up.

Anita Arrowsmith

Such 'practices of the self' (Rose 1990) are used to negotiate the change in
environment and preserve their relational, refracted selves. It is through
creating a network between the way they are constructed by the prison and
the way they affirm continuities with the self, i.e. their life before prison, that
the elders make do in prison. They are aware that through active disengagement, they are re-configuring the way they present their needs within a
system where their voices are often unheard.

The harsh discordant sounds of prison life, the bullying and the vulnerability that elders feel within this environment are salient features of prison life.
Once in the system, elders describe the process of acculturation and inculca-

tion of prison life as one which starves the body from being a receptacle of experience and knowledge to the point of creating a catatonic form. Alison succinctly argues this point:

AA: You have to try and be different and break the pattern – not be like a zombie and just follow everyone around and do what – You see, that is what they [the prison] want, when you are put in prison, they want you to just accept everything. They want full control. If you're fighting, if you are appealing, if you just don't float through the system like they [the prison officers] want you to, they [the prison officers] don't like it. They [the prison officers] hate it when you say you are innocent and you are fighting. And you've got people on your side fighting for you. They seem to resent people who have got support. People who do have regular visits, regular phone calls. People bringing them things in.

Alison Anwar

The harsh surfaces of the prison architecture, the regime, the use of time in prison and the process by which their refracted selves become the property of the prison service, disorientate women in later life. For some it is the language used by other women that is threatening, while for others it is the way some of the younger women look, covered in tattoos or carrying open wounds resulting from self-harming, that prevents elders from participating in communal spaces. Alison Anwar finds that the prison environment is very much:

AA: Dog eat dog in here. I have been bullied. I have been threatened. You get pushed to the back of the queue. People push in. I've never ever come across *such ignorant, bad-mannered, foul mouthed, crude* – You know I have never ever heard things like it in my life. [emphasis in original]

Alison Anwar

Types of punishment

The tense atmosphere, the jangling of keys, the blaring of music and cries of distress encourage women in later life to resist the homogenising effects of prison life by withdrawing from every aspect of prison life to the haven of their cell:

AA: They like come alive on a night. But as I say I don't bother, I just go in my room and just lock the door behind me and that's it.

Anita Arrowsmith

ZZ: Too many rules and regulations here. I just keep myself to myself here. I don't really bother too much here. I just get up in the morning, work, go to bed at night. I don't really bother. I don't ask the officers for *nothing*. I don't really talk to them if I don't have to. [emphasis in original]

Zadie Zing

Yvette Young, a first-time offender in prison for a non-violent offence, averred that:

YY: You get treated the same as the younger ones. *Well you do.* I think I'm not going to jump the fences at my age and things like that. And you still get treated the *same*. I don't like the way us older women are treated. I don't know really I – I feel as if I am always looked down upon. [emphasis in original]

Yvette Young

Effects of punishment

Although ground down by the system, the governance of the self deflects the institutional gaze, sealing an inward face. The strategies of subversion employed enable a preservation, a protection and the closeting of refracted selves from the prying gaze – for example, by transposing the prison world into a world of scholarship. Another woman copes with the prison regime by reinventing and transforming a humiliating and degrading experience into one which allows her to take control of the gaze, the violation and the situation. Nevertheless, Julie is being controlled by the necessity to transform her personality; the prison produces the quality of 'brazenness', so the act of resistance/transformation itself also 'scorches the body'. This is how the prison does its work of inscribing 'on the body':

JJ: The [first time you] strip off. It is a *really degrading thing.* For a long time it used to bother me. And if I knew I was due for a search or if you knew the wing was closed down, I'd think, '*Oh God, they'll be coming in a minute. They'll be coming and I have to take my clothes off*'. You see how I have changed. I've changed and I've become stronger and I think to myself, I whip it off. And they say, 'Don't take your bottoms off before you put your top back on'. I think, well, *blow you*, because what's the difference, I'm being stripped stark naked. So I just throw everything off now. I can't say I like doing it. But it's my *bravado.* If you do it like that really quickly I feel as if *they* take a step back. They are more *embarrassed than I am.* [emphasis in original]

Julie June

The strip-search is a disempowering experience, a technique which renders the woman helpless, reinforcing her lack of control over those who survey, gaze, police and govern the most intimate surfaces of her body. The profaned bodies as constructed by the corporal reality of the prison world negotiate the disciplinary gaze into purloined looks. Wan-Nita Williams found ways to subvert these techniques of control by controlling the strip-search. Again, the prison experience is inscribed on the body via the medium of the woman's act of resistance:

WW: Somebody said to me once you know, because I used to get very upset when I had to strip and they said to me, what you do is; if you do it really quickly, you peel off all your clothes right, you quickly rip off your knickers and hand it, and as you're handing your knickers, just twirl around and you're in *control* of the spin. That day I had this white lacy body on me, all in one thing, so I slowly took off my clothes, peeled off my blouse, peeled off my leggings. [emphasis in original]

Wan-Nita Williams

It is through these bodily practices that the elders transformed their gendered habitus, thus creating identities for themselves which transgress the boundaries of what it is to be an elder female in prison. The bodily betrayal of the ageing body furthers the pains of imprisonment when women are subjected to a degrading violation of privacy. Many of the women find the process of being strip-searched by a woman half their age exacerbates the pains of punishment. Because women of this generation grew up with femininity embracing modesty, this punishment in effect is robbing elders of their femininity and reinforces their loss of dignity. Consequently, elders are further punished for their lack of femininity by a procedure whose punishing effect is specifically tailored for women. The extract above illustrates how the women control how the strip-search is conducted. The performance controls the watchful disciplinary gaze, the time taken and the manner in which the strip-searches are conducted, undermining the disciplinary effect of official regulations governing the procedure:

WW: I stood for a moment in this white lacy body and I thought I'll just let them see how well I look for the age of fifty, and then I peeled it right off and handed it, twirled around, carried on laughing and that is the first time ever I've dealt with a strip like that. Whereas before I used to get really distressed and everything.

Wan-Nita Williams

The above section describes how the capillaries of institutional power intersect and intrude upon the lives of the women reaching into and onto every part of the 'body', processing the outside refracted selves through to the institutionalised prison body. Moreover, these responses to the strip-search, or withdrawing to uncharacteristic solitude, are examples of taking power which is equated with doing something which may be perceived as a 'violation' or 'distortion' of the habitual self-image. To the women concerned, this may feel like a behaviour which is 'not-self' but voluntarily chosen to protect the valued aspects of self, as an enforced act of 'not-self' eroding the sense of personal integrity, or as a positive addition to the personal repertoire, a sort of enrichment of self by discovering new ways of coping.

Servers of prison time

I try to hide behind a mask,
So no one else can see.
I even make believe you know
that I am *really free*.

I just pretend that it's not real.
Then I know that I won't feel
the sorrow that comes in my head
when I wish that I was dead.

Wan-Nita Williams

As we have seen, the women survive by constructing a mask motif which is seen initially as something which is put on by the women, but is also separate from the self and is very much a response to the social world of the prison and the expectations placed upon them by the system and by the other women. The mask motif is employed to interpret and give meaning to their environment and ageing bodies. Thus, as the mask motif becomes inscribed within their performativity, it raises the question of what the regulatory impact of stereotypes of criminal/deviant women is on the behaviour of other women inside prison. The inscriptions placed upon the performing outward mask can in turn counter/resist/subvert hegemonic discourse. Furthermore, this engagement connects the varied/multi-faceted technologies of corporeal, carceral and self inscriptions. The meanings inside and outside prison connect women in later life to the outside world by which they manage the meanings of the prison world. Identity management is vital in order to survive the inmate culture through providing the means to recede from the prison gaze, creating a space that allows women across the life course privacy of the self. This tacit knowledge re-creates women in later life as knowing agents within a system which attempts to suppress the sense of self by re-creating their identity and their knowledge of the outside world, in order to 'produc[e] and shap[e] an obedient subject' (Foucault 1977b:225). Prison becomes a project of the body, one of perpetual surveillance subject to indefinite discipline and an interrogation without limits:

TT: You had to show people that you weren't going to be sort of bullied and that. You had put on a false front, if you know what I mean. If they [saw that] you were vulnerable and that then you would probably get picked on by the youngsters. If you are new in, people sort of intimidate and, you know, have this off you, and want that off you.

Tokwan Thomas

The women respond to the writing by the penal scribes on the body by utilising a masking insignia. The mask mediates the relationship between the appearance and the essence. This is not to argue that they are separate identities but one in which the governance of identity boundaries blur between the appearance and the essence creating new possibilities. In other words, the body becomes a resource, which can be managed in a variety of ways in order to construct and protect a version of the self from the gaze of the prison jigsaw:

AA: The way to survive in prison is to put on this *mask*, a tough exterior. The more you swear, the more you shout, then nobody takes advantage of you because they are too afraid to. But when you are quiet and they know you are not going to say anything to them that's when they know they can get away with it you see.

Alison Anwar

The mask becomes not only a shield from the intrusive glare of the prison machine, but a survival strategy, a coping mechanism in a turbulent and violent environment. One can argue that the mask becomes an extension of refracted selves, the sartorial outward facing mask (Biggs 1999; Connor 1999; Tseëlon 1995). In other words through force of circumstance, an element of the refracted self becomes an organising feature of the coping persona:

PP: I think that um you have to learn if you like to cover your emotions quite a lot, you appear to be perhaps more passive than in fact you are inside [laughs]. I think sometimes that it works against older women because we don't shout loud enough, a lot of time. We tend not to be catered for if you like.

Petra Puddepha

The last two quotes contrast the kind of mask they refer to. In the first, the mask is the tough exterior, but in the second the mask is 'more passive than you are inside'. Therefore, in the first quote, shouting is seen as a cover-up; in the second it is seen as an expression of the real feelings. In both cases the elder is a public object, who physically keeps quiet, keeps out of the way and is also at the same time being invisible, pushed to the periphery and placed in the shadows. It is by not being 'catered for' that the subjectivity of the elder is hidden, marginalised, regardless of behaviour. The outward mask manifests itself in a multi-faceted way.

PP: Most of us are walking round with masks on. The real people underneath, you very seldom get to see.

Petra Puddepha

The body, a malleable receptacle, produces mechanisms which aim to reinforce, preserve and protect life in prison even in the most extreme conditions. Molly Mossdale describes the degradation and humiliation of having to slop out in the mid-1970s:

MM: At Penjara we had to slop out, it was disgusting. We were potty trained again. We had a bucket of cold water, you had your flask and if you came on – *God help you.* There was nothing you could do about it. You couldn't clean. You couldn't do anything. You can't have a woman who is on and not clean. Privacy was non-existent because the officers could come round when you were sitting on a bucket. It was disgusting – it was so degrading. We had to be searched every single week and all your belongings, clothes were on the corridor, for all to see and you had to put it back again. [emphasis in original]

Molly Mossdale

It is because of the constant invasion of personal space that elders find ways of maintaining their own private space. In this example, Molly refuses to discuss her illnesses with her personal prison officer and she 'keeps [her] nursing things for the nursing staff':

MM: We haven't got much privacy. I would rather keep my nursing things for the nursing staff and not spread around the prison. There is no privacy here, everyone else gets to know, it gets too much. You are not a person, *you are a number.*

Molly Mossdale

As the carceral reality ambushes her physical and spiritual being, she resists the penal re-coding of her body[5] to the recess of her mind. It is her body which is placed in the public domain of carceral

power, a visible aspect of the person as distinct from the 'private', the subjective self:

MM: In the mean time they took away all my self-esteem and self-dignity. At least
they can't take away my mind, they can't take away my academic achieve-
ments. They can take everything else away. You know, it is hard to respect
yourselves when you have to undress in front of people. It is hard when you
have to be searched every single week, and your possessions are touched by
people and they are messed around and every letter is looked through, day
after day you are reminded you can't be trusted, you can't have any responsibility. It wears away after twenty years. I don't think I'll ever really lose that.

Molly Mossdale

The proliferation of the gaze, the incommensurability of generational discourse, and prison nuances polarise the frightening culture of prison life and
encourage women in later life to withdraw into their cells. Throughout, the
mask metaphor is used by the women to describe a series of tactical game-like
moves to ensure survival. It is indicative of how the body resists and negotiates
the social meaning produced externally and internally by the women:

AW: What are the mind games?

WW: Just making you strip, making you squat, holding back your mail, repeating
what's in your letters to other people, loads of little things.

Wan-Nita Williams

The process of finding techniques capable of negotiating the iron cage of
prison bureaucracy, the jail craft of the 'locks, bolts and bars' make demands
on sometimes fragile and limited personal resources. As Cath Carter describes:

CC: Psychologically it is very tough. You are in a community. You need community skills to survive. You also need a strong sense of self-esteem which we
don't all have by any means. So you have to work on it, otherwise you will be
pushed and prison seems to be geared to grinding you down.

Cath Carter

Conclusion

The elders have shown their ability to draw upon different life threads to resist
and modify the capillary force of prison life. It has been demonstrated
through the voices of the elders that shared and conflicting discourses can be
woven together in different ways, just as numerous patterns can be made from
a few colours on a single loom. In this battle there are none who come through

unscathed. Inevitably, some fare better than others in negotiating the capillaries of power.

The elders' accounts illustrate how the effects of the total institution are mediated by the women's own attempts at maintaining a conception of themselves as active, controlling agents. These acts of resistance are experienced as sources of strength and personal power, but also as necessary and resented accommodations, alien to self.

Notes

1   For Foucault, 'juridical' power produced the category of criminal – i.e. it deals with acts and their punishments, 'carceral' power produced the category of 'delinquent' – i.e. it deals with personality types, their genesis and their treatment (i.e. it deals in the disciplining of the person). One of Foucault's points is that juridical discourse has been infiltrated by carceral discourse because 'punishment' is seen out of step with the hegemonic discourse of pathology and rehabilitation. It has to couch itself in the same terms, thus leading to differential application of the law to different people (i.e. sentences influenced by social/psychological factors as well as the illegal status of the act. It is in this area that the analysis of 'normality' and 'pathology'/'deviance' as applied to women fits in well with Foucault's analysis – i.e. the influence of the carceral ideology on the application of judicial power giving rise to the effects of the discourses of femininity and of 'chivalry' etc., producing anomalies in the sentencing of women. It is interesting to note the infiltration of juridical power by outside discourse in the way the concept of legality becomes (and always has been) a battlefield between conflicting discourses. These days, the conflict is often between the discourse identified by Foucault which manufactures 'pathological types' and rehabilitative practices, and the popular practice of demanding retribution (c.f. the media-orchestrated campaigns for retribution against the killers of Jamie Bulger and Sarah Payne), which inevitably resulted in a political over-riding of the juridical and carceral side.

2   Each prisoner is allocated a personal officer who has a duty to look after that prisoner's interests and share work with the prison probation officer and other personnel in relation to sentence planning, etc.

3   Prison colloquialism for when they are called to sign the check list.

4   'Shipped' means being moved to another prision, often without warning, sometimes as a disciplinary measure, but often for operational reasons.

5   I am using the 'body' to denote the public, visible aspect of the person as distinct from the 'private' and the subjective self.

Chapter 4

Running Out of Time

The use of the word 'time' in the title of the book is deliberately ambiguous. Time is multi-dimensional and can be used as a form of disciplinary control and at the same time it is harnessed by the women. This chapter will explore how conceptions of time in prison were structured and how time was used and managed by elders in prison. The oscillation of time from the outside to the closed world is feared, relished and relinquished, a medium which gives a different meaning to age. What this chapter will attempt to do is to make visible the time-frames in prison, although these are difficult to describe, to get hold of and ultimately to pin down.

Challenging time

A number of commentators have noted (Giddens 1981, 1987, 1991a) that there is a limited discussion about temporality in sociology, criminology and in gerontology. The former (sociology), at least in the past and excluding the work of Adam (1990, 1995) and Davis (1990), lays emphasis on the grand narratives such as structural functionalism rather than on conflict, change and progress (Sorokin and Merton 1990; Thrift 1990; Zerubavel 1990). It has been argued by Clark (1977 cited in Hassard 1990a), that the sociological research process has been 'synchronic rather than longitudinal' (1990a: 110): that is, it has stressed the enduring features of structure rather than the flux and dynamics of change. The latter (gerontology) has been reduced to the study of rites of passage: life begins, we age, and then we die which is the only certainty we have in a post-modern world (Dollimore 1999; Elias 1978, 1992; Erickson 1983). The march of time structures our biological 'living clocks' (Ward 1971 cited in Gervitch 1990), which in turn control our physical biographies. Heidegger stated flatly, 'there is no time without man' (cited in Lewis and Weigart 1990:78) and it is precisely this that this chapter will be analysing within the framework of prison time.

Our everyday communications are littered with references to time: we speak of clock time and winter time, good times and bad times, of the right time, of a time that flies and time that takes its toll. We live in, and by, and are caught in time and it is thus not surprising that 'time' is one of the most frequently used nouns in the English language. We are also surrounded by pictures of time. The iconography of time has been appropriated to a male persona, changing over time from the Destroyer associated with death and destruction, or the Reaper equipped with the sickle/scythe, to that of the omnipotent, benevolent patriarch, Father Truth and Old Father Time (Davis 1990). Despite changes in iconography, time never changes gender and this idea of gendered time is under-theorised in the latter two disciplines (criminology and gerentology) (Davis 1990, Olsen 1980; Osborne 1995). It is noteworthy that in Greek mythology two distinct, albeit related aspects of time are represented by the male god Chronos, god of chronology, successive time, and his sister Karios, god(dess) of cyclical time as observed in the changing of seasons and the reproductive cycle. Interestingly, it is the former which survives in contemporary European languages, and which arguably predominates in a culture structured by consumer capitalism (with its emphasis on 'progress' and obsolescence, and the commodification of the person which gives rise to the sense of old age as a time to 'give way' to the more valued younger members of society). This is not to say that there is something 'essentially masculine' and 'feminine' about these two aspects of time, nor that the structuring of time-consciousness under capitalism can in any simple sense be explained as residing in its 'patriarchal' character. Nevertheless, given the continued cultural (and economic) centrality of reproduction, parenting and grand-parenting in the lives of most women, and the continued association of masculinity with the public world of status acquired through career progression and increasing authority over younger men (which is then lost on retirement or through skill-obsolescence), it is still meaningful to argue that the dominance of chronological, external, commodified 'clock-time' serves to distort or under-represent female experience and values. Perhaps a more relevant way of putting it is that women's experience of time in the sense of progression through the life-span is typically structured by 'generational' roles (e.g. daughter, mother, grandmother) which constitute core aspects of identity. As we shall see, the experience of imprisonment thrusts elder female offenders into a temporal order, whereupon time becomes a quantifiable commodity to be taken away, or ingeniously endured, and where clock time and calendar time become the key technologies for stripping offenders of autonomy, identity and self-definition.

The history of time

The concept of time in sociological theory was directed by what is generally termed the French tradition, in particular the writings of Durkheim (1961). In *The Elementary Forms of the Religious Life* (1961), Durkheim illustrates how the ordering of time is a product of the collective consciousness, a 'rhythm of collective life dominat[ing] and encompass[ing] all particular durations' (1961:69). For Durkheim, then, time is an abstract, objectively given concept derived from social life interlocking into a plethora of temporal activities.

The point here is that the experience of time is structured by the knowledge of our mortality, which imparts an urgent need to value our use of time. Time is thus experienced as an ordered, sequential development, which travels in one direction, more often than not is perceived as a movement from the past to the present and then on towards the future (Rabinbach 1992). Thus, the essence of time-punishment is time which cannot be recaptured.

The dualism of cyclical and linear time mirrors other naturalistic dualisms, for example: old/young; female/male; good/evil; reversibility/irreversibility; mind/body; and nature/culture (Davis 1995; Duncan 1998; Gervitch 1990; Hawking 1988). In the words of Elias (1992: 8) 'time cannot be understood on the basis of a conception of the world split into "subject" and "object".' The separation into natural and cultural time, he continues, is an illusion, the 'artificial product of an erroneous development within science' (ibid).

The contemporary industrial way of work and its fundamental dependence on clock time is associated with the development of cities and urbanisation. More than 50 years before Thompson's (1967) seminal essay, *Time, Work – Discipline and Industrial Capitalism*, Weber (1930), in *The Protestant Work Ethic and the Spirit of Capitalism*, identified a link between capitalist principles and practices and capitalism's utilitarian, economic approach to time. Franklin expressed the commodification of time in his famous adage: 'Remember that time is money', which was placed on the one cent coin (Lash and Urry 1994:226). Time became a valuable resource tied to work, capital and gain. It became an economic variable like labour, capital and machinery, a resource that had to be handled economically. The contemporary approach to time clearly denotes a historical move away from working *in* time towards working *with* time which has now moved to working *for* time. Marx comments that 'man is nothing; he is, at most, the carcass of time' (Marx and Engels 1976: 127).

During the industrial revolution there was a growing workers' conscious-ness of labour in which 'time' became assigned a specific value intruding upon identities, disciplining the body into regimes and sequences of activity. Within this development of industrialisation, time became a valued commod-ity. Through the seminal work of Marx and Engels (1976), Postone (1978, 1996) and Thompson (1967), one can trace how labour time became socially necessary – constituting, mediating and conditioning identity (Giddens 1981, 1991b; Nyland 1990; Urry 1991). The development of modern capi-talist society in Western Europe gave rise to the dominant conceptions of time. Adam (1990) argues that this change, in fact, suggests that rather than time being money, money became time.

The possession of time varies according to differences in status, power, money and freedom: 'The wealthy can buy the labour, service and skills of others as time, while agents of the state and persons in positions of authority have the right to time-structure the lives of those under their control' (Adam 1990:114). In relation to prisoners and as a criticism of Adam's (1990) point that it is only if one has very little time that time is valued, surely it is whether or not that time is owned by the person that will determine its value. In many cases having a lot of time is of little value to people who have no time of their own, such as prisoners in a total institution (Goffman 1961). The 'value' of this time is measured in terms of time lost. The value of time is based on two terms (rather as the value of a commodity is based on the relationship between supply and demand). Time is more valuable when the time available for a certain activity is not as great as the time desired for it. Thus, in terms of prison time, time is not valuable because the prisoners are not in a position to 'spend' it on a desired activity. However, the time 'lost' to them is of great value, albeit in a negative sense, because it represents the things they would be *doing* if the time was theirs to 'spend'. Thus, one needs to take account both of quantity and of ownership or control. In *Psychological Survival*, Cohen and Taylor (1972) make a similar point in that an 'unlimited time does not have the same subjective appeal for the prisoner as for the hippie drug user' (1972:53). Time presents itself as a problem. It is no longer a resource to be used, spent or saved but rather it is an object to be managed in an undifferentiated landscape which has to be marked out by time-frames that connect prisoners with the outside world (Sapsford 1983).

With the rise of capitalism and urbanisation we see the separation of time and labour, and time itself becomes a craft which universalises, homogenises and regiments activities (Grazia de 1964; Whitrow 1972). The linear, urban, industrial system dominates and inculcates the interstices of modernity, reproducing and simultaneously constructing time into a series of repetitive sequences. The linearity of time becomes coded upon the subjective rhythms of the workers, translated into the governance of self (Bell 1992; Foucault 1977a, 1977b, 1978; Osborne 1995) and is used in terms of the prison to govern, police and survey the prisoners with the hope of eliminating idleness by 'producing good habits of industry' (Prison Rule 1, cited in Fitzgerald and Sim 1982; Scraton, Sim and Skidmore 1991).

Giddens states that:

> The commodification of time…holds the key to the deepest transformations of day-to-day social life that are brought about by the emergence of capitalism. These relate both to the central phenomenon of the organisation of production processes, and to the 'work-place', and also the intimate textures of how daily social life is experienced. (Giddens 1981:131)

Time elevated to an a priori has been cast out and trawled, inscribing the structure of industrial time upon the consciousness of the populace. The techniques of time usage are exemplified, 'when some of the worst masters attempted to expropriate the workers of all knowledge of time' (Gurvitch 1990:153. See also Marx and Engels 1976; Thompson 1967; Thrift 1990; Zerubavel 1990). As the new time discipline was imposed, workers began to fight, not against time, but about it. As the currency of time gained meaning:

> The first generation of factory workers were taught by their masters the importance of time; the second generation formed their short time committees in the ten-hour movement; the third generation struck for overtime or time and a half. They had accepted the categories of their employers and

learned to fight back within them. They had learned their lesson, that time is money, only too well. (Giddens 1981:131)

Time becomes, as Giddens argues, 'the most direct expression of class conflict in the capitalist economy' (Giddens 1995:120). Thompson avers:

> This measurement embodies a simple relationship. Those who are employed experience a distinction between their employer's time and their 'own' time. And the employer must *use* the time of his labour and see it is not wasted: not the task but the value of the time is dominant. Time is now currency: it is not passed but spent. (Thompson 1967:21, emphasis in original)

A salient point expressed in *Being and Time* (Heidegger 1978) is the concept of time as moored in a particular place/structure, and it is within the execution of time that it has different effects depending on the location of the person. Therefore, time through the voices of women will be described as a 'cat's cradle', interlinking, and interdependent on every thread, unlike the linear notion of time moving in one direction, or time as purely cyclical like the seasons. The cradle's web can be cyclical on one level, yet linear on another, and these leads can be rarefied, subdivided but ultimately linked together in a constant state of movements, moments and places.

The multi-dimensional aspect of time leads the reader back to the onto-logical question of time: what does it mean? What lies beyond the origin of time and beyond the end of time, if time is structured on the premise of the 'now', the 'future' and 'past'? Because what was 'now' has immediately 'passed', and what has passed has opened up the future (Foucault 1986; Gervitch 1990; Jaques 1982). The acculturation of the self into and through the triumvirate of the 'past', 'present' and 'future' illustrates the reflexive rela-tionship we have with time and the significance of time in everyday life (Bergson 1997; Bourdieu 1990; Giddens 1981, 1991b, 1995).

The meaning of the time of incarceration

The prison became an experimental laboratory of the whole design.
(Foucault 1977b:130)

It was during the 'great age of confinement' (Foucault 1977b) that time was enlisted as a tool in the networks of the structural dimensions of power and knowledge (Giddens 1987, 1995; Harvey 1990). Although Foucault does not analyse time *per se*, one can develop the concept of capillaries of time which, as we have seen, have become a definable feature of a time-discipline society (Thompson 1967). Foucault (1977b) demonstrates that prison was the paradigmatic institution, representing distillation of time discipline, as of the other disciplinary techniques pervading society (Foucault 1989; Goffman 1963a, 1963b, 1971; Rabinow 1986). The landscape of disciplined industrial capitalism became dominated by bells, by the 'time sheet, the time keeper, the informers and the fines' (Thompson 1967:82. See also Giddens 1991a, 1991b). These markers of time became techniques which induced surveillance, normalised the day and sequestrated the formation of identity into sequences and motions. As discussed earlier, linear time supported the rise and development of capitalism within generalised labour. Melossi and Pavarini (1981:26) argue that, simultaneously with this development, the prison emerged as a technique of punishment (as opposed to mere incarceration). 'The modern prison had to transform itself into the laboratory', for transforming the violent and troublesome and impulsive criminal (real subject) into an inmate (ideal subject). Furthermore, one must remember that work discipline and 'habits of industry' lie at the core of the Victorian notion of a 'good and useful life'. This premise led to the belief that prisons could transform the offender by work and discipline. This in turn became a major aspect of 'rehabilitative training': however, a paradox comes to light when work is not only considered as a privilege, something that helps to make time pass in prison, but also as a scarce resource in prison. As a result of this contradiction the criminal could not be cured solely by the institutional disciplines of solitary confinement or penal servitude; thus, new techniques of discipline arose to rehabilitate/cure the offender through physical, psychological and chemical means of control in order to discipline the body. Prison then became not *for* but *as* punishment. Foucault (1977b) makes the distinction between the juridical discourse, in which the punishment was deprivation of liberty for a set term (i.e. prison *as* punishment), and the carceral discourse within which it was the techniques and regimes employed within the prison which constituted the 'treatment' or rehabilitation (subjectively, prison *for* punishment). He points out that the language of rehabilitation has also seeped into the juridical system as judges seek a humane rationale for sending people to prison.

However, the reality lies with the paradox in that prisons do not have the resources to practise the rehabilitation techniques (disciplinary techniques) that they espouse in theory, so prison returns to being *as* punishment in that the punishing effect lies within the fabric of prison life itself. Prison regimes exist to maintain the disciplinary effect on prisoners which is largely viewed as an unlooked-for and unfortunate side-effect by liberals, and by others is seen as deserved retribution (a concept Foucault erroneously regards as politically defunct).

The use of time as a mechanism of surveillance and control is more pervasive in prison than in wider society. Time acquires a different meaning under the carceral gaze, where time is defined and controlled by others. It is something over which the elders have no control and yet it is something they do negotiate, and work within. The effects of time in prison penetrate, contaminate and regulate the body through time-tabling and the regimentation of the day. The most distinctive effect comes from the process of 'doing time' which has to be learned; learning to 'do time' is having the ability to suspend the self from the free world.

'Watching the clock'

UU: [Time, in here is] quite different because you're *watching* the clock inside prison whereas you don't necessarily *look at* the clock on the outside. I mean the clock was there and you might glance at it, but here *clock time* means *everything*. [emphasis in original]

Una Ulrich
Age: 61
Time spent in prison: 2 months

Time use in prison is embodied in the institution's philosophy, practice and types of punishment which are inflicted upon the body. Time is neither tangible nor real but an ontological curiosity that divides 'reality' into seconds, minutes, hours, days and years. However, in its myriad of forms the capillaries of time in prison govern possible 'freedoms', representing the 'past', 'present', the 'now' and possible futures. This exploration will take us into the triple-edged world of time in prison, where time is a measurable, tradeable commodity, a form of 'currency' and further punishment.

The extract below explores the coterminous nature of time in relation to the new order of time i.e. prison time, remand time, sentenced time (psychological time), actual sentence time, the doing-of-prison time (physical time). In this extract Wan-Nita Williams eloquently discusses how within this island of prison time (i.e. prison structural time) she becomes lost within seas of timelessness (subjective prison time), separated but aware of time passing and time changing on the outside:

WW: My life on the outside has already *gone* because from the very first day when you come into jail; first of all you are on remand time, you live in a *make believe world*, because you think you're going home. So for that year, you think you're going home. Then you get sentenced and you've got a year where you know you're not, you're still undecided as to what's going to happen to you. You know you've got a life sentence but you don't accept it. You see you still think a miracle is going to happen, and each day your life slips away from you a little bit and then one day *you wake up in the morning and it's all gone and that's the worse day of all, when everything before has gone.* I was writing, it was like a diary effect, I was writing about present day and past and it was all mingled in together, it sort of made you cry and laugh at the same time, and that's what happened to me along that way. It *all* just slipped away. *You can't keep it, you can't hold it.* It's like my Clare, my baby, who's not a baby anymore. Toni's a young lady. You can't hold that life there because it doesn't mean anything. [emphasis in original]

Wan-Nita Williams

Time passes and stands still as elders are temporally and spatially isolated from wider society. Their normal patterns of life are both materially and ideologically severed over time. This time of incarceration, time standing still yet passing away, permeates the self and through the severance of life threads to the outside world, creates a new temporal order. Julie June argues that:

The role of time on the outside runs out but 'never in here because we are serving it'. (Letter received on 14 July 1998)

Time becomes part of their lives which elders revolve in and around, in which they are captives too; check (prison colloquialism for when prisoners are called to sign the check list), visits, canteen, everything. In a letter dated 18 April 2002, Kate King eloquently highlights the irony of time and the ownership of time in prison:

KK: Association time[1] – our time when we should be able to do what we want – again everything is regulated by the regime and we cannot go to the gym when we want, cannot go for a walk, cannot go down to the pub (ridiculous I know but just a point to show we cannot do what we want with our time).

Kate King

In 'doing time', time can be harnessed, disciplined, forfeited (remission days lost), gained (added days), negotiated, managed, survived and feared. Throughout the extracts, prison time becomes the enemy, insidiously penetrating all aspects of social life. The prison day is essentially empty and one day closely resembles another. Molly Mossdale describes the passing of time:

MM: Time has *stood still* whilst I have been in prison. Time has *stood still* in that everything goes *on* and *on* in the same *repetitive way*. It is as if the twenty years could have all been fitted in one year.

Molly Mossdale

Another elder, Orla O'Reilly, who is serving a mandatory life sentence and has served 14 years explains,

OO: [It is] the boredom and isolation, I think because every day is the same. *It is just dreadful. Every single day is the same.* It drives you mad! I don't know how you come out of prison and you're sane. *Because every single day is just actually the same as the day before.* Your meals are the same time. *Everything.* Oh it's horrible. I'm telling you. It really is. I mean you've got to do your time because you've committed a crime. But the fact that it goes on and on and on and on – There is just no end to it. You are thinking to yourself my God when is this going to end? So it does wear you *down.* [emphasis in original]

Orla O'Reilly

Elders in prison severed from the outside use of time live in a world of dead time, devoid of 'meaningful' social interaction which allows for:

> Minutes, hours, days [to] slip away with terrifying insubstantiality. Months will pass away like this, and years. Life! The problem of time is *everything.* Nothing distinguishes one hour from the next. The minutes and hours fall slowly, torturously. Once past, they vanish into near nothingness. The present minute is infinite. *But time does not exist.* (Serge 1977:7) (my emphasis)

One must stress that matters of time, work, privacy, freedom and deterioration are also serious issues for those on the outside; however, they lack the salience they have for offenders growing old behind bars. It is not purely their sense of time passing which is problematic but their relationship to the prison world. The pain of prison time arises from the tension between self, prison self (the effacement of self) and reality (Goffman 1990).

> Without something to belong to, we have no stable self, and yet total commitment and attachment to any social unit implies a kind of selflessness. Our sense of being a person can come from being drawn into a wider social unit; our sense of selfhood can arise through the little ways in which we resist the pull. Our status is backed by the solid buildings of the world, while our sense of personal identity resides in the cracks. (Goffman 1961: 320)

'You are up against it all the time'

The analysis of time in prison, in effect, becomes a discussion of the presentation of identities in, through and by time. However, time in prison is constructed within the boundaries of the institution, imposed from above by a system of explicit formal rules. Prison time becomes meaningless as elders find ways of surviving prison time. The routine of daily activities comprises a single rational plan which has been designed to fulfil the official aims of the institution rather than the needs of individuals. It is the use of time as imposed that eliminates choice, which in turn disables the self to create meaningful and symbolic relations with prison time and external time. Time as discussed above has been constructed to discipline and bring about the social death of the outside self through temporal and sensory deprivation (Christie 1981; Cohen and Taylor 1972, 1992; Foucault 1977b).

Olivia Ozga, a first-time offender serving an eight-year sentence, reiterates how time in prison becomes a psychological punishment from which there is no escape and it seems as though

OO: Some days I just climb the walls. I have a lot of sleepless nights as well – it seems *never-ending*. It seems as though it is never going to happen when you are going to walk out of that gate for good. It is just damn hard to cope with some days. It is very hard and when *you are up against it all the time* and you wonder how much more you can *take*.

Olivia Ozga

Through the voices of the women the trajectory of time is 'never-ending', and is systematically welded into types/forms of punishment. For example, Alison Anwar, who is at the beginning of her sentence, has experienced how punishment on an informal level is distributed by time:

AA: You see the way they can get back at you if they take a dislike to you is they'll go over for your visits late. So that cuts the time down for you. What she used to do is she used to make me stay on the Wing and take the others through and say my visitors wasn't there.

Alison Anwar

'Catching time'

Although time is a basic structuring principle of prison life, the elders find innovative ways of catching time. It is by creating meaningful and symbolic activity that elders find ways of tracing, connecting and maintaining life threads on the outside.

Julie June, who is actively fighting against her conviction, describes poignantly how the outside world begins to recede when one serves time:

JJ: But the longer it goes on the more painful it is to be apart from them. I want my children and my friends to get on with their lives but sometimes, especially when it comes to like Christmas time and things like that, it's like as if you are *on a thread and that thread is* getting *finer and finer.* Somehow you feel that you are losing contact. As I said I get loads of letters and they say we don't like telling you but we've booked a holiday. I write back and say, *please* tell me because there is *life outside this prison.* You can become cocooned by the prison environment and I don't want that. *I want to know.* I mean *every day* I watch the news. *Every day,* I try and get hold of a newspaper because I want to still hold on to what's on out there. [emphasis in original]

Julie June

To compensate for the loss of those feelings and activities performed in daily life on the outside, elders like Alison Anwar find ways of resuming those life threads through visualisation and memory of personal spaces and loved ones. She disciplines time through fantasy, of putting herself in another space and time.

AA: You have to try and visualise and remember. Like at nights, when I start saying my prayers, it is as if I go home. I go through my front door and I go round the house and then finally go up stairs and into the bedroom and I get into my own bed. Being with the person that you love, you don't forget how that feels. But you forget what it's like to just get up and go and have a *bath. Or a shower. To cook a meal. Or* just to put the kettle on and make a drink. Instead of having to drink out of a flask. A luke-warm drink out of a flask. *Just to be able to choose what you eat. Eat when you want to eat and food that you want to eat.* [emphasis in original]

Alison Anwar

Others find an escape route through studying, sleeping or mentally living outside prison. Cath Carter evocatively states:

CC: This is *life* after a while. The outside world recedes and this is more real.

Cath Carter

In these circumstances, prisoners have to sustain their lives in some way and look around for ways of marking time (Roy 1990). While forced to 'mark time' in terms of serving their time, most attempt to make prison time meaningful. Each woman finds ways of differentiating and dividing time. The elders interact with time by making time digestible, ticking months off, weeks off and even days off, placing time around visits or parole dates.

For Gertie Grangley, her strategy for surviving time in prison is to make her sentence time digestible. It is through punctuating the months that she makes the months seem shorter and the passing of time quicker by marking off the days and months. Gertie here holds on to a time of 'the real' through the calendar but she also makes this time move faster through marking March off and turning to April before it actually arrives:

GG: Oh yes, yes, I was crossing them off and then I was leaving them to the end of the month. I've got my calendar and I thought to myself now I'll mark half of March off. Tonight I'll mark the other page off and turn the page off to April and see if it goes any quicker that way instead of doing it day by day.

Gertie Grangley

Of course, days come and go, but they do not pass as they do on the outside. It is not just the division of time which concerns elders but the rate at which time passes. If anyone has watched a kettle boil, in the same way if a letter or a visitor fails to arrive, the experience of waiting gives monotony the upper hand, joined by its inevitable, constant companion, fatigue.

Disciplining discipline: Catching time

An important aspect of time in prison is its currency in terms of days left to serve, remission or days gained. This time discipline is enacted through the compulsory time-tabling of a prisoner's location which, on the one hand, is used to structure the operational needs of the prison, yet on the other can be used as a form of disciplining the elder who is out of sync with prison time. The artificial, abstract construction of penal time inscribes, governs and penetrates into the intimate bodily functions: the biological functions of sleeping, waking and using the toilet become regimented by the prison order of time. This use of time in prison illustrates the multiplicity of 'time' and techniques used in governing the inmate, but also provides possibilities for using time in order to survive and negotiate the prison-time machine. Inasmuch as prison is an oppressive institution, the positivity of power creates prison as a site of resistance (albeit within externally determined boundaries). Moreover, in this particular timescape elders show a facility in 'knowing their way around' time, acquiring knowledge about the role time plays and how they can mark out time in prison. Cath Carter manages her time by:

CC: Um, for me it is partly how to avoid being in the cafeteria longer than possible. You've got to eat in order to survive. So how much can you buy from the canteen once a week in the form of Ryvita and things. So that sometimes after you've trekked in the dining room you can just leave and be by yourself – just listen to the radio or read. Rather than sit like a lot of cattle waiting to be fed. I find it a very unpleasant part of the day. I try to avoid it. So I occupy myself in planning what I am going to buy. So that I don't have to sit in that place more hours than is absolutely necessary. That gives me a sense of autonomy. So that's a strategy – yes.

Cath Carter

As time passes, by constructing prisoners as 'other', some elders retain a sense of self as a sense of what not to become. Through their loss of role once in prison, the ambiguity caused by the severance of relationships with significant others is a disabling process, making it harder for elders to hold on to the world they have left behind. For many it is the fear of being institutionalised into a series of routines, ruled by prison-clock time which they battle against. Julie June catches herself, as do others in the study, falling into a routine. It is this awareness of repetition which makes many of the elders in the study make a conscious choice to change their routine in the fear that they might become institutionalised. The conscious subversion of prison time becomes immensely symbolic as an act of self, and of resistance to the loss of will (Pawelczynska 1980). It also gives form and meaning to daily existence:

JJ: Um…I still try to retain thoughts about outside. I mean obviously, um I think you have *to work hard* at *not becoming institutionalised.* You see people *being* institutionalised. And sometimes you are finding *yourself* – I mean sometimes you go for a shower at the same *time* every day, because you know you've only got so much time left. And sometimes I'll say to myself, '*I'm not going for a shower tonight*'. Just because I know I always go at such a *time* and sometimes it just *stares* you in the face. I think you fill your flask at a certain *time* because it is ten minutes before lock in. And I think, 'Oh, no' and you know it's a *battle*. It's *a battle* not to become institutionalised because everything is regimented.

Julie June

Although actively resisting the synchronised movements of disciplinary time, many of the elders recognised that they were slipping into the rhythms of prison time. Julie June recounts how, although she does 'battle' against falling into a set pattern, she also finds herself affected by prison life:

JJ: When I first came into prison I couldn't *stand my time* in cell. The *first* time the cell door shut I had to purposely turn my chair I had in my cell towards the window. Because I couldn't stand, I couldn't sit looking at the closed prison door.

I sometimes think, 'Oh I'll be glad to be locked in tonight to get away, to be on my own.' Whereas I never used to be able to cope with that time in the cell.

I would *never have thought* I was a person who enjoyed solitude, my own space. I often wonder now, because we've been um *programmed*, I supposed to being on your own. I think maybe when I get out there will be times when I've got to go off somewhere to find my own space. [emphasis in original]

Julie June

Serving and resisting time

The vagaries of time change depending on the nature of the institution. For some there is a discontinuity of time created when one moves from a closed to an open prison. Time, according to the participants in the study, is more structured in a closed prison. Although an open prison involves greater movement around the building, and more contact, which means greater 'freedom', it also lends itself to more opportunities for petty surveillance, stricter control and punishment. Thus, the more activity there was, or more 'free flow', the more closely regulated they were. This movement requires analysis of why and how similar but different institutions demand different things. The majority of the elders acknowledge that, as Ellen Evergreen states, 'time in a closed prison goes quicker'. Ellen, who has spent 11 years in prison, has been imprisoned first in a maximum secure prison, then in a closed, and finally in an open prison. The impact of this regime illustrates a contradiction between the 'appearance' of more freedom and the mechanisms conditioning the subjective sense of freedom. It is the constant control and surveillance applied in an open prison which create a sense of time slowing down. Molly Mossdale's account shows that, although an open prison implies greater freedom, 'nothing has changed':

MM: In this respect nothing has changed, when you go to another prison the rules are the same. There is still lock-up. You have still got to abide to the times when you go to work, the times you come back, they never vary. Sometimes you can go to work on the outside early, or you might like a stroll to work, you don't have any decisions here. Everything is decided for you.

Molly Mossdale

These extracts illustrate the multiplicity of time in which there is a dominant time order, but how within the different categories of prison lie vagaries of time. Edith Ellis, who found herself in prison after selling two E's to undercover police officers, explains the time differences in an open and closed prison:

AW: You said that time goes slower in here than it does in a close prison, why is that?

E.E: I don't know. I think its because after you've been in bang-up [prison slang for a close prison] you're told what to do, waiting on the door closing. You come here, you're just left to wander around and find out for yourself what you've got to do. If you ask anybody, they say 'Just a minute', and you're left *waiting* and nobody else comes and you're just a bit lost really. [emphasis in original]

AW: Was it easier to do time at the beginning of your sentence rather than now?

E.E: I think it was, but that was probably with it being a bang-up jail. You were locked up for a certain time in the morning, and then you were let out for your dinner, and then back again. I think it was just like a habit you got into, you just expect to do the same things every day.

Edith Ellis

Molly Mossdale recounts her first day in an open prison after spending 15 years in a closed maximum secure prison:

MM: I remember getting up for the first time and looking out of the window. I spent over an hour just looking at the rain changing the colour of a twig. The twig started out as a dull brown but pale like a tan, and suddenly as it got wetter, it got darker, and darker and I thought my God, what am I doing here? I spent over an hour just staring at a twig. Then you look at the grass and the green and you can go on, and the smell of the flowers. I haven't smelt flowers for over fifteen years, and it was just fantastic.

Molly Mossdale

For many of the elders in the sample their stay in an open prison represents the final leg of the prison circuit. Like many of the elders Davina Devlin found that the passing of time took longer on the inside than the outside because they were always in a process of just waiting for an answer:

D.D: Waiting. You have to *wait* for everything. You have to *wait* to put in an application to have clothes brought in for you. You have to *wait* for an application to go and see the Governor. You always have to *wait*. [emphasis in original]

Davina Devlin
Age: 54
Time spent in prison: 3 years

The passage below illustrates the movement and the medley of time which is neither coherent nor linear. Unlike some of the women, Molly Mossdale found the movement from the closed world to an open prison allowed the experience of time to gain momentum because, as she argues, 'there is a hell of a lot to learn out there':

MM: In an open prison, we are really interested because we are going out on home *visits for two days, then three days, then four days, then five days,* and it sticks to six days until six months before we leave, it goes up to seven days. So when you are *going out all the time* and you are having days out – so suddenly there is a hell of a lot to learn out there. [emphasis in original]

AW: Do you feel that the longer you are in here the more distant you become with what's happening on the outside?

MM: Yes, the longer I am in. But I am now getting frustrated because I know what the outside world is like, I know from the outside visits. I want to be *out* all of the time now. [emphasis in original]

Molly Mossdale

The closed prisons represent the severance of the outside and an existence in a closed world of marginality but, in Molly's case, the movement through to the open prison shows how her life threads begin to look towards what lies beyond the gates. Prison time, structured, disciplined and routinised, differentiates itself from the outside world. Prison time steals on, procrastinating, in contrast to time on the outside where we run out of time. The women, once knowledgeable agents in the outside world, have become strangers in time; for example, they are strangers to the currency (the new pound coins) and technological innovations such as the cash machines. Molly Mossdale recalls her amazement at the technological and monetary changes that have occurred whilst she has been in prison:

MM: For me, I am *raring* to get out and *to start living.* I find it frustrating at the moment. Once you have been out you know what you are going out to at long last, for example the currency has *changed.* I have never come across the twenty pence piece; the new ten pence piece which is half the size of the other, or the five pence coin. You have a tiny *little* thing that you can hardly see. *The currency is different.* The prices of everything outside are *different.* I find people less friendly than they used to be – you go out shopping and everyone is rushing around. People now keep very much to themselves, they read their paper, they are on their mobile phones, and it's totally different. I have *slowed down* here as there *is nothing else to do.* Everything is at a walking pace, or a leisurely pace. Outside everyone is *rushing.* The time concept now is totally *different.*

I have never seen credit cards before – now everybody is using them, you don't carry money, you just carry them. When I went out it was with great excitement. I thought banks had telephones but of course it was where the money came out [She laughs].

I thought it was a telephone, '*Where do you speak*', I said.

She said: 'Don't be stupid Molly, don't show me up.'

'So tell me, where do you speak?'

'You don't, that's where you get your money out.'

'But the banks are open.'

'It doesn't matter, you don't have to go into banks any more, you just press these things.'

'I thought it was a telephone.'

I get excited when I go out now, so many new things to find out about, *everything has changed so much.* [emphasis in original]

Molly Mossdale

As outside time becomes less significant with the passing of time in prison, new life threads emerge, replacing familial networks on the outside with ones on the inside. It is the acceptance of playing prison time which allows for routines and camaraderie to emerge, creating a form of dependency on the system which in turn controls very intimate aspects of the body, e.g. bodily functions. Furthermore, it creates a space where individual roles and responsibilities emerge, *governed by the tyranny of time in prison.* Although the realities of prison life are harsh, friendships emerge and camaraderie exists. For example, Molly finds it difficult to walk without the aid of her crutches. Her friends help her in various ways:

MM: My three really good friends do everything for me. When it comes to tidying my room, I do everything I can do on the surface, and then my friend – she'll do all the sweeping.

Molly Mossdale

Prison time is different from time on the outside, and different depending on whether you are an offender or a member of staff, the length of sentence, the time already spent in prison, age, outlook and people's experiences before imprisonment, and so on. For those who have served long sentences and are close to release, such as Molly Mossdale, the predominant feeling is of:

MM: Raring to get out and to start living. I like to think young. I am going to try and enjoy myself and see as many places as possible. Make up for lost time.

Molly Mossdale

Although they are aware that their prison time consisted of time in waiting, and that the lost time can never be replaced, this period of new time, of post-work, post-menopause brings new freedoms, new roles, new opportunities and new fears grounded in becoming dependent on the state in an age-discriminatory society. Molly, although 'raring to get out and to start living', eloquently describes her anxiety about being released:

MM: When we get out, that's when we start our sentence. That's when we really start our sentence. Are we going to be accepted? Will we be found out? Will they find out what we did? Will we be able to assimilate without too much difficulty? *That's when it starts!*

Molly Mossdale

The question of time in prison has often been referred to in literary texts, biographies of ex-offenders and memoirs of revolutionaries. In some form, everyone does time or is doing time. The landscape of time blurs the edges of the life course into a running stream of the past, the future and the present (Wood 1989). The women's experience and fear of time in prison is eloquently stated in a letter from Julie June who has already spent several years behind bars and has another eight years to serve:

JJ: Had I been told a number of years ago that I would have to spend time, even a year within prison I would most certainly have said that I could not survive such an experience. It would have seemed an impossibility. In fact I am not sure how I have come through.

Time seems to take ages and ages, every minute like an hour, every hour a day, every day a week. Yet when you look back, it seems to have passed by so quickly and nothing has happened. Prison is very much a waiting game, a wasting game. The survival battle is very much a battle against time, of how to live your life. When time is escaping away… Endless time. It is like being stuck in a time warp. Outside is the real time, inside is the physical containment. Prison not only robs you of your freedom, it attempts to take away your identity. The indignities of prison are demeaning, they humiliate and demoralise.

Not everyone copes, some flounder and diminish. They resort to medication to 'solve' their problem of time and will be encouraged because this aids control. No help is given and often it is left to the other prisoners to guide and encourage those in difficulties. Time in prison for many could be so worthwhile, quality time, but it is time wasted. It is best to fill your time with constructive activities, write your thoughts down, escape into literature, help others and feel worthwhile.

Only through seeking your inner liberty and having a free mind, can you break through this deadly time set!

(Letter received: personal communication with Julie June)

Julie June

Life which is lived primarily in the linear plane of time, is suffused by perpetual anxiety about what the future may bring. It will however never be entirely without hope. The question of time then is a paradox embodying a union of opposites and it is therefore an expression of the 'past', 'present', 'futures' and that which lies beyond the 'eternal' (Bell 1992; Eliade 1989). It is by unravelling the tapestry of time and its appropriation on a macro, micro and mezzo level that one can deconstruct the socially constructed nature of time in prison (Adam 1990; Hassard 1990b; Wood 1989).

> If Being is to be conceived in terms of time, and if, indeed, its various modes and derivatives are to become intelligible in their respective modifications and derivations by taking time into consideration, then Being itself (and not merely entities, let us say, as entities 'in time') is thus made visible in its 'temporal' which can no longer mean simply 'being in time'. (Heidegger 1978:401)

After identifying the time threads, the durée of daily time use in a total institution, one can understand the relationship time has with the self (Bergson 1997; Castoriadis 1997; Dreyfus 1991). Julie June describes her personal struggle to hold on to her family:

JJ: *I love my family dearly and they do me.* The *longer* I'm *in* the more *painful* my visits get. *I long and I crave to see them.* But sometimes I also think I'm better off if I don't see them. I *feel so* emotionally drained after the visits. That I think perhaps I'm *better off, if I don't* have visits. I mean that's not the case of course. I always want my visits and I want to see them every day if I could. But the longer it goes on the more painful it is to be apart from them. Time and things like that. It's like as if you are on a thread and that thread is becoming *finer* and *finer* somehow. [emphasis in original]

Julie June

It is through their unbending belief in a beginning and an end, life and death, that the elders in prison feel that once they are released, time is a scarce resource to be savoured, lived and experienced. This is also an indication of time based in the future which can be marked and rationalised, in terms of past dreams, lost hope, transitions from zones of exclusion, the prison to zones of marginality in wider society.

The use of time in prison is a salient example of how techniques and modalities of power are embodied in the process of reconstituting the criminal into an 'ideal' subject. This is achieved, as Foucault argues, by the intensification of the technologies of surveillance and discipline which are manifested in society through education, careers, therapeutic interventions; but what actually happens in prison is an exclusion from these things, with the result that the prison is modified in unintended ways, partly by prisoners missing out on the 'normal' institutional immersion which is productive of 'normal' disciplined identities.

In the voices of the women we hear that, in order to survive the new order, they create transgressive spaces in which they can suspend the outside world but in an unprecedented fashion float between the prison and the outside world (Deleuze 1973). Time is regulated and punctuated by the calls for check, medication and meals. Gertie Grangley describes this process as being wound up and then left to run down, like a robot.

GG: Yes, yes, well you're just like robots aren't you really, just like a wind up robot really. You just wind it up and you just let yourself run down at night. It's just that every day, is the same. You get up, it's just so boring, so terribly boring. And you just like wait for your visits you know?

Gertie Grangley

The stories of the women show how they are exposed to a type of punishment which is underpinned by time discipline. They are caught within the movement and motions of time and space, both within the time of 'the real' on the outside and in terms of prison time. This is the in-between space of carceral time within which women live and which they negotiate. The following chapter will discuss how the elders articulate the ageing process within a secure setting.

Note

1   Association is the time when prisoners are allowed out of their cells to meet, talk, watch TV, etc. It is regarded as a privilege and can be withdrawn as a punishment. Prisoners not allowed association have to remain locked in their cells.

Chapter 5

Health Care and the Cost of Imprisonment

I think if you were old and in prison and ill it would be a serious problem.

Julie June

The previous chapters landscape[1] the transition elders are forced to make as they move from court to prison. It is within this movement from wider society to the closed realm of the prison that we see a series of regulatory techniques in operation, working upon and indeed within the 'old' female body. This chapter will focus on how the lack of health-care provision multiplies the pains of imprisonment. The feeling of loss, lack of exercise and of primary preventative health care results for some in an overwhelming fear of becoming ill. In part this is because

MM: The only thing we have control over in here are our bodies.

Molly Mossdale

The intimate intrusions of the prison gaze can be diverted and arrested by employing strategies such as selectively choosing what officers should know about their bodies. For elders in prison, the intimate, private lines of the body are revered, sacred in an environment that aims to efface the importance of the private and the personal. This provides one of the many life threads that link elders to the outside world. Hence, the fear of being ill in prison is grounded in the knowledge that whatever privacy and control they have over their medical condition must be relinquished to the penal system. Should hospital treatment be required, it is the mask of the inmate which takes precedence and hence the woman becomes in yet another way a commodity to be dealt with by others:

AA: I get the feeling because you are a *prisoner*, and you go to the hospital; they *know* you are a prisoner. They don't *care* about you. They do it because *they've got to do it, that's the feeling you get.* [emphasis in original]

Alison Anwar

The journey from prison to the hospital, the process of seeking and receiving medical treatment, becomes an ordeal in itself. The inhuman treatment, the omnipresent power of the penal 'scribes' begins before they leave the prison walls, as officers deride Alison's medical condition and her body, not only between themselves but to a complete stranger, the taxi driver:

AA: They were cracking jokes about me. They were saying about my weight, you know, about my breasts. Even before I went. Even here on the wing, they were making jokes about *what* I was going for to the *male officers.* Things like, um *she's going to see if she can find her breasts – they'll be lucky!* That type of thing, you know, meaning that I was so thin that I didn't have any. [emphasis in original]

AW: And how did that make you feel?

AA: Oh, *it makes you feel terrible. Really terrible, you know.* You just feel that you are going to curl up in a heap. You are upset and you are choking back the tears and you know you've got to walk into the hospital with all of this. This particular time, it was something to do with this lump in my breast and they took me to the hospital by taxi. They take you in a van now. The taxi driver, he was only a young man. We got in the taxi, and the prison officers [were] saying [things] like, '*Don't worry, there's no need to be frightened. She's having the top of her head opened up. She's a psychopath but she'll be all right.*' [emphasis in original]

Alison Anwar

Being talked about in this way, while present, and already anxious and vulnerable, reinforces the process of being silenced, effaced by the system. In her versatile ability to 'make do', Alison insists that, regardless of the dominant signifier of criminal/older female offender, she is entitled to a degree of 'care' as stipulated by the European Convention of Human Rights. By referring to her life before, she re-identifies with her life beyond the walls. Alison's life threads remind her that the world she has entered is unfamiliar, alien and unnatural:

AA: I am *a normal human being.* I've been taken from a *normal family environment with children, grandchildren. To be treated like that is – In fact* when I went for my mammogram, I said to the officer, *'have you any idea how upsetting* and *degrading* this is?'* [emphasis in original]

Alison Anwar

Women in later life are further humiliated and stigmatised by the visible signifiers of discipline, the jailers' tools. The women complained about being put in handcuffs and chained to an officer when they went to and from hospital. They found the process degrading and felt it showed no respect for their maturity or medical condition, which in many cases would have made it physically impossible to abscond when taken outside the prison for treatment. Alison recalls her experience of receiving hospital treatment on the outside:

AA: First of all you've got these really great big cuffs on and they are really heavy, thick and made for men. Then they put another pair on you, cuffed to the officer. You can't move. You can't even blow or scratch your nose. You can but you have to get down like that and if you lift your arm up the officer's arm comes up. You are like that all the time until you come back. You have to be stripped before you go, completely, in front of two officers. And then when you come back the same again even though you've never been off the cuffs or out of sight of the two prison officers.

Alison Anwar

This treatment reinforces and affirms in their minds their status as only prisoners which rationalises for them the way in which they are treated by the other women and the prison estate:

AA: You go and you are double-cuffed. *Great big cuffs on. Really heavy ones. I don't mean the ordinary pair of cuffs. They are really solid cuffs.* You have two pairs on and you are cuffed to the prison officer. And *there is no way they'll take them off. So how do they expect to treat you?*

It's really, really degrading and upsetting just to walk into the hospital in the first place *shackled to another human being.* [emphasis in original]

Alison Anwar

It is the knowledge of how things were before imprisonment, their life threads from the past to what is now, and present, which makes the imminent process of receiving treatment an emotionally as well as a physically painful process. It becomes an intense attack on who they are as people, a process of producing the body under the prison gaze as a *tabula rasa*.

For others, the process of being punished in a public, outside space can be subverted by reversing the public gaze onto the jailer. Rather than surreptitiously cloaking the visible signifiers of punishment, the counter-technique is to make them public. This process enabled Kate King, in the example given below, a means of controlling the viewers' gaze.

KK: Those screws that leave the handcuffs on, I'll embarrass them in the hospital. I would hold my hand up and make sure that everybody in the hospital saw them. The screws take them off in the end because they [are] embarrassed. I don't let them get away with it. You just have to play them at their own game, don't you?

Kate King

This is a good example of how 'profaned bodies' of elders and purloined looks of the outsider gaze can be reversed.

Una Ulrich, a first-time offender in her early sixties, was recovering from a heart attack brought on by the stress of the trial. She found herself handcuffed and chained to two male officers, suffering from a coronary attack and unable to move. The measures of restraint used were excessive and inappropriate in relation to her medical condition:

UU: I was taken onto the coronary unit from the hospital. The family came in and I'm wired up in the coronary unit and my daughter just burst into tears because I was handcuffed and chained to an officer. There were two officers sat at the foot of my bed. I will *never ever forgive* the system for that.

She later goes on to ask,

What security risk did I pose? The doctor pleaded with them to take the handcuffs off and the answer was, 'We can't, we're sorry, it's the system'. But what does it do to your family to see, when they know I've never hurt anybody in my life.

AW: And did you have your own room?

UU: No. It was obvious to the rest of the ward.

Una Ulrich

The shackling of prisoners in hospitals is a common occurrence yet the media have only focused on women who give birth in chains. On 9 January 1996 the then Shadow Home Secretary, Jack Straw MP, stated that 'in a civilised society it is inhuman, degrading and unnecessary for a prisoner to be shackled at any stage of labour' (*The Guardian*: 10 July 1998:4). Surely, this also holds true for any woman hospitalised and chained after suffering major operations. The humiliation of being handcuffed and the indignities of being strip-searched when moving to and from hospital prevents many from seeking vital medical treatment. These examples display the intransigent power of the penal system, impressing on both prisoners and public that not only do prisoners have no rights, but that not even the usual professional prerogative exercised by doctors and nurses holds sway when the patient is a prisoner.

Treatment

It is through catering only for the able-bodied offender constructed by the prison gaze that the elders' needs and experiences of the life course are dismissed and subsumed by the dominant discourse. As shown already, this holds true for the above elder hospitalised and chained after undergoing a major operation. Thus, elders in the study often preferred to lay low, avoiding the medical gaze through fear of further punishment and to elude the omnipresent penal gaze. The same woman not only had to contend with being placed in an open ward shackled to male officers, but also suffered from the lack of after-care provision:

UU: I was in a room for six weeks. I didn't get out for association because there wasn't the staff. The windows were whitened up. The food was served through a hatch in the door. The only time I got out was to see a visiting specialist. That was for six weeks and that was my first six weeks introduction to prison.

Una Ulrich

Already excluded from mainstream society by her imprisonment, Una's illness and incapacity to work led to further exclusion and became yet another technology of discipline exercised by the carceral machine. She was denied association and exercise, and incurred a loss in pay, reinforcing her sense of dislocation and isolation. The distress caused by such traumatic experiences cannot assist the convalescing ill. In these circumstances (and such experiences are not uncommon) can the prison service support its vision, of a 'service…which the public can be proud of'?

UU: Because you are ill, you are locked in a room for six weeks. You can't even see out of your door, your food's fed to you through a door, even when you get your canteen stuff, that comes through a door. You don't get out of that door for anything. Your shower's in the room. So you're stuck in this room for six weeks because you are ill and nobody will ever tell me that is justice. You'd take an animal out to exercise. But they [the prison service] get away with it and I feel very angry about that.

Una Ulrich

Thus, in addition to loss of liberty, older women are further punished by the lack of adequate facilities to cater for age-related illnesses. For elders who are too ill to receive treatment from an outside hospital, the process of bringing treatment and expertise into the closed institution becomes a battle with the prison authorities. Yet delaying the period of treatment may have serious consequences for the women's life-expectancy. In addition, it has been well researched that environment significantly influences the course of illnesses, both psychologically and physically (Arber and Gilbert 1983; Bond 1993; Bond *et al.* 1993b; Booth 1989; Chaneles 1987; Gillespie and Galliher 1972). The unknown world of prison, the different use of time in prison and the lack of care received can and does damage health as well as increasing feelings of anxiety, isolation and dislocation. It is the fear of being ill in an alien environment in which bureaucratic, prison time ticks slowly which reinforces for elders a common fear: dying alone in prison (Kerbs 2000; Krane 1999; Marquart, Merianos and Carroll 1997). Alison explains:

AA: Since I came into prison I have had lots of problems with my health. My family have had an *all out battle* to get it sorted out. You know, you go to the doctors, and a year later you are still waiting. It's really quite frightening actually the thought of getting ill in prison. Like I got a lump in my breast and *nothing* was happening about it. Eventually, after a long period of time they did something about it. Fortunately, it didn't turn out cancerous. But had it been cancerous the amount of time that passed while it was being sorted out. *I could have been dead and buried,* you know? [emphasis in original]

Alison Anwar

The metaphor used throughout is one of being at war, where the battle against institutionalisation – the replacement of the outside inscriptions with meaning codes pertaining to the status of 'inmates' – in some cases amounts quite literally to a battle for survival. In Alison's case, with the help of her life threads on the outside, she managed to make do:

AA: They sent a specialist because of the fighting done through my family. The specialist actually came in here to me.

Alison Anwar

Nevertheless, her defiance, her agency and her insistence on the continued relevance of the outside status and resources, was punished by the institution and the deliverers of care, leaving her feeling infantilised and less than human. It is also indicative of the lack of appropriate provision of adequate healthcare facilities for women at HMP Penjara:

AA: When the specialist came, they didn't tell me what day he was coming. I wasn't prepared for it. I just that minute came back from work and they shouted me. They didn't give me time to go and have a shower, change my clothes or anything. I just had to – when they shout for you, you have to go. That day he did a biopsy. There's a hospital on here. I don't know whether you know that or not. It's for the men really. But they do take the women over there for X-rays. The place where they did the biopsy is like a cell that they done out like a treatment room. The specialist came and there was no nurse present. It was just a prison officer who stood at the door. The cell was filthy. There wasn't even a towel. No swabs. That day, I felt like some [pause] *trollop* who had gone down some back street alley for an abortion. *That is just how I felt.* [emphasis in original]

Alison Anwar

The prison officers are employed 'to look after [the prisoners] with humanity'. This description in theory implies that they are not administrators of state-legitimated pain, the punishment being the simple deprivation of liberty. In reality, through enactment such as the above, the prison stage becomes an area of punishment, and the officers' role becomes that of deliverers of pain. The denial of privacy, cleanliness and the protection of modesty implied by the presence of a female nurse all constitute violations of the dominant construction of 'femininity' – especially of the 'respectability' normally deemed appropriate to the older woman. This illustrates how the construction of offending women as 'other' than female (Carlen 1983) contributes in a concrete way to the pain of imprisonment when created through punishment techniques which have a disproportionate impact on these older women.

The power to punish – The role of medicine in prison

The withholding role of medicine and medical treatment prescribed on the outside and the over-use of psychotropic drugs provide two of many illustrations of the ways punishment can be delivered and in which prison regimes have been adapted for (but are not accommodating) female prisoners (Allen 1987; Sim 1990). The underlying set of beliefs is that women are more mentally unstable than men, are by definition mentally disordered and so react in a more neurotic way than men. One worrying, indeed dangerous effect of this assumption is the dismissal and trivialising of women. Molly Mossdale recounts an incident when:

MM: For instance, we had a woman in here who had a stroke. The officers thought she was fooling around, her arm was completely rigid, it was a stroke. The doctor was sent for and he said, 'You have only got a migraine and sometimes it affects your arm, so just lie down.'

Half an hour later, she started shaking all over, one of the nurses who happened to have worked with geriatrics suddenly realised it was a stroke and then they took her to the hospital, that was six hours later. We are all frightened of being ill in any establishment like this. You can query a doctor on the outside, you cannot query the doctors in here.

Molly Mossdale

For many of the elders in the study the fear of becoming ill that results from having inadequate medical provision in prison is highlighted by the attitudes of the (predominantly male) prison doctors. Many, indeed, are reluctant to report illness when this would mean being forced to see a male doctor.

MM: I would like to see a female doctor but there aren't any. *No choice.* In the twenty years, I haven't seen a female doctor in any of the prisons I have been in. You don't have a choice, some of us do really object. That is my main grievance about the medical in any of the prisons I've been in. You don't have a choice. The process of going to a male doctor and the nature of the regime is a degrading experience.

Molly Mossdale

One of the many complaints is that when the women genuinely feel ill, their request to see the doctor is refused. Illnesses are trivialised on the basis of an out-dated typification of women as hysterical hypochondriacs, or as 'nothing more' than a gynaecological problem:

MM: I can approach the medical staff but the doctor is set in his ways. Anything wrong with a woman it must be menstrual, the time of the month or her age.

Molly Mossdale

The women who required medical help frequently feel belittled, infantilised and frustrated when medical notes go missing, lost in transit as they are shipped from one prison to the next. This results in their medication being delayed or withdrawn, causing quite serious and humiliating situations to arise. In the extract below Rebecca Rose, frightened and silenced, withdraws from help. She says:

RR: This is the second time now I keep wetting myself. Well, you know I had this trouble on the outside. And I've been waiting now. I didn't see him the first time because he was busy. I still haven't seen him. So I'll just wait and see. *I shan't push it.*

I came in with it [the tablets] but they stopped all the medication when I first came into prison.

AW: So how long did you have to wait to receive your medication?

RR: Three months. I had problems with my waterworks, I was going to the toilet every half-an-hour instead of possibly every couple of hours.

Rebecca Rose

Quite serious medical conditions were trivialised when women were sent away with two paracetamols. Tokwan Thomas, after three months of being turned away, was eventually diagnosed as suffering from pneumonia. Her lung was on the verge of collapsing before she was admitted to an outside hospital. On her return she went several days without receiving any medication because of mistakes, such as the information not being written on the nurse's file or the tablets not being put on the trolley:

TT: I was supposed to take twenty-nine tablets a day, and I think it was for the first three days they [the prison medical staff] said they *hadn't got them.* Then they stopped them all of a sudden and said you'd finished them and then a week went by and they [the PMS] said, you know, you've still got this course to take, you know, and turned up with another load of tablets.

Tokwan Thomas

The lack of facilities and inadequate care serves as a constant reminder of their status as prisoners who become lost in a system. It is also indicative of how age-related illnesses are not adequately understood, catered for or even acknowledged. The discontinuation of long-term medication is problematic for women, having unforeseen and unacknowledged side effects:

ZZ: I'm on HRT. When I first come in they took my tablets off me when I went to [HMP] Lager. I hadn't had a period for twelve months, you see and when they took them off me in Lager and then I came here they never gave me them. So I got up one morning and I was flooding. It was just running down my legs – I didn't know what was happening to me.

I told the nurse and all that, and the doctor said, 'well you haven't got the name of them, you can't have them'. I couldn't remember the name of them.

He [the doctor] said, 'If you don't know the name of them, I can't help you'. I said 'Lager took them off me and kept them'. And it wasn't until the next day when the nurse did a bit of tracing, called me up and gave me them.

Zadie Zing

The situation reflects a lack of awareness of what it means to be menopausal and places a question mark over the policy of not offering women the right to see a female doctor in prison, which becomes an obstacle for elders seeking help about gynaecological and cytological issues. For women who were born in the 1940s, maintaining their modesty is imperative. Anita Arrowsmith was yet another elder whose HRT tablets were taken off her when she was received into the prison system. As she states:

AA: I am worried now that I have had the show[2] because at my age I don't think, after eight, nine year, it's not a very good thing is it? I've got to see the doctor and I don't know whether I'll mention it to him. If it was a lady doctor I would. I don't like talking to a male doctor.

Anita Arrowsmith

Another doctor decided to withdraw Yvette Young's HRT because he thought she was receiving too many hormones. Yet as she states:

YY: But I had taken them for fourteen years.

Yvette Young

Another elder, Gertie Grangley, suffered the effects of her medication being withdrawn when she came into prison as a first-time offender for cheque book fraud, when

GG: I was on medication, strong medication but I'd been on it for a long while because my own GP prescribed it for me and they [Lager] took it off me.

AW: Can you tell me what they are?

GG: [They are DF 118]. It's like a very strong painkiller, they're morphine base you see, and that, but they think you're going to abuse drugs because you see they class everybody *the same* in prison. They treat you as though you're a druggie and that does my head in. I don't think they should do that. I had very severe pains in Lager, very bad, and when I needed the DF, he took me off them, he took me off them. I was very bad, for months I suffered without them pills.

But when I have very bad pains I need to take them. I get very bad facial pains, I've got spondylitis in my shoulders caused by my arthritis and it goes in my face and when it goes in there it's horrible. It really is bad and it goes in my chest. I have these shooting pains that go right through to my back. I just need to take one and it then goes in a couple of minutes. The only thing I could do in Lager [was to] rock. I rocked on my bed. I just rocked for comfort.

Gertie Grangley

In contrast to the medicines prescribed on the outside, which were often with-drawn, a major purpose of medication prescribed in prison is to discipline and normalise; the emphasis on control and change through coercive treatment does, from the examples, invariably thwart any notion of rehabilitation and reform, as is illustrated by the high dosages of sedatives women in general receive. This disguises the fact that rules and regulations are enforced in women's prisons with such rigour that a greater number of disciplinary offences are recorded for women, at least twice as many compared with male prisoners (Fitzgerald and Sim 1982; Home Office 1985 cited in Carlen and Worrall 1987). This results both from regimes that aggravate and multiply the problems many of the women have, and from discriminatory social ideologies that, in general, demand higher standards from women than from men. The prescription of psychotropic drugs provides one of many illustrations of the ways in which prison regimes have been adapted for female inmates. Genders and Player (1987) recorded that, between January 1984 and March 1985, over 145,000 doses of anti-depressants, sedatives and tranquillisers were administered to women in prison, proportionately five times as many doses of this type of medication as men received in prison.

Molly Mossdale succinctly argues that the reason for this is that:

MM: It is easier for them to have quiet people around, not people crying their eyes out, not people emotionally disturbed, give them night medicine. It's how to keep people quiet.

                                                                           Molly Mossdale

Yet, for elders who have been on medication for years, the medication is either withdrawn, delayed or a substitute is given. Many felt aggrieved that their maturity, wisdom and knowledge of their own bodies and health experience were not taken seriously. They felt affronted when treated in a derisive manner by the doctors or in the same manner as women with known drug addictions.

Elders in prison were concerned that they had never been called for a mammogram or cervical cytology screening, and those who did obtain tests complained of the time it took to get their results back, compared to the waiting time of a maximum of ten days on the outside. Cancers of the breast and reproductive system kill one in 12 women, and the National Health Service encourages all women over 50 to be tested for cervical cancer and breast cancer every three years. Of the establishments included in the research, not one conducted systematic cervical cytology or breast screening, despite the HMCIP Thematic Review stating that 'women prisoners come from a group with many of the risk factors for cervical cancer' (1997:108). Another example of the discrepancy in treatment is that it is recommended practice for women on HRT to have a gynaecological examination on a yearly basis. However, some elders in this sample who were on HRT found that they were placed on a repeat prescription without further examinations having taken place. It has been argued that the long-term use of HRT increases the risk of breast cancer and the British Medical Association (BMA) is still unaware of all the possible side-effects.

The lack of adequate health-care provision, regular check-ups, or systematic screening, and the frequency of misdiagnosis of illnesses, leaves many elders vulnerable and afraid of placing themselves under the gaze of yet another expert, the doctor, for further reassessment when, as often happens, their files are lost as they move from one prison to the next.

The lack of adequate provision, i.e. a health centre, turns being ill into a form of punishment when women find themselves locked behind a blank door and excluded from association, the use of the phone and a decent wage, all of which are necessary to be able to maintain links with the outside world. The National Health Service is supposed to apply equally to individuals serving custodial sentences, maintaining continuity with provision in the community.[3] Yet, the literature on the treatment of health problems in women prisons focuses on younger women and the needs of young children, not elders *per se*. The *Thematic Review* (HMCIP 1997) and the follow-up of 2001 (HMIP 2001) mentions elders only in the context of the problems presented by younger women.[4] However, Yvonne Wilmott, Director of Nursing at HM Prison Service Directorate of Health Care, stressed that 'women in prison require health care services to be tailored to their needs. There is great scope for health promotion and illness prevention as well as care and treatment. The impact of successful intervention can go much further than the woman herself into her family and society' (Lyon and Coleman 1996:15).

The notion of health care tailored to women's needs should be seen in the context of a long-term trend towards a larger female prison population, and an older population in society at large. The prison environment accelerates rather than arrests the deterioration of their health. For some, their eyesight has weakened from the constant glare of fluorescent lights. Replacement dentures are of poorer quality, leaving elders in some discomfort, and in extreme cases preventing them from being able to eat. The draughty corridors of the old Victorian fortresses sets off arthritic pain. Sasha Sibley acknowledges that:

SS: I was suffering with it on the outside, but not as much. I was in Holloway, it was very cold there. It is an old heating system. And there were all these little, little windows – you couldn't shut them properly. No matter if the heater was working. The wind blew in. It was very cold there.

Sasha Sibley
Age: 54
Time spent in prison: 13 years

As the prison population ages, the costs of keeping older women will increase (Bernat 1989). This can include special diets, physiotherapy and long-term medical care, through to help with personal care, which is another reason to consider alternatives to custody for elders, who are a low re-offending risk category. The lack of adequate physiotherapy and through-care once released places the responsibility to motivate themselves and find means of keeping their body active on the elders themselves, sometimes through a risky process of trial and error:

SS: I feel heavy because there is nothing to keep me active – there's a *gym* here but for somebody like me it's no use. Because I went there once, and for one week I couldn't get up after that because of my arthritis.

Sasha Sibley

A common theme was that the diet they received was nutritionally inadequate. This wasn't compensated for by vitamin and mineral supplements. For some, supplements were a necessary requirement to maintain a reasonable quality of health, yet they are denied this basic preventative measure:

MM: What happened with going in prison some people stop their periods. But I didn't, I just started running. It went on and on and on. It just wouldn't stop. By the Monday, they rushed me in and did me the hysterectomy. They said I had to stay on iron tablets *all* the time, *constantly all through my life*.

Holloway gave me the iron tablets. I went to Penjara with a month's supply of iron tablets. They took them off me and said you not having iron tablets. You are not allowed vitamins in prison and I have never had an iron tablet since. But now we are allowed to buy them, my friend of fifteen years sends them me. But I have never been allowed a vitamin tablets from the health centre, none of us have. Silly isn't it. [emphasis in original]

Margot Metcalf

Many couldn't afford to buy the vitamin supplements sold by the prison service, which in any case are barely adequate, and of poor quality. The lack of minerals and vitamins available to women meant that they relied on vitamins being sent in from the outside (Wahidin 2003). The lack of supplements for women going through the menopause or for those whose ovaries were removed early on in the life course accelerated the onset of osteoporosis and arthritis (Shapiro 1993). It has been documented that the removal of the ovaries will cause a cessation of oestrogen production and a consequent premature reduction in bone density (Gannon1999). Molly Mossdale, who has lived behind the bars since her late thirties and is now in her late fifties, found herself at the age of 40 undergoing a hip replacement and now suffers from rheumatoid arthritis and osteoporosis.

The lack of after-care she received after she underwent a hysterectomy in her thirties has accelerated the ageing process and age-related illnesses. Owing to her versatility in 'making do' in an environment which does not cater for anyone other than the able-bodied, she chose to do textiles as:

MM: It helps my legs when I am using the peddles. It gives them some exercise.

Molly Mossdale

A further potential cost of keeping older women in custody is that of adapting buildings for those with limited mobility. In practice, women with mobility problems found that once inside prison such measures were not in place, and they were expected to 'make do', arrive on time for 'check', work, etc. This meant that elders with impaired mobility had to leave earlier to avoid being put on report. Some were walking further than they would do at home without the equipment to assist them with their disability. Once in prison, they found that they had to walk up and down three flights in order to be able to go to work. Even though in some prisons a lift was in place, in one establishment it needed to be operated by a member of staff. Owing to staff shortages the operational needs took precedence over the woman's physical needs. Consequently, women with mobility problems were excluded from exercise and other facilities, fostering feelings of isolation and increased regulation, and creating further obstacles to maintaining a tolerable level of health.

Punished for being ill

While not all older prisoners are in need of high levels of medical attention, many may suffer from the chronic ill-health experienced by elders in society as a whole: emphysema, arthritis, cardiac problems, hypertensive disorders, osteoporosis, etc. The questions which fuelled the women's fears were, 'what happens when women become infirm? Who looks after them? How do they get about, is there adequate provision? And if not, what are the alternatives?' Their fears were confirmed when they saw other women in later life 'making do', with the help of other prisoners but not of the prison system. Alison, who had been seriously ill for the first two years of her 14-year sentence, raises these concerns:

AA: I mean what happens when women become infirm, or incontinent? Or, who brings them their food? Who looks after them? How do they get about? What happens if you have got osteoporosis? There just aren't any provisions for that kind of thing in prison.

— was here, she had osteoporosis. She was very slow at getting up and down the stairs. She used to get other prisoners to do things for her. The stairs are also quite narrow. You just have to come down to the boiler and fill a flask full of boiling water and then struggle back up the stairs with it, while other people are pushing past you.

Alison Anwar

For women in later life the lack of careful assessment of their health needs, or provision for their disability, and the cursory and dismissive attitudes of some of the doctors, have led to serious cases of neglect, increasing and fostering feelings amongst older prisoners of isolation, humiliation and fear of the consequences of being ill in prison. It is evident that the operational needs of the prison are imposed on the individual:

AA: If you are ill, and you don't go to work, you are locked in your cell. So you are punished for being ill. You can't phone home. You lose your association. So even if I'm feeling ill I still make the effort to go to work. Because I know I need to ring home every day.

Alison Anwar

Elders who were convalescing depended on other women to assist them in their survival, instilling a sense of rolelessness and helplessness:

AA: And if it's not for the other prisoners filling your flask there is nobody to do anything for you.

Alison Anwar

This can create a tense atmosphere, impinging on the rights of others and putting the elder in a potentially very vulnerable position. Julie June recalls a time at Penjara where one elder who was on crutches depended on the other women to assist her:

JJ: It wasn't ideal, people were having to help her and people were getting fed up of carrying her things up for her.

Julie June

In these circumstances the needs of elders must be taken into account to fulfil the mission statement and avoid accusations of injustice and lack of care. Yet, the structure of prisons in organisation, architecture and training fails to address the diversity of need of those who are other than able-bodied. The kinds of problems women in later life may, and do, experience in the prison system largely result from the fact that prison is geared for the young and able-bodied male (Caldwell and Rosefield 2001), and has not previously been designed with the disabled or elderly person in mind. For particular prisons it is the absence of basic facilities, such as having a medical centre on site, and ground-floor rooms, which emphasise how women throughout the life course are discriminated against within the penal system. Add to this the discourse of the essential woman, the malingerer, which informs health-care practices, discriminating against women throughout the life course, and the sentence for older women becomes harder to bear. It is through these discourses and the invisibility of their need that techniques of discipline have a cumulative effect based on ageist discourse. Likewise, it is a salient feature of the text that problems of overcrowding and the restrictions on numbers mean that higher paid jobs, and education classes tended to favour the younger women.

A further effect of being ill in prison is that the person is paid at the basic rate and has little chance to buy phone cards to maintain contact with the outside, thus compounding the sense of dislocation and isolation with the feeling of rolelessness in society. Even when women showed exemplary behaviour and were placed on an enhanced regime, they could be excluded from the privilege because of their age-related illness and the lack of adequate facilities in prison to cater for their needs. Thus, many felt they were punished further because they were excluded from earning a higher wage and from moving to better parts of the prison even though they were entitled to. Una Ulrich describes it as follows:

UU: I mean being enhanced here means absolutely nothing to me because I am in a medical room on the ground floor which is not an enhanced room. It is a shared room. It's a six bedded room.

Una Ulrich

Although she is entitled to enhanced privileges,[5] Noleen's medical condition and the lack of adequate ground-floor facilities has meant that she is in a shared room with younger women, where she has to abide by the rules of the basic regime. Many elders felt embarrassed changing in front of younger women, having to reveal the calligraphy of age upon the body and the marks from major surgery. In order to avoid changing in front of younger women, elders are forced to find a space in the prison, which arrests the gaze. Noleen Norton found sanctuary from the gaze changing in a toilet which was used by the whole prison:

NN: When I get changed, I go and get dressed in a toilet but I don't really like doing that because it is quite hard to find places to put your clothes and things. It is not so bad now that the weather is getting warmer and the clothes are thinner. You can fit them on top of the cistern. But when it is bulky things and then you sort of take off your dressing gown and where do you put that? This is where having a health problem actually sort of works against you here, where the discrimination comes in. There are two toilets available for us to use. But they are also used by everybody else.

Noleen Norton
Age: 69
Time spent in prison: 10 years

Although she finds ways of making do, she argues that they shouldn't have to; this necessity reflects the lack of appropriate facilities. The categories of risk, need and conduct become subsumed under the operational needs of the prison. In terms of risk she is treated with unnecessary methods of restraint. Her health needs are marginalised by the lack of appropriate after-care provision, and her good behaviour loses its currency under a regime of 'privileges' designed with the young and able-bodied in mind. Although there is a room on 'the flats' (ground-floor accommodation in prison) obviating the need to use stairs, she is denied the privileges that accompany the enhanced status, e.g. a single room with a television and the sole use of a toilet:

NN: We have a room – bedroom downstairs here on the ground floor. We are enhanced. But we can't have a television. Up on the 3rd floor where they're enhanced, they can have a television. But because this takes other cases, other people who perhaps aren't on enhanced, we can't have a television.

She goes on further to say:

NN   Now to me that is – we're being discriminated against. Our lights go out at eleven o'clock, the same as young offenders. It doesn't happen for other enhanced but because we're down here, it happens.

Noleen Norton

Elders' existence on the periphery becomes more salient when their illness becomes punished not only by the lack of facilities but by the direct cut in their wage if too ill to work. The effect of this upon what is an already meagre wage in prison prevents many from seeking help or allowing themselves adequate time to recuperate fully. It is the worry of not being able to keep in contact with the outside world and the family, not being able to afford to be ill, that prevents many from using the time in prison to convalesce, thus exacerbating their condition. Anna Arnold found that although seriously ill:

AA: I was more concerned about [being] put on Basic[6] and I was only on £2.50. So obviously, I couldn't buy the stamps when I wanted to. I couldn't keep in touch with my family as much as I wanted to. It was coming up to Christmas and I wouldn't be able to phone my kids. So what I did, I was off for about six or seven weeks and the week before Christmas I was on sentence planning, so they asked me if I'd got any problems and I said I [would like] to go back to work.

You go to Basic, if you get bed rest. If you're ill then you're only on £2.50. Then if you go on long term it goes to £3.25 but it's *nothing*. It just so happened like I'd got a stock of toiletries anyway, otherwise I mean I wouldn't have managed. I'd got my mate who was here, she was good and she helped bath me; well shower me, you know she give me little bits and bobs. She did help me through it.

Anna Arnold

The lack of standardised care and an adequate wage mean that women in later life can only survive via the support of others who themselves have very little to give. Without other prisoners assisting them to bathe and sharing toiletries, some elders become forgotten, neglected and cut off from the outside world. Elders also complained at the lack of information given to explain the wage system and the criteria of what makes a person eligible for Labour 1, 2 and 3.[7]

Although Petra Puddepha fulfils the criteria for the enhanced regime, her illness prevents her, like many others, from accessing the benefits of that level. She states that:

PP: Because I am not A 1 category health wise, I can't go on to the hostel. A lot of the jobs are closed to us. It really causes a lot of problems.

I think it is two sitting which may be three. Some people say it's a non-worker, which is three, and some people say it is two sitting only. So I don't honestly know quite which one it is.

Petra Puddepha

In one prison the criteria for moving onto the hostel are mobility and length of sentence. Petra Puddepha fits the latter but the lack of mobility prevents her from getting onto the hostel.

PP: To get on the hostel you've got to be a Category 1 worker, which I am not. I very much doubt if I will persuade them to up-grade me to Category 1. So the hostel is closed to me.

I really could have done with getting on the hostel or at least having the opportunity. I asked for instance if I could possibly go on a town visit into Whitstable, to the Job Centre, to see if there were any jobs that I felt that I was capable of doing. I was told, 'Oh no, you can't do that until you are on the hostel'. But you can't go on the hostel unless you've got a reasonable prospect of getting a job. [Laughs]

Petra Puddepha

Similarly, Molly Mossdale, who suffers from arthritis and osteoporosis, has found herself although eligible, excluded from the pre-release hostel and forced to disengage from certain activities because of her lack of mobility. Molly states the reasons for this:

MM: How would I get to college or get onto the pre-release scheme? Once the taxi forgot to wait for me. It took me seventy-five minutes to walk back to the prison – most people do it in twenty minutes.

Molly Mossdale

For older women in prison becoming ill is one of their greatest fears. It is a fear based on the loss of autonomy, and the knowledge that they would be left to serve their time on the periphery dependent on a system which is over-stretched and under-resourced. This hidden minority will pose challenges to the jurisprudence and due process system, which is failing to prepare elders to 'lead law-abiding and useful lives in custody and after release', and not providing adequate and suitable facilities to enable elders to live a reasonable quality of life behind and beyond the walls.

It is imperative that the prison system provides not only comprehensive opportunities while in prison (Edwards 1998) and appropriate resettlement programmes (Dugger 1988, 1990), but also alternatives to the traditional custodial framework in which older women find themselves growing old. The possibility of housing older women in a specialised area of prison, albeit with access to common areas, will be discussed in a later chapter. By taking account of their specific needs and the obstacles that elders face in prison, the prison service would be reversing the process which up to now has served to render the experiences of women in later life marginal. Petra Puddepha was emphatic about what was needed to improve the situation:

PP: There's nobody here with responsibility for older people in prison. I would just like to see a working party set up to look at women over fifty and disabilities as well.

There's so many things that we can do, but there is no expertise, or no age or disability policy here at all. Just thinking in broader terms of what we can do. It's just short-sightedness [on the part of the prison service]. What I'm advocating is the appointment of somebody who looks at the whole broad issue of disability and age. Because they are disabled or infirmed, doesn't mean to say that they're written off so that *they wander around here for years doing nothing.*

What are their needs? Whether it's physical, mental they have different needs and there are avenues which haven't been explored. We have an officer for bullying, we have a racial discrimination officer, but there is nothing in here, or anywhere else that I've come across, that looks at the needs of women in their fifties.

Petra Puddepha

Conclusion

The heterogeneity of elders in prison makes understanding the health status of the elderly prisoner a perplexing endeavour. Special barriers contributing to this dilemma are associated with the vast differences in prison populations and the lack of research and statistical information available – for example, regarding the health-care expenditure per head of prison population by age (Personal communication, Dr Mary Piper: Directorate of Prison Health-care).

As people age, certain physiological changes take place. While these changes may vary from individual to individual, they generally affect body tissue, sensory perceptions, circulation and other physical and mental functions. Tissue changes include the decline of lean body and bone mass and the increase of fat mass (Henwood 1993; Holtzman, Brauger and Jones 1987). Bones become brittle due to decreased mineral content and joints lose elasticity. Muscle strength decreases and susceptibility to debilitating injury from falls increases.

Older prisoners in England and Wales report chronic ill-health at much higher levels than their peers in the community (Personal Communication, Dr Mary Piper, Directorate of Prison Health-care). Studies have indicated that this health profile matches that of the older prisoners in the USA who have been found to exhibit 'accelerated biological ageing' in prison, and 'to have aged roughly 10 years beyond the average citizen'. A typical 50-year-old prisoner is physiologically similar to an average 60-year-old person outside (McShane and Williams 1990:202–208). The Florida Corrections Commission (1999:17) adds that on average each inmate over the age of 55 suffers from at least three chronic health problems, including hypertension, diabetes, alcoholism, cancer, emphysema and stroke. These prisoners have a higher incidence of disease and significant functional disabilities (http://www.dcor.state.ga.us/research). Though exact costs are difficult to determine, most estimates calculate the cost of housing an older inmate as three times that of a younger prisoner (Georgia Department of Corrections 2002; Florida Corrections Commission 2001 Annual Report).

The cost of medical services for prison elders is estimated to be four to five times more expensive than that of the under-50s. In 1997 daily medical care for the general prison population cost $5.75 per offender nationwide (Neeley et al. 1997). American research shows that the cost of caring for prison elders was nearly three times higher at $14.50 (ibid.). Care for an increasing number of older prisoners will dramatically strain health-care resources as well as increase prison medical costs. Over the past ten years the cost of health care has been rising in society at large, and concurrent to this there has been an increase in the number of persons going to prison. In addition we are seeing in England and the United States the general ageing of the prison population. Despite this fact, little systematic planning has been conducted to address the multitude of attendant issues.

Elders who have fallen ill or are living with an age-related illness are acutely aware of the lack of provision in prison. As already discussed, it is vital to provide adequate and suitable internal spatial arrangements for elders with mobility impairments or age-related illnesses. While a single cell is viewed as a luxury in prison, the elders in the sample would argue that it is a privilege which should be potentially available to all women, since it offers the possibility of privacy, and enables an expression of self-identity in the form of personal territory. It would prevent some of the bullying and victimisation experienced by elders in the study. It is also important to address how elders lose this privilege when ill.

Allowing elders privacy and autonomy and the maintenance of their privileges regardless of age-related illnesses, would empower elders to take control over crucial aspects of their lives. It would encourage elders to seek medical attention when they need it and allow themselves adequate time to convalesce without the fear of losing their income. It is clear from this chapter that the health-care needs of elders must be addressed to avoid accusations of neglect (Cavan 1987; Chaneles and Burnett 1989). It is in this process of 'making do' that the elders draw on prior (and indeed stereotypical) qualities of the women – e.g. resourcefulness and stoicism around medical and domestic difficulties and also having the ability to withdraw and keep to oneself. Some elders draw on qualities which are stereotypically associated with the female *offender* – e.g. rebellion and refusal of 'feminine' modesty; and some create qualities new and hitherto alien to the women in question, so that (perhaps 'perverse') aspects of institutionalisation may be increased rage and flexibility of the 'self'-repertoire.

It is interesting also that this is an interactive process – just as the women's experiences and enactments of self are constrained by the environment, so the environment is also a product of the various responses and adaptations of all the 'actors' (inmates and staff). A good example of this are the fictional portrayals, such as the BBC drama *Bad Girls*, which focus particularly on the institutional as a created culture, which both changes and is changed by each person, event and configuration of relationships, although obviously the structural and political determinants provide the ultimate constraints as well as containing inbuilt bias towards certain outcomes, many of a tragic nature.

The essence of this chapter demonstrates how female elders are further punished by a system which fails to accommodate the differing needs of the women in their 'care'. It also demonstrates how elders construct scripts/a prison repertoire in order to make do. The next chapter will illustrate how externally imposed restrictions on education, training and employment lead to a severance with the outside world.

Notes

1   Urry's definition of 'scapes' is applicable as it captures the fluidity of time and how the women are not in stasis: '*Scapes* are the networks of machines, technologies, organizations, texts and actors that constitute various interconnected nodes along which *flows* can be relayed. Such scapes reconfigure the dimensions of time and space' (Urry 2000: 193).

2   By 'show', she means that after nine years of taking HRT on the outside she was no longer menstruating; however, with the withdrawal of HRT she begun to menstruate.

3   National Service Framework for Older People 2001 Section 15 states, 'The NHS and Prison Service are working in partnership to ensure that prisoners have access to the same range and level of health services as the general public.'

4   Para: 3.33: 'Younger women prisoners, like younger men, are, in general, the more volatile group and present greater control problems: older women prisoners have become part of the strategy to manage them.'

5   Under the Incentives and Earned Privileges Scheme (IEPS) introduced in 1995, prison regimes are divided into Basic, Standard and Enhanced levels, and prisoners move from one to the other according to their behaviour. Some women's prisons house Basic regime prisoners on the bottom landing, known as the Flats. (For further details see Appendix C: Incentives and Earnable Privileges table.)

6   Prisoners on a Basic regime are allowed to spend only £2.50 a week and their visits and phone calls are severely limited.

7   Classification of work prisoners are judged to be capable of – Labour 1 is any kind of work, however heavy. Labour 3 is the lightest.

Chapter 6

Within These Walls: Older Women in Custody

The experiences of older women in the criminal justice system are determined, as we have seen, by the structural, political and economic constraints that characterise the prison system (Carlen 2002). Furthermore, in terms of their gender, older women are placed in an aggregation of conflicting and contradictory discourses. Women offenders are assumed to be different from men (the criminal norm), while at the same time failing to meet the criteria for 'femininity' imposed by the dominant culture; parallel to this is imposed an age-neutral rule, which ensures that elder women's specific needs are not catered for, alongside (and in apparent contradiction to) practices which quite explicitly discriminate on the basis of age. Nowhere is this more apparent than in the area of education and training, broadly thought of as 'rehabilitation'.

This chapter will examine the impact on older women of the lack of appropriate educational facilities. In addition, it will closely consider the related issues of the employment opportunities available in prisons, and their implications for the subjective experience of prison. Historically, educational training in women's prisons has been part of the disciplinary regime based on returning offending women to their essential roles. Education in prison is linked to 'traditional' conceptions of women's roles. Women are less likely than men in prison to receive education, pursue leisure activities and access training, and they are more likely to have to carry out domestic tasks. Thus, the ideologies of the family inseminate the prison regime and condition the meaning of women's imprisonment as part of a wider discourse that defines criminal women as 'doubly deviant' (Carlen 1983; Dobash *et al.* 1986). Educational facilities in women's prisons are still based on 'female subjects', such as home economics and other domestic skills (Hamlyn and Lewis 2000). These discourses of the 'essential' woman are not only responsible for the economic dependency – inducing domesticity inherent in penal regimes and prison education for women (Carlen 1983; Dobash *et al.* 1986) – but also negate women's skills, and aptitudes for life-long learning, thus failing to take women's employment needs seriously. Prison for women is experienced as the inculcation of dependence, deferment and, for women in later life, invisibility. So what happens to women in later life who are deemed by the prison and wider society to have had their life?

For women in later life the prison regime fails to address the commitment to *helping* these women. Instead, the women are faced with cumulative vulnerabilities in an uncertain and changing society which are based on ageist discourse and stereotypes of later life and of femininity. They are ascribed secondary status in terms of accessing facilities in prison. Yet, they are also expected to govern others, to maintain order by virtue of their age, even as they are constructed and treated as the same by the jailers. The experiences women in later life have gained through the life course become negated, forgotten and invalidated in the prison environment. Rather than being celebrated for her academic acumen and having specific courses tailored to her needs, Olivia Ozga, who is serving an eight-year sentence, was told:

OO: I was over-qualified and there was nothing here for me but I would have thought that when you are doing a long sentence that you need some form of stimulation and you just cannot continually find that stimulation on your own. I found it quite soul destroying in many respects. You know, the government continually prattles on about rehabilitation and preparing people for when they leave prison but they never do anything constructive about it.

Olivia Ozga

Although education facilities varied from one female establishment to the next, the overriding issue was the lack of adequate provision compared with the facilities and training for male offenders. For example, at Penjara the women were limited to five educational sessions a week in comparison to male offenders who on average spent three months in the prison and were given access to full-time education. In addition to the limited number of sessions, women found themselves on a waiting list because of the lack of space and computers available. Their frustrations resonate with the sentiment voiced in the *Times Educational Supplement* (1998) about the limited education provisions in prisons against which women's fare worse. 'Hundreds of hours are being slashed from prison timetables by governors…in the face of funding cuts'. The article further comments on the irony of the cuts, 'just when the government is emphasising life-long learning for all. Surely ministers could justify spending money on a system which would send offenders back into society better educated' (ibid.). Prior to imprisonment, Rosie Robottom worked in human resources as a trainer, but found that prison, rather than harnessing expertise or constructing tailored programmes for women of all abilities, had just one educational programme aimed at basic numeracy:

RR: There's a lot of things [older women] could be involved in. When I came here, the same as when I went to the other prisons, I was given an educational assessment. I was given a sheet of paper and asked to fill in the missing words, which was so basic, that I understood why they were doing it. But if you fulfil that basic requirement that you had the core skills of reading and writing that was it! That's the end of the story.

Rosie Robottom

The work which women do in prison has in the main little to do with acquiring skills for waged work outside, but is instead for the benefit of the instituion; i.e. cleaning and producing goods for sale (Giallombardo 1966; Mandaraka-Sheppard 1986, O'Dwyer *et al.* 1987). The Prison Reform Trust in 1995 conducted a study of prison education and concluded that 'it is to be regretted that no new policy statement on the education of women prisoners, which recognises the contribution of vocational skills, has been forthcoming from the Prison Service' (see Prison Reform Trust 1995). Any training that occurs is mainly a secondary by-product of this process of providing domestic services within the prison. Penal institutions reinforce the stereotypical and traditional sex-role of women which will return the criminal woman, who has offended against the 'nature' of her sex as well as against society, to her essential being.

The lack of appropriate work or training intensifies the sense of the loss of self, individuality, affirmation by others, and the disengagement with the outside world, which in turn reinforces the prison identity and the sense of rolelessness in prison. This is a good example of the punishing effects that prison embodies, which are based not solely on the deprivation of liberty but go deeper, and in this case are based on the *failure* of the 'disciplinary' function of the prison, to identify a 'normality' to which elders in prison can be returned. This reflects the lack of status and of positive roles for elders in society at large. It is the absence of facilities for an acknowledgment of this significant minority which constitutes further punishment. This contrasts with Foucault's view of discipline as technology for producing types of persons and behaviours. What we have here is exclusion, absences of a definition of desired characteristics to be produced by disciplinary penal power, or if this is a desired characteristic it is the negative one of refraining from dissent, acquiescing in invisibility. Olivia Ozga found herself in an open prison but in her

OO: Ten months [there] I haven't done anything constructive to keep my brain stimulated in that ten months other than what I do in my own room

Olivia Ozga

However resourceful they may be, the women find themselves in the direct path of the mechanistic prison machine which fails to accommodate difference, need and ability. The poor educational facilities combine with the general lack of provision and the disciplinary power of the prison jigsaw to infantilise women in later life by imposing a prison inscription, rendering them powerless while at the same time disciplining their resourcefulness. To combat this assault on their identity, some have written to funding bodies outside prisons in order to get recognition and support for their studies. The bureaucracy and the time it takes to set the wheels in motion when beginning a correspondence course reinforce their sense of helplessness and of being alone. For Petra Puddepha and others like her educational facilities and educational opportunities were limited:

PP: The educational opportunities, no. I think you tend to be treated as though you have an age of somewhere between the age of five to fifteen, most times. I don't think the education either here or in Lager takes into account people's various abilities. It tends to cater for the lowest common denominator. They give lip service to being helpful but it's not really that helpful. Um, yes, you can apply to courses and I am on an Open Learning course at the moment. But I find there isn't really – if I get a bit stuck with it there isn't really anywhere I can go. And as I say, I just feel as if I am butterflying from one thing to another and achieving absolutely nothing, which I find very frustrating.

Petra Puddepha

Many women felt that the prison system overlooked their need to be rehabilitated in order to lead law-abiding useful lives. Olivia Ozga was initially denied a place on education on the basis of her age. However, with insight, initiative and resourcefulness she did without 'luxuries' such as chocolate and phone cards to fund and further her studies:

OO: I think prison activities tend to favour the younger prisoners. I mean with regards to education I get a bit fed up when a place is given to a youngster. They don't use it to the best of their ability. They mess about a lot of the time and they don't take their placement seriously enough and then someone like myself is longing to get on to a placement to be able to do something positive. I've had to wait on the sidelines for so long. And that was put down to my age.

Olivia Ozga

The women regularly complained about the lack of fulfilling educational and employment facilities and the deleterious effects this has on their self-worth and sense of identity. There was a pervasive feeling of despondency about the role of employment and education in prison for them. They were resigned to the fact that the employment opportunities on the outside, once released, would be limited because of age discrimination and where others perceived them to be in the life course. It is by internalising age discrimination on the outside that elders rationalise the discrimination involved in prioritising the needs of the younger women over their own. Thus, their need becomes secondary in 'a culture built on youth'. Ellen Evergreen typifies this sentiment when asked:

AW: Do you think that's fair?

EE: No, I don't. I would love to work. But still – you've got to be thankful that the young ones get the jobs. That's the main thing isn't it? *Give them a chance.* [emphasis in original]

Ellen Evergreen

This raises the question of who perceives a woman in later life as too old for education and why, and what does this say about the prison's statement of purpose and the role of rehabilitation for women in later life?

Rosie Robottom makes sense of this overt form of discrimination in prison by placing it in the context of ageism in wider society, 'No – well I was *too old* for education. I won't work because I would be lucky if *I can get a job at my age.*'

By rectifying these discriminatory practices, the prison estate would have the opportunity of assisting older women to combat the age discrimination they will certainly meet on the outside, rather than merely reinforcing it by denying them the opportunity to acquire competitive skills and by encouraging them to believe that they cannot, and should not, expect to have a productive role in society, once released. Discrimination in work and education produces an 'excess' of punishment for older women, not least by further eroding self-esteem and painfully intensifying the frustration of wasted time, placing additional obstacles in the way of rehabilitation to an independent and useful life.

The work provided was based on the confining stereotypical role of domesticity. Lorna Langley, in her mid-seventies, felt humiliated, 'silly', when the activities consisted of making jewellery boxes, baking cakes, T-shirt painting, knitting, etc. As she says:

LL: They had sewing. I felt a bit silly, making little boxes, cardboard boxes which is rather silly for me, but there you go. Little boxes and you cover them with a cloth and put a lid on, for jewellery. I suppose the younger girls would say this would do for their jewellery, you know, but I think they could cater more in education for older women.

Lorna Langley

Jane Jobson describes the regimes of femininity, illustrating how these gendered strategies of control enforce 'traditional' modes of femininity by policing women's behaviour regardless of age and ability. Female prisoners are thus offered predominantly gender specific tasks and activities like sewing and 'third-form cookery':

JJ: I mean for instance the cookery is like third-form cookery. You know making Victoria sponge cakes and scones and everything is the lowest denominator. For older women that can cook it would be nice [to do] something a bit more interesting. I would like to see something about women's lives and their role in society.

Jane Jobson

Veronica Vicar asks why the prison can't have classes which are relevant to their lives:

VV: Well, classes about women and *their lives* and things that relate to them would be to me very stimulating. I am not saying, don't have a soft toys class, because there are people with children and babies. But I mean, how many soft toys do you want to make? [emphasis in original]

Veronica Vicar

Such offerings represent not only an extreme of stereotyping and patronising infantilisation, but also an apparent denial and devaluing of the 'feminine' skills the women *have* learnt, i.e. it is not merely that they have to learn how to cook, but there is no acknowledgment that they already know how (an assumption that, as prisoners, they must be deficient at the skills supposed to be typical of real women). There is no recognition of cooking as a complex craft from which someone could earn money (e.g. analogous to mechanics). This is an interesting example of the way some crafts become a trade or profession in the hands of men, while others are treated as a trivial hobby or 'accomplishment' for women. This tendency has its history in the bourgeois denial of the economic validity of 'women's work' and the notion, conversely, of economic work as unfeminine. Thus, what this elder is describing is also a class bias and reminds one of the history of bourgeois ideology as 'discipline', with its particular ideas about gender difference and morality (Atwood 1997). This enforced cult of domesticity continues as an ideological force associated with situating the female offender into dependency and into the home (Carlen and Worrall 1987). Tokwan Thomas reiterates the need for the female estate to have in place adequate educational provision so that women across the life course after imprisonment 'lead law-abiding and useful lives after release'.

TT: I mean I'd rather be out there doing something constructive you know, woodwork, something like that. [laughs] Why do they give *women, women's jobs sort of thing*? But they've never thought maybe they probably would like to learn something else. But all we have are sewing rooms and *laundry*.

        I also think a lot of women in my age group would like to do something more than the knitting group and creative design. I think a lot of women would like to take up something quite different to the stereotype. [emphasis in original]

Tokwan Thomas

It becomes apparent that imprisonment for many women in later life answers the first part of the statement of purpose, i.e. 'Her Majesty's Prison Service serves the public by keeping in custody those committed by the courts'. The second part of the statement of purpose would be answered by providing a milieu therapy. One can argue that the failure of the latter is indicative of the failure of the prison system to acknowledge the needs of elders in preparing for release. Rather than being enabled to feel that they have a fulfilling life to lead once released, they instead feel, as Molly Mossdale does, that:

MM: For elderly women nothing – *they have had their life I think* that's really bad. You see, the special facilities are for the youngsters going out so they can start to lead more useful lives. Over fifties, who *cares*, whether you lead a *useful life or not. You are over fifty – you have had it!* [emphasis in original]

Molly Mossdale

The sense of rolelessness and the lack of empowering activity is a pervasive feature of prison life for elders. Molly argues that,

MM: For the youngsters the gardens are excellent and the garden is good. They are out all the time in the fresh air; you've got painting parties, works parties, ever so good for the youngsters. But for our age, there is only the work room – it is tedious work [she whispers] – and then there is textiles – but apart from that *there is nothing else.* [emphasis in original]

Molly Mossdale

Tokwan Thomas raises a pertinent question when she states:

TT: I'm sure there's lot of women and youngsters who'd like to do courses on this, bricklaying, plumbing. *I mean it's equal opportunities now. Why are prisons not doing the same thing?* [emphasis in original]

Tokwan Thomas

In addition to addressing this blatant gender stereotyping and discrimination, Petra Puddepha argues that:

PP: There needs to be more provision for um if you like – it seems to me that *unless you are really fit you are totally disabled.* There doesn't really seem to be any provision very much mid-way. [emphasis in original]

Petra Puddepha

As these accounts show, elders in prison have concerns at how they are marginalised within a space which claims to enable women across the life course to 'lead useful lives' in custody and after release. Their exclusion from the limited activities is a disabling practice, which makes them feel that they have no role to play. It enforces dependency and engenders a sense of stigma around their ageing bodies, merging with the stigma of the prison label. This process of institutional infantilisation of elders into a second childhood and the denial of their rights as adults is dehumanising. The routinisation of daily activities, formal rules and the block treatment may prompt elders to feel as if they are marooned in an alien environment, forcing them to disengage rather than having the choice of refusing to engage in activities (Kratocoski 1990; Mackenzie 1987; Moore 1989).

Although the elders confront assaults on their identity daily, they also devise ways to keep control by subverting the techniques which attempt to normalise the inmate. Over time the physical and social forces limiting such challenges become progressively stronger and the protective mask becomes ingrained upon the space beneath the outward face. Their resistance is one which attempts to thwart the contamination by prison codes.

KK: You just have to put the mask on really. I don't let anybody see the real me. They need to see the face. The happy face, smiling and joking.

I was on the yard yesterday with two other girls. One is only twenty-one and I felt so depressed because it is so sad to hear her talk about what drugs they could get, how and when. I think maybe a lot of it is a way of coping and I think they also do it for the attention. Each day they find another ailment to talk about. Oh, we *can get this and take this...*

Kate King

JJ: I was walking around with them and they were discussing their own medical things. The young girl said, 'I'm on Amitriptyline[1]', and another name. I can't remember what it was. She was saying, how much she got for each and who to go to get other things. I asked her why and she said they took her baby away. They just float around like der, de, de, you know. Prison is a sort of fantasy world. What we are living in is a *moment* in prison. It's so sad. [my emphasis]

Julie June

Yet for those who don't subvert and negotiate the prison glare the fear is that the 'soul, personality and life of this being has been amputated, to leave the carcass, able to function in an animated yet somehow strangely lifeless way' (Probyn 1977:109–110).

The social structures and processes that create dependency in prison, coupled with the demands of the institution's regime (for example, of eating at set times), create a state of institutional dependency and have long-lasting effects on the individual's experiences and the subjective meanings of ageing and imprisonment. As Cath Carter argues:

CC: Prison is about taking away your dignity. So you have to strive to maintain your dignity in spite of all the assaults on it. *By other prisoners. By certain officers. By the system.* It is into *grinding you down* and some of them will tell you that you are the *same as everyone else.* [emphasis in original]

Cath Carter

It is important to note how the prison gaze on the one hand attempts to homogenise women in later life with women as a group, and on the other excludes, discriminates and constructs elders as 'other'. The paucity of activities for women *per se* serves as a constant reminder of their status as prisoners. Elders in prison can be seen as living life on the margins. It is the feeling of dislocation both with the outside world and the prison culture that make prison life for elders in later life become an 'existence both within and without a life'. This is a salient point in that women exist within this structure but don't, in effect, live. The quote below illustrates the way in which women feel frustrated that prison is failing to acknowledge and value their experience and knowledge which could be 'put to good use'. Rosie Robottom, quite rightly, states:

RR: I am fifty-seven next week. *I've got a life too.* I have got a wealth of experience and skill that I can put to good use out there. [emphasis in original]

Rosie Robottom

To curb feelings of despondency, rolelessness, depression, worthlessness, loneliness, and so on, women in the study want their experience and knowledge to be acknowledged and harnessed by the system so that both they, other women and the individual prison can benefit by using their experience, to facilitate more enabling forms of care and rehabilitation throughout the system. The time in prison should utilised, and, as Una Ulrich argues, the women should be given:

UU: A chance to be able to use *our* expertise, *our* ability, *our* experiences that we have; a chance to use *our* strengths. There's a lot of expertise in the prison, [which] isn't harnessed. It *isn't* used. They've got people here now who have very good academic records. They don't use it. They could give us much more. One of the things that's missing here is when you come in you get a pack of set information that's been prepared, telling you what the routine is and whatever. There is not a prisoner's handbook that gives the information such as, when you go on resettlement, wear the same clothes that you go out in as you come back in. That's the prison rules. Its only a little thing, but there's hundreds of those little things that we, as prisoners, know, and we've gone through the pitfalls. And an ideal project for me, and a few other women, would be to sit down and actually put one of these handbooks together. *Our expertise and experience is not used.* [emphasis in original]

Una Ulrich

For some the prison machinery over the years has stripped them of their agency and creates, as Probyn (1977:109) puts it, a catatonic state that looks neither beyond nor within the prison gates but which, as Molly Mossdale explains, is also based on a material reality:

MM: I have *no future.* I have *no future.* I can't go to a job, I can't go into the community as I would normally. There is such a gap between when I came in – I have to account for twenty years. So that means really getting lost on the outside. [emphasis in original]

Molly Mossdale

It is the interminable monotony of doing mind-numbing jobs year in and year out which discourages feelings of self-worth and motivation, and makes prison life unbearable, resulting in self-mutilations, suicide attempts, being placed on psychotropic drugs and feeling that their time in prison is a mere existence:

MM: I was given sleeping medicine the very first night here. I was given Chlorpromazine,[2] it looks like a clear liquid and it burns your throat. They then suggested that I was going through a bad time just take it for a week, and that week lasted for five years. By then I was not speaking coherently, I was doing everything very, very, slowly. After that I couldn't play badminton, I couldn't even see the shuttlecock, I couldn't move. I couldn't play table tennis. I was a complete zombie. It is easier for them to have quiet people around, not people crying their eyes out, not people emotionally disturbed. Give them night medicine. It's how to keep people quiet.

Molly Mossdale

The majority of the elders had at one time or another contemplated committing suicide or had made suicide attempts. Kate King, who for a time looked after the prison animals, recollects how her final suicide attempt was stopped:

KK: I'd swear, it was my goats that stopped me because I was on this bucket with a chain around my neck and all I had to do was kick the bucket away. But my goats were sitting there looking at me.

Kate King

The boredom which is unavoidable in such an environment intensifies a most personal fear of their physical health and mental capacity deteriorating. For women suffering from mobility problems, arthritis, rheumatoid arthritis and so on, choices that are available to other women are denied them. The following extract illustrates how the elders' sense of well-being goes unnoticed, resulting in more suffering because the prison system fails to address the differing bodily needs as one ages. Sasha Sibley's account is indicative of the prison officers' lack of training and awareness of needs of women in later life:

SS: There is nothing to keep me fit – there's a *gym*. But for somebody like me it's no use. I went there once, and for one week I couldn't get up because of my arthritis. So I was advised to walk round the garden every day. That's all I do. [emphasis in original]

Sasha Sibley

Out of the four prisons visited only HMP Avida acknowledged an ageing female population. However, the activities provided there for the over-fifties were in actual fact the same activities as for the under-fifties. An hour set aside with tailored activities for elders would have enabled those who were self-conscious about their bodies to benefit. Frightened by the verbal intimidation from the younger women, ridiculed and unable to go at the same speed as their younger counterparts, elders were dissuaded from using the gym. Tailored programmes specifically aimed at the over-fifties would decrease the potential for victimisation and bullying, and would encourage health promotion:

AW: Does Avida provide special facilities for the over-fifties?

MM: They used to. Last year there was an over-fifties. There isn't really – although they say there is an over-fifties gym. The fifties gym does exactly what everybody else does, so you do bums and tums or you do weightlifting. If you're over fifty you don't want to do weightlifting, you don't want to be walking on the trapeze.

Molly Mossdale

Ensuring that women in later life have access to appropriate facilities would do much to restore to them some level of control and responsibility over their lives. It would help eliminate the frustration and sense of helplessness engendered when attempts to attain personal worth, or even just stay fit and healthy, are blocked by the lack of adequate provision. Prisons would need to have policies in place reflecting the needs of women over fifty who are other than able-bodied. Petra Puddepha argues:

PP: I do think that they [the Home Office] should have a plan of action for what they *are going to do with older women*. It seems to be something that they *haven't* really addressed at all. I think they should have some kind of plan for older women. I mean at the moment actually there is a fairly high proportion of older women in here. There is a fairly high proportion of us.

But I certainly think in terms of Gefangnis and I suspect of other prisons, that no specific thought is given to people who are in this age category. It is given to sort of other categories it is not really – *they don't really* think about people of *our age group and our families*. And yet – I mean I appreciate we are a minority but I think a number of people you have to interview would say we are a *significant minority*. And presumably will continue to be! [emphasis in original]

Petra Puddepha

Petra and others like her, 'who although are not one hundred per cent fit on the outside had a normal job'. In prison elders found themselves being dismissed, despite having led active lives outside, because:

PP: If you are not fit you are totally disabled. There doesn't really seem to be any provision very much mid-way. When it was decided that I had to have a sitting only job it was sort of – Well, it was sort of well I don't quite know what we are going to do with you. We'll have to find something for you to do I suppose, were the words that were used and they were used by a Senior Officer. Um to me that means that nobody had really addressed those needs.

Petra Puddepha

Two questions arise from the above extract where there is nothing between 'fully fit' and 'fully disabled': where are all the ordinary sedentary jobs which the majority of people in the general population do which do not require high levels of fitness, strength or mobility? Why are the same standards on the outside not enforced in prisons, such as employment law as it relates to disability access and discrimination in recruitment? To prevent prison *for* punishment comparable standards should be enforced in prisons.

One has to acknowledge that, although the prison system rarely achieves its stated objective, many of those working at the various prisons are of a high calibre and show great commitment to reducing the pains of imprisonment. They are restricted, however, in a climate of cut-backs and the unprecedented growth in the prison population (Councell and Simes 2002) which in turn produces unintended perverse consequences. A prevalent feeling amongst the elders in the study is echoed by Alison Anwar:

AA: There's been a lot of cut-backs. It's getting worse. Come a time when they might as well just shoot everybody. [chuckles] They *just want to keep us alive*. How do they expect you to want to carry on? [emphasis in original]

Alison Anwar

Conclusion

Once in prison, elders are marginalised/excluded by their location in relation to wider society on the basis of being convicted and through their age and gender status. It is the sense of the loss of self and of individuality, the lack of affirmation by others, and disengagement with the outside world which reinforces the prison identity. A principal thread running throughout the book is how elders in prison remove themselves from a position which reinforces their situation of helplessness. Some elders become more self-reliant and resourceful, perhaps retreating to scholarly activity and to their cell. Elders who are illiterate are left to utilise their time/fill their time in any way they can. Molly Mossdale pointed out that, although living in open conditions, elders who are unable to read or write or lack the means to buy batteries for the radio or phone cards to maintain contact with the outside world are left with few resources for survival. In her account of an elder who fits this category, her way of surviving in prison is by:

MM: Moving her room around three to four times a week because she has nothing else to occupy her mind. I think it is a terrible waste of a human life when the only thing she can think about is moving her room around three to four times a week. There has got be more to life in prison then just re-arranging your room.

Molly Mossdale

This chapter shows how the women become observed in terms of their ageing bodies rather than their capacity as active agents with a life to lead. They are also excluded because of the lack of facilities and rendered invisible by the absence of acknowledgement of external (to prison) roles and responsibilities. As prisoners, females elders suffer from discriminatory practices, which result, for instance, in receiving fewer leisure, work and educational opportunities than male and younger female prisoners. Although we have seen them to be resourceful, the women found themselves in the direct path of the operational needs of the prison machine, which fails to respond to difference, need and ability, in enabling offenders to lead a useful, law-abiding life in and out of prison.

The prison service, penal reformers and the general public must rectify the invisibility of elders' experiences of prison. It is only by making visible the ignored and the forgotten that we can begin to address the needs of this particular group in prison.

Note

1   Amitriptyline is a sedative used to alleviate some types of depression.

2   Chlorpromazine is an anti-psychotic drug more commonly known by the brand name Largactil. Largactil is a 'major tranquillizer once commonly used to control severe psychotic conditions, such as schizophrenia. It is hardly used on the outside because of the side-effects, which include the slowing of thought and speech, numbness and difficulties with motor coordination' (British Medical Association, Royal Pharmaceutical Association of Great Britain, *British National Formulary,* September 1999, Vol 38:168).

Chapter 7

Forget Me Not: Older Women in the Criminal Justice System

The previous chapters demonstrate that the journey from court to prison is a brutalising process where the operational needs of the prison are imposed on the individual. This chapter will demonstrate how the prison label takes precedence over their life outside. It is in part through a process of losing reference points on which to hang their identity that they as women in later life are rendered invisible, punished in ways which go beyond mere incarceration and beyond simple material hardship and deprivation. It is the loss of role and status brought about by a range of experiences from being over-regulated and spoken to disrespectfully to having their responsibilities in the outside world blatantly ignored. The organisation of the prison is in itself the creator of punishment and within that the officers become servants and operatives of the penal machine (Carlen 1983; O'Dwyer *et al.* 1987). The quote below illustrates how punishment goes beyond the deprivation of liberty.

SS: The prison would improve by letting the officers treat you with a bit of respect for a start-off. They just treat you as the young ones.

Sasha Sibley

SS: They talk to you, like you're *nothing*, as if you're just *nothing*. Not all officers, don't get me wrong but they talk to you as if you're *nothing. You have done a crime, you're in prison now.* [emphasis in original]

Sasha Sibley

A salient feature of the above quote is when Sasha notes that 'not all officers' engage in punishing the women, implying that, although working within the prison machine, the regimes can be negotiated. The carceral and juridical stare together encompass the requirements of punishment, and the carceral not only holds prisoners but also manufactures networks of institutional power which penetrate into all aspects of the women's lives; consequently, the deployment of punishment takes many guises, from the intimate intrusions of being strip-searched by women half their age to how much toilet roll they are allowed to have on a monthly basis. This is degrading and problematic for all women going through their monthly cycle, or who are menopausal or incontinent. Julie June, who is fighting to clear her name, poignantly discusses the techniques of discipline used by the system and the officers so that women in their 'care' become dependent on the system and their carers. The extract provides an example of how punishment is manufactured and delivered within the carceral system:

JJ: We are being dished out so many slices of bread. That's never happened. *We are grown women.* The bread was left in the kitchen and we helped ourselves. Now we are only being given so many slices of bread. It's *oppressive* in that, if you run out of a toilet roll, or tampax, or...you could go down more or less at any time. It's got a bit more – it was stipulated times like unlock after tea time. You could go at any time and ask, 'May I have a toilet roll?' Not any more! You are given monthly supplies and *if you run out of those supplies, God help you.* I brought that up at the council meeting. I said, one girl in particular here, who is very sort of withdrawn, would be too embarrassed to ask. [emphasis in original]

Julie June

For elders – in particular for women – their place within the generational order is central to their personal identity, as a result of their close identification with generationally based, care-giving roles, and the disruptions to this generational order are experienced as infantilising and alienating. Throughout the chapters this is a thread linking the disparate lives of elders:

AA: I'm old enough to be their mother. To be spoken to, like they speak to you is really degrading. I've never been spoken to like it. And the young girls [officers]. Younger than me. I've never been used to be calling them 'miss', which is quite degrading really. There was one officer there. I'll never forget she was very loud mouthed and the vile language she used to use. She was terrible. Just because she had a uniform and key on.

Anita Arrowsmith

Some elders are carers of elderly parents, grandchildren, elderly husbands and children. The discontinuity of outside reference points increases the pains of imprisonment. The women argue poignantly how they resent and resist the infantilising process. The process can take many forms from the way they are expected to address members of staff, calling officers 'Miss', to the way younger officers respond to their requests. Petra Puddepha encapsulates the infantilisation process and the indignity of being placed in a system where age and experience become worthless commodities.

PP: Um, they don't seem to allow us any scope for us to use our *own* common sense in matters. I feel that they forget sometimes that we have actually lived lives outside before we came to prison. [emphasis in original]

Petra Puddepha

The pains of punishment would be alleviated, as stated by Cath Carter, by simply not 'treat[ing] you as if you are some kind of half-witted three year old'. As elders withdraw from the prying gaze, they simultaneously withdraw from help in order to do their time quietly, with minimum interaction with the structure of the prison jigsaw. This act of withdrawal reflects an awareness or a tacit 'knowing' (Goffman 1983, 1990) of the environment on the part of the elders. Owing to the unpredictability of the other women in prison and the transitory population, the new set of mores within prison disrupts the boundaries of what is known in and out of prison, which encourages women to withdraw, re-creating themselves as knowing agents.

Cath Carter, a former teacher, said that life in prison would be bearable if:

CC: Well I would like to be treated as an adult and given some consideration that I have had, whether I am guilty of this offence or not, I've had fifty years in the world, *offence free* and that hasn't been given any credit.

I'm not given any credit for that. I'm not *treated* as an adult. I'm *not* given *responsibility* and I am *not trusted*. I think the older you are, the more you resent all those things being taken away because you are used to having them. Whereas younger people are not used to responsibility yet. [We] wear many hats and in here *it's regression time*. You know, you have to go back to *being a number* – you have a *prison number*, and you have to remember it, and a lot of women find that very hard. [emphasis in original]

Cath Carter

The women interviewed said that they found the hardest thing they had to endure in prison was the fact that they had been stripped of their dignity. Most of them had worked all their lives and, at a time when they were retired or coming up to retirement, they were suddenly being treated with little respect by the staff and ordered about as if they were children. Cath Carter poignantly describes this variant of punishment:

CC: A lot of us have had children, some of us are grandparents. We are used to being in charge, we are used to running our own homes, looking after elderly parents. I mean, it is a great ordeal to come into an institution and to be powerless and for your autonomy to be taken away entirely.

They make no differentiation between the young offenders and the old offenders and that is something which is very irksome. As I say, a lot of us have had not only responsibility – important things to do in life. And to come here and to be sort of bossed around and fingers wagged at you and all kinds of trite bits of home-made philosophy trotted out. It's very irksome indeed. I would like to be treated like an adult, even if I am in prison.

Cath Carter

Some likened the experience to being put in a residential home for the elderly, where having still retained their full mental faculties, they were being treated as if they suffered from senile dementia. It was incredibly embarrassing for elders to endure regular strip-searches by women the ages of their daughters or granddaughters. Some of the elders at the time were going through the menopause, which wasn't taken into account, and the irregularity of their periods led to humiliating situations. Elders who couldn't manage the stairs were placed in a dorm with younger women who looked upon their aged bodies with mirth and derision. Thus, their aged bodies become an object of the younger women's gaze, labelled as 'other', revealing the frailty of their body and bodily functions in an environment in which youthfulness and the ageless body is viewed as the norm. The lack of recognition of women's lives outside becomes a source of anguish for women, who are constantly reminded that their seniority and experience is a worthless currency in prison.

Any positive connotations of seniority current in wider society are lost in this carceral reality. To survive, elders in prison forge together a visage, a countenance which immobilises the prison gaze, revealing nothing to their captors. However, over time the decomposition of their outside identity is dependent on the length of sentence, the degree of contact they have with the outside world and the types of medication they receive once in prison.

Elders in the study resented, resisted, negotiated and subverted the infantilising process. Their seniority in terms of age and their role on the outside become defences against the onslaughts made upon them. Their outside status as mother, worker, carer, grandmother, responsible adult, gives meaning to their understanding of who they are in a system which attempts to render the voices and experiences of women in later life silent. Alison Anwar experienced further punishment and disciplinary control on a visit:

AA: It started by being told not to kiss Tony on my visits. It made me feel like *some dirty little teenager, who'd been caught in some door-way, down some dark alley, doing something awful.* I was only giving him a peck on the lips. He was about to get up to get me a cup of coffee. You *should* be able to have contact with your loved ones. You should be able to hug them and give them a kiss. I'm not somebody who goes in there and wants to be feeling their bodies or bum. It's like I said to her, I said at the time I was fifty. I said, *I am a fifty year old grandma* and I said, you've made me feel like some a dirty little teenager. [emphasis in original]

Alison Anwar

Femininity denied

Prison, as we have seen, is a place *for* punishment rather than merely *as* punishment. The cumulative pains of imprisonment already described compound the feelings of estrangement from the outside world. But, as the extract below shows, prison doesn't have to *do* anything 'extra' to women in order to be *for* (and not just *as*) punishment – confinement and separation from their life context *per se* result in continual guilt and anxiety about people they are responsible for. In this sense prison *as* and prison *for* punishment are one and the same thing. This may be particularly severe for older women who have spent their lives coping with responsibilities for others and have built their self-esteem upon being competent and reliable carers and partners. Although Olivia Ozga is confident that her bills are being taken care off, it doesn't stop her from worrying, as she says:

OO: I'm lucky, I've got a good partner. But that doesn't mean to say that there's not problems outside and when another problem hits you, it's like a brick bat and there is no one you can turn to for help. [Gets tearful] And so therefore you get so wound up and then you start blaming yourself again and you go through so many deep seated emotions and it becomes almost unbearable and you just don't know how to cope with it. And it's hard and it's having, I think quite an adverse effect on my self-esteem.

I mean there was a stage when I just wanted to sit in a corner of my room and never get up again. But what can you do? You have got to get up and you've got to get going and carry on. But believe you me your heart's not in it.

AW: Would you like us to stop? [at this point she was getting quite upset]

OO: No, it's fine. Your heart's not in it. But I think it's the bits along the way you know – you just think – you just get on a nice smooth run and you think good – you know everybody is well at home and the bills are being paid and the visits are not too bad and all of a sudden there is a glitch. What might seem very trivial to somebody outside becomes a mountain in here. And no matter how intelligent you are, how logical you look at things they won't go away whilst you are in here. You feel so helpless. You just feel that you are bound and gagged from head to toe and there is no escaping that situation. I think with prison it's not just taking you out of society to say you've done this thing and you've got to be removed from society and be punished; the punishment just continues on. It starts from the day you are arrested and just continues on and on and on. But it's not just the punishment of being away from home. If only if it was that easy. *But it is the one hundred and one things that happen every day of the week that is the punishment.* [emphasis in original]

Olivia Ozga

The pains of imprisonment are achieved through a myriad of techniques and technologies (Foucault 1977b). This process defines women in later life as 'outwith', sexuality, femininity and domesticity. The work of Carlen (1983) shows how, in practice, conceptions of femininity contribute to the 'pains' of imprisonment. For Olivia, it appears her self-esteem has been of a recognisably 'feminine' nature: highly 'merged' with her partner/family, perhaps used to being the one who could always sort things out for them – in other words, defined by self and others in terms of this distinctly 'feminine' characteristic of feeling responsible for others and basing one's self-esteem on the ability to 'make it right' for everyone else. Yet, through being in prison she is treated as though these qualities and this typically female life situation does not apply to her. She is rendered powerless to enact the role upon which the meaning of her life rests. The result is guilt, depression and low self-esteem. Thus, we have a paradoxical situation whereby, even while the prison regime pursues its agenda of producing docile and domesticated females, there is an unarticulated process of punishing through the denial of, and refusal to respect and respond to, the gendered, 'feminine' nature of life experiences which results in additional trauma for women in prison.

Although the structure of prisons in organisation, architecture and training is slowly but progressively changing, the philosophy behind it remains the same. Today prisons are without the brutal conditions of the old Victorian penitentiaries, but are prisons nonetheless, not therapeutic communities. This reveals the tension in the work of Foucault who in *Discipline and*

Punish argues that a total institution represents the ultimate in carceral discipline, e.g. a planned, sophisticated technology for shaping human output; yet, what the elders are voicing is that the most severe effects of prison are far less planned than this, largely consisting of 'spin-offs' of unexamined assumptions about the nature of age, femininity and so on. The very crudeness of the means of responding to them, and the interaction of the fact of incarceration in itself with prison conditions, the psychologies of those involved, and so on, are determined on the outside.

The process of infantilisation, denial of autonomy and substitution of more disempowering (and irrelevant) modes of femininity within the prisons is evident, but ultimately the best training or help in prison can achieve little if women are returned unaided to the same conditions or to face the same difficulties which caused their 'downfall'. Molly has seen over the years women come back to prison because of the lack of through-care.

MM: The other needs are groups whereby we can see what is available for us on the outside, because the majority of us are not going out to jobs. And if we were, we couldn't get it, not at our age. What do we do about basic needs, like how to sign on for dole? What can you get from the social service: furniture, flat, anything like that etc.? To be prepared for the outside world, how are we going to cope as an old person living alone outside? Most of them are going out to nothing. I'm not but a lot of them are. When they go out they'll be alone, they've got to start all over again.

AW: Do you think from your experiences they can cope?

MM: No, they can't cope, because you see the sad part is they have offended once before, unless it is an old lag. But unfortunately, when they go out they are starting afresh, because their flats have been raided or their houses have been raided and everything has been emptied because there has been no one to look after it. So they've got to start all over again. They can only do that by going back to the crime again, they have not the money to survive.

Molly Mossdale

Women in prison: Forgotten roles

Women across the life course are structurally located differently from men in both the public and the private sphere, and the prison population reflects these differences. For example, the majority of women in the study are mothers, carers of elderly parents or grandchildren. Studies conducted so far focus on the needs of female offenders with younger children. The studies illustrate that women are less able than men to trust that their responsibilities will be taken on by their partners (HMIPP 2001). The then Chief Inspector of Prisons, Judge Tumin, in his 1989 report stated that 'it is often said that imprisonment is a punishment for both the offender and the family, that if a man goes to prison things are hard on his family, but the wife will *hold things together — she will cope*; the reverse is not necessarily true' (NACRO 1994b: No.24, my emphasis). In 14 years very little has changed.

Women in later life describe in detail how they are further punished by the informal social controls based on ageist and sexist assumptions which configure to deny them the continuation of their role as carers on the outside (Edwards 1994). Julie June's experience of imprisonment typifies the sentiments of the elders in the study when she explains that punishment is not just directed at the offender, nor does it stop at the prison gates, but has wider implications:

JJ: I feel like it's a whirlpool and I'm there in the middle. I know this has happened to me and my family know it's all wrong. Friends know it's all wrong, and it doesn't *just affect* me. And it doesn't *just affect my children*. It goes on and on until it affects a wider circle. It's like a whirlpool going out. It's like my son's getting married, the birth of my grandson Alfie are events which can never be gone over again. [emphasis in original]

Julie June

Women in later life argue forcibly that the system renders them invisible and attempts to sever the life threads that provide a conduit to the outside world. The cumulative punishments faced by women in later life result from the system failing to recognise their needs by prioritising and acknowledging only women with younger children. Wan-Nita states that:

WW: My children, oh yes, well the *forgotten children*, well they are because they think that because your child is older they're not a child any more. My Debbie is twenty-seven going on eighteen, she's a baby but not my baby any more, she's still my child and she still has great needs. She wants a hug and a cuddle and understanding, the same as a little child does. It doesn't *stop you being a mum, it doesn't stop you being a daughter*. You should be able to have a family visit day for the older child, not just for the younger child.

Jail has made her grow up a lot faster than she would have done, but at the end of the day she's still my baby and she's the forgotten one, where visits and things are concerned for children. I mean you want to be able to go on a visit, a little child on a visit can sit on your knee if they come to visit, but because of the seating arrangement I can't sit in close contact with my daughter. [emphasis in original]

Wan-Nita Williams

Motherhood and familial responsibilities do not end at the prison gates or when the child reaches the age of 16, but according to the elders in the study the prison rules assume they do. Petra Puddepha emphasises this point and explains how this in itself comes to constitute further punishment:

PP: Um, I think we tend to be not catered for if you like for the needs of our families who are although grown up still need us in a different way every bit as much as the younger people who can go out and get compassionate leave.

Although I might not be able to cure the problem at least I know what the problem is rather than leaving it to my own imagination. But because she is over sixteen. Well, she is thirty this year. But because of that I'm not considered to have a *need*. You *never stop being a mother*. You are a *mother 'til the day you die*. Um, your children remain – they may be adults but they are still your off-spring and your worries and concerns change, um, over the years but it doesn't stop them existing. But as far as the prison system is concerned, it would appear that once you've reached the arbitrary age of sixteen then you no longer have the need of a mother. [laughs] Regardless to her age she stills needs a hug. Somebody to confide in, and to talk over her problems with. Um, and I still have a need to be a mother as well. *The prison system as it stands for me certainly doesn't address those needs.* [emphasis in original]

Petra Puddepha

The hostile space of prison does not cater for the fundamental differences that define the situations of women in later life. One can argue that, although their needs are different, elders in prison are not perceived as having needs at all, reflecting attitudes to female elders on the outside. I would claim that this is a reflection of common perceptions of female elders as lacking a role because they are perceived neither as objects of desire nor as persons who are productive, economically or reproductively.

In my view this leads on to a very practical recommendation: that female elders should be encouraged or enabled in every way to remain in touch with their outside responsibilities and identities. (However, it is imperative to recognise that, unless men are also treated as though they have family responsibilities, it will reinforce the stereotype of caring as a predominately feminine role and also discriminate against the families of these men, 'holding it together' on the outside.) The ideological myth of age neutrality, rather than age discrimination is reproduced by officers, stipendiary magistrates and medico-legal discourses. By addressing the needs of older mothers with older children, by providing equal and adequate visiting facilities for children across the life-span (including the forgotten grandchildren), the prison system might result in women in later life feeling acknowledged. Current regulations can result in women losing contacts and roles in the outside world, or in returning to families in which they have become an outsider, a misfit, literally a stranger to its younger members; at best, perhaps uneasily accommodated and 'at worst' meeting outright rejection. Not only is this in direct contradiction to the meaning of rehabilitation, not only does it construct these women as 'burdens on society' and their families, but it constitutes a punishment of unimaginable emotional pain and loss which is not just for the duration of the prison sentence but for an entire lifetime.

Conclusion

The exploration of the women's stories highlights the pains of imprisonment, the resentment of the criminal justice system and in particular of the prison as it fails to harness and acknowledge elders' experiences and responsibilities. The great majority of the elders were carers of ageing parents, children and grandchildren; yet, there has been no systematic study of the responsibilities elders leave on the outside and the impact imprisonment has on their lives outside. I have argued throughout this book for the importance of engaging women across the life course in purposeful activity in prison and providing suitable through-care once released. Using the voices of the elders we can see how the criminal justice system is producing women that nobody wants.

The problems of overcrowding, the shortage of employment and resources for training and education result in a policy where higher-paid jobs and education classes tend to favour the younger women. As one woman says, this is because they have a 'life to lead' in contrast to their elders who are deemed by the system to have 'had their life'. The effect of unemployment is that they are paid at the basic rate and therefore have little chance to buy phone cards to maintain contact with the outside, compounding the sense of dislocation and isolation with rolelessness. The lack of constructive educational and employment opportunities leaves many with an overwhelming fear of being placed as a lone older female in another institution – the residential home (Bernard and Strange 1986; Johnson and Robert 1996; Ovrebo and Minkler 1993; Tinker 1997). Therefore, it is vital that the prison service ensures that elders in prison are not 'slung out' of prison but are given advice and support to make that transition from prison to the outside world.

TT: No, I think if you're going to cater for older women you've got to look at giving them some positive things to do inside. So when they get to the end of their sentence, no matter whether it's a large sentence or just a few months, they've got something to go out to, you know, to work towards. There isn't enough for them, you know? You can spend years in this place and be none the wiser when you get out, you're just thrown out into society. It's a very alien sort of situation, you know, because everything's taken off you, everything, rights and everything. You're just *slung out* into the street and expected to cope with whatever happens to come along. Instead of trying to teach people about what is going on; money situation, you know, everything about what's going on in society. [my emphasis]

Tokwan Thomas

It is fear of being alone once released, having to start afresh in a changing world that has rendered them unemployable, that for some makes staying in prison a preferable option. They are reminded that they are beginning to outlive their familiar social worlds and will return as strangers in time. It is imperative then that the prison system provides not only comprehensive resettlement programmes but alternatives to the traditional custodial framework in which older women find themselves growing old. It is the lack of rehabilitation to an ever-changing world which renders elders as forgotten; lost to the welfare contract and lost in the penal system.

The sense of loss suffusing such accounts relates to the notion of prison not *as* punishment but *for* punishment. It is through the loss of youth, of health and hence of hopes that the years spent in this closed prosthetic environment bring punishment far exceeding the 'mere' abstract loss of freedom. As time passes, the visible signs of imprisonment become inscribed upon the body. There are many who are in a similar situation to Wan-Nita, who 'have lost everything' and in this case, as she states, her life on the outside 'has gone on a car boot sale'. She, like many, will have 'to start afresh', where for them, time is running out.

Chapter 8

Concluding Comments: Responses to Ageing – Women in the Criminal Justice System

No specific thought is given to people who are in our age category. Thought is given to young offenders. It is given to lifers. It is given to sort of other categories, it is not really – *they don't really* think about people of *our age group* and *our families*. I appreciate we are a minority, but I think a number of people you have interviewed would say we are a *significant minority*, and presumably will *continue to be*. I do think they [the prison estate] need to address some of those aspects. They [the prison estate] need to address the problems of people who aren't *one hundred per cent fit*, but who on the outside had normal jobs. [my emphasis]

Una Ulrich

This book is based on the narratives of older women in prison in the UK. The principal aim of the book is to rectify the invisibility of elder females in prison by analysing their subjective experiences of imprisonment. The book has examined how gendered assumptions and stereotypes and gender-specific elements of the life course play a pivotal role in the experiences of elders in prison.

The argument throughout this book demonstrates how time is running out for elders in prison and how more and more women encounter the criminal justice system later on in the life course. As mentioned earlier, the two key thematic reviews (HMCIP 1997, 2001a) fail to address the ageing female population, despite the fact that the female prison population is likely to double by 2009 to 6900 (HO 2002).

Throughout the book the women have argued that it is through the lack of acknowledgement, facilities and general provision for female elders in prison that they are further punished. The elders in the book have shown how they become caught in a nexus of ageist and gendered expectations which for some bear little resemblance to their experiences, needs and future aspirations once released. By addressing the subjective experiences of female elders in prison one can identify how female elders move from the initial reception in court through to surviving prison life. This enforced severance with the outside world, with the effacement of key roles and responsibilities, has perverse effects upon the women's sense of self.

This concluding chapter will suggest how, by moving away from block treatment to differentiating need in prison, one might alleviate some of the pain elders in prison endure. It is within this hybrid of a residential home constructed and governed by the penal gaze that private lives are indeed placed in public places. If prison is about enabling offenders to lead law-abiding and useful lives, the prison service should be looking at ways to maintain the elders' sense of self.

Reclaiming agency – Old bodies in prison

The relationship between the elders, power, punishment and the prison is a complex one, which needs to be investigated further in gerontological, sociological and criminological research. Central to this book is the role of agency and how elders mediate self in a total institution, the prison. Relevant here is the idea of social life as a performance, associated with the work of Goffman (1961, 1963a, 1963b, 1971, 1983) and Butler (1987, 1990). In *The Presentation of Self in Everyday Life* (1990), Goffman argues that performance constitutes everyday life. He defines performance as: 'all activity of an individual which occurs during a period marked by a continuous presence before a particular set of observers and which has some influence on the observers' (1983:19).

In effect, for Goffman displays of the self are performed through agency. Butler (1987), in contrast, suggests a more textured idea of how our actions incorporate the interpretations of our audiences. She writes about gender that:

> I not only choose my gender and I not only choose it within culturally available terms, but on the street and in the world I am always already constituted by others, so that my self styled gender may well find itself in comic or even tragic opposition to the gender that others see me through or with. (Butler 1987: 139–140).

It is necessary to find ways of understanding power, agency and resistance in order to challenge the stereotypes, the discourses which attempt to construct elders on the inside as lacking, by virtue of their age, the ability to be active, rational agents with a life to lead once released. Throughout the book, elders have shown that surviving in prison becomes an art of existence. Moreover, this art of existence behind the walls is performed through, and by, discursive understandings of appropriate conduct in any given situation. Within any given performance of the self, choices are informed by a repertoire of scripts governing action (Wahidin 2004). This is not to suggest that there is a predisposition towards certain ways of acting, since this would deny elders agency, the ability to act and to make a difference. I suggest that through the discourses and the performances of the elders it is these choices which constitute, condition and make possible the identities and existence of elders in prison. It is within the elders' performances and within the strategies of subversion that elders draw upon their experiences and understanding of age, gender, sexual orientation, ethnicity and so on, in order to negotiate the prison setting. Within this conceptualisation, the elders in the study are illustrating how agency is a practical accomplishment that can challenge, negotiate or maintain power relations.

The experiences of elders in prison

Prison in itself, as I have argued, is a mechanism for state-legitimated pain delivery: imprisonment and the experiences elders face at the hands of so-called 'carers', agents of the state, is a debilitating process. The word 'care' in this context provokes many questions – in particular about the needs of the users of the services. Prison is, to a greater or lesser degree, a concentration of debasement, symptomatic of the system itself rather than the system's victims, in which all those who enter collude with the institutionalised violence which in turn produces the fecundity in which violence breeds. In any system where the operational needs of the institution take priority over the needs of the users, the potential is great for direct and indirect abuse to flourish unregulated (Biggs, S. 1993, 1989, 1990, 1999; Hearn and Parkin 1983). Furthermore, the lack of continuity of programmes from the outside, such as health care, structured activities for the non-working prison community, and of an 'adequate' living allowance for women who are of pensionable age in prison, increase the pains of imprisonment as the disparity between the working younger prison population and the non-working populations is magnified (Age Concern 1997a, 1997b, 1998, 1999a, 1999b; Hancock and Sutherland 1997; Phillipson 1991).

Resonating throughout this book are the material consequences of obscuring the needs of elders and how, by acknowledging this significant minority, we can move in the direction of alleviating some of the pains of imprisonment in the future. The lack of facilities catering for individual need increases the pains of imprisonment where the prisons focus resources and facilities on the younger women. In this study and the current work in which I am involved there is a pervasive feeling of despondency about the inadequacy and inappropriateness of the employment and education provided in prison, and about the occupational roles once released. Many elders felt that they were discouraged if they showed interest in an educational programme. Prison officers believed that the limited resources available should be offered to younger women who were more likely to benefit occupationally from them. Often the staff were reluctant to place elders on educational or training programmes on the basis that elder ex-prisoners, once released, would have less opportunity than their younger counterparts to be employed. This inequality reinforced the discrimination in training and employment which is likely to face the older woman on release, as well as ignoring the vital role played by work and education in mitigating the effects of isolation, frustration and despair.

The lack of help and rehabilitation to an ever-changing world renders elders as the forgotten minority, lost to the welfare contract and lost in the penal system. Once in prison, the vulnerabilities of age become exacerbated by the lack of adequate facilities to enable elders to lead 'law abiding and useful lives in custody and after release'. Once released, they will suffer the effect of the discontinuity of pension contributions. In the United Kingdom pensionable age is currently 65 for a man and 60 for a woman; recent legislation passed by Parliament will raise the pensionable age for women to 65. The change will begin in 2010 through to 2020 and will not affect anyone born before 6th April 1950. The basic pension is premised on the accumulation of contributions (as opposed to receiving credits). However, if you have grown old in prison, or spent your youth in and out of prison, it will leave you with insufficient contributions and consequently you will be in receipt of either a partial pension or none at all. The raising of the state pensionable age for women to 65 (for those born after 1950) will have particular consequences. Ginn and Arber (1995:206) argue that this measure will almost certainly reduce the amount of women's state pension income. They point out that this change will mean that the majority of women will now have to wait an extra five years to receive their state pension. Among those with no private pensions entitlements, the majority of non-married women will be dependent on Income Support. This will mean that they will forfeit their basic citizen's right to be catered for 'from the cradle to the grave' (Midwinter 1997).

The current wave of anti-social legislation such as the Housing Act of 1988 (reducing the housing available for ex-prisoners), the Criminal Justice Act of 1994, the Crime and Disorder Act of 1998, and the diminishing value of the basic retirement pension and the complexity of the forms which need to be completed, have in turn led to low take-up rates of benefits by elders. The Housing Benefit, Council Tax Benefit and Income Support (Amendments) Regulations 1995 ended the previous practice of using housing benefit to meet rent payments of convicted prisoners serving up to a year in custody. Assistance is now confined to prisoners serving sentences of up to six months who receive conditional discharge subject to good behaviour after 13 weeks in custody. These changes are bound to increase homelessness among released prisoners by causing a substantial number of prisoners to lose their homes during periods in prison between 13 and 52 weeks. A report, *Housing Benefit and Prisoners* (Penal Affairs Consortium, March 1996), estimates that 5000 additional prisoners could be released as homeless each year as a result of this change (Devlin 1998:42). This will lead to savings for the government and create yet another poverty trap for the needy (Bytheway 1983b; Chaiklin 1998). Moreover, it will perpetuate inequality, homelessness and poverty, encouraging dependency and other forms of abuse, which deny autonomy and agency and also increase recidivism. In effect the prison is creating prison-made prisoners, destitute, homeless and dependent on the state.

Restoring to women some level of control and responsibility during their time in prison would at least give them direction over their lives. A basic initiative would be to introduce independent advice centres in prisons, ensuring that the prisoners had information about available benefits and access to legal resources. The continuation of National Insurance contributions while in prison is an obvious necessity. Furthermore, a network of halfway houses needs to be established, and facilities/schemes for women introduced comparable to those at Grendon Green and Latchmere House[1]. Such schemes have already been successfully introduced, but far more are needed to ensure that all eligible prisoners are able to access this kind of support. Women in later life need improved health services, better pensions, different types of housing and a variety of aids when they become disabled. But they also need a reason for using these things. 'In our society the purpose of life in old age is often unclear… Old age is seen as a "problem" with the elderly viewed as dependants; worse still, they are often described as a non-productive burden upon the economy' (Phillipson 1982:166). It is not surprising that elders experience isolation and alienation when they are denied access to the sources of meaning, which are valued by the society in which they live (Phillipson and Walker 1986; Turner 1988).

Women, old age and the criminal justice system

> Of course being an older person in jail you're in a bit like *no man's land*.
> [emphasis in original]
>
> Wan-Nita Williams

Although little research has been undertaken in England and Wales into the health of older female prisoners, Wahidin (2000: 55–56) found that women prisoners over 50 considered themselves disadvantaged in terms of ill health prevention and health awareness schemes. While not all were in need of high levels of medical attention, some did suffer from 'chronic ill health' and for those too ill to receive treatment from outside hospitals, the process of bringing in specialised treatment was described as 'an all out battle'.

In the USA Kratcoski and Babb (1990, cited Kerbs 2000:219), found similarly that older female prisoners were less likely than men to participate in recreational programmes, and reported significantly higher levels of poor or terrible health (46 per cent against 25 per cent), with depression and generalised 'worry' being the two most persistent health problems they experienced.

The former Chief Inspector of Prisons, Sir David Ramsbotham, voiced concern about these issues in his Annual Report for 1999–2000, identifying 'totally inadequate care for the increasing numbers of elderly prisoners...too many of whom are, inevitably, confined to Health Care Centres (HMCIP 2001a: 7/8)

The *National Service Framework for Older People* (cited in DOH 2001b), is one of the few policy documents in the UK to refer to older prisoners, it states:

> The NHS and Prison Service are working in partnership to ensure that prisoners have access to the same range and level of health services as the general public. [Elders] have a wide range of health and social care needs, both while in prison and on release. It is important that there is good liaison between prison healthcare staff and their colleagues in health and social care organisations in the community to ensure that prisoners who are being released are assessed for, and receive services which meet their continuing health and social care needs. (2001b:4)

It is in a climate of cut-backs and under-funding that a Prison Service Instruction, (referred to as PSI) outlining the requirements of the NSF to governors, concludes that, 'there are no additional staff or non-staff resources required to implement this PSI' (PSI 2003). In addition it states that programmes for elders should begin at 60. Studies have indicated that elders would benefit from wellness programmes and health initiatives targeting the 50 plus population. Moreover, the NSF fails to address the social care needs of older prisoners during sentence and after release.

A policy document, *A Report of the Working Group on Doctors Working in Prison* (DOH 2001b:51) averred that 'social care and support is required and that they should review the needs of older prisoners...and take steps to ensure that they have access to the same range of professionals and services that are available to these groups in the community'.

The discourse of less eligibility permeates throughout the stories of the women and becomes the basis for delivering types of punishment. Although the *National Service Framework for Older People* (DOH 2001b) advocates equivalent health-care standards beyond the prison gates to that of society, governors are finding it had to implement. Sim (2002) argues that New Labour's commitment to new partnerships, realised through *The Future Organisation of Prison Health Care*, published in April 1999 (HM Prison Service/NHS Executive 1999), and the National Service Framework (DOH 2001b), has failed to dent the prison's disciplinary armoury and is unlikely to alleviate the gendered nature of the pains of imprisonment (2001b: 10). Prison health care remains low on the ladder of state expenditure.

The health-needs profile of the ageing offender is hard to map, given 'that expenditure cost for age cohorts in prison, is not known, the cells are not a data set used' by the prison health service (Dr Mary Piper, personal communication, August 2003). Without UK data on current health care expenditure, one has to look to studies conducted in the States to understand the future resource implications of an elderly prison population. In 1997 daily medical care for the general prison population in the States cost $5.75 per offender nationwide (Neeley *et al.* 1997). The cost of caring for prisoners over the age of 50 was nearly three times higher at $14.50. Elderly prisoners are significantly more costly to care for than their younger counterparts. Several nationwide studies have indicated that the elderly prisoner costs, on average, approximately three times as much to house (Fazel *et al.* 2001; Gallagher 1990). Despite making up only 8.5 per cent of the total prison population, prisoners over 50 were responsible for 19 per cent of the costs paid for ambulatory surgery episodes; 17 per cent of costs for non-emergency room episodes; 31 per cent of costs for ancillary care episodes; 20 per cent of costs for specialty care episodes; and 29 per cent of costs for inpatient care episodes (Florida Corrections Commission 2001). One Federal prison in Otisville, Iowa, spends $980,000 a year out of its $425 million budget on dialysis for 20 of its prisoners, or $449,000 per prisoner for just this one health-care expenditure (Henderson 1994).

McDonald (1995) identified several conditions that have forced prison health care costs in the States to rise (Anno 1991; Krebs 2000). A similar pattern is emerging in the UK prison system. The factors influencing the increase in expenditure are:

- the rising cost of health care in society at large
- the increasing number of prisoners in the prison system
- the general ageing of the prison population
- the higher prevalence of infectious diseases among prison populations.

Increasingly, prisoners coming into prison need immediate medical services. Like prisoners in general, ageing prisoners have not had proper access to health care on the outside. They come into the prison system with numerous chronic illnesses and consume multiple medications. In a paper presented to the Virginia Department of Corrections, Jonathan Turley, Director of the Project for Older Prisoners, noted that 'the greatest single contributor to the high costs of older prisoners is medical expenditures. On average, prisoners over 55 will suffer three chronic illnesses while incarcerated' (Turley 1990: 23–28). Prisoners as a population traditionally have medical and social histories that put them more at risk for illness and disease than their non-inmate peers (Marquart et al. 1997, 2000). Many prisoners have substantial health needs and engage in a number of risky health behaviours. Statistically, they have higher rates of HIV/AIDS, sexually transmitted diseases, tuberculosis and other infectious diseases than the population at large. As the number of older prisoners increases, the prison system will be even more challenged to provide adequate health and social care provision.

With a predicted rise in the number of offenders who are older, sicker and serving longer sentences, coupled with institutions' stretched resources, it is reasonable to argue that if we fail to address the needs of elders in prison we will be facing an inevitable crisis (Prison Reform Trust 2003). As more cohorts enter the latter stages of life, the age revolution will significantly affect all facets of the criminal justice system (Age Concern 2003).

Age-sensitive policy recommendations

To alleviate some of the pains of imprisonment, the prison authorities should be turning their attention to residential literature (Atherton 1989; Cantor and Cantor 1979; Coleman 1993; Hockey 1989; King, Raynes and Tizard 1971; Parsloe and Stevenson 1993; Thane 1983). There are many simple measures which could be taken and which would allow elders control over their immediate physical environment – for example: installing doors and windows which could be opened easily, and radiators which they could adjust themselves; replacing the harshness of the prison corridors with appropriate carpet tiles; use of electricity plug points which would allow all elders the opportunity to listen to the radio; and replacing the glare of the strip light with something less harsh. Such measures would at once make prison a less hostile and more accessible place. In addition, with the impairment of sight, hearing, memory and reflexes and also the general slowing of movement and mental responsiveness, elders need to be cared for by staff members who are specifically trained in the needs of elders in prison. As Molly Mossdale states:

MM: I think too many of the officers have no respect for older people. We are all lumped together as criminals. They don't realise that we have got separate needs. They don't realise that we are getting older and their day will come as well. We can't do the things at the speed that everybody else does.

Molly Mossdale

The USA has been at the forefront of delivering special programmes for persons over 50 and in prison (Aday 2002; Aday and Rosefield 1992; Krajick 1979). In this sense, 'special programmes' constitute the distinctive treatment of the elderly prisoner housed in an age-segregated or in an age-sensitive environment. Segregation provides a concentration of specialised staff and resources for the elderly, thereby reducing costs (Florida Corrections Commission 2001).

Previous research supports the notion that participation in a specific group increases self-respect and the capability to resume community life once released. A choice of age segregation or age integration provides the older prisoners with the opportunity for forming peer networks, while at the same time reducing the vulnerability and violence that they may encounter in the mainstream of prison life. Fattah and Sacco state:

> The concern for their safety and the need to protect them against victimisation, exploitation and harassment outweigh any stabilizing effect their integration may have. (1989:101)

Elders illustrated the benefits of being able to choose whether they lived on a particular wing or had access to specialist provision which had been designed with elders in mind. Petra Puddepha discusses the advantages of having designated areas for women in later life:

PP: If it was a wing or an area in Gefangnis which meant access to every other part of Gefangnis I would then go without a doubt. I think that a lot of our interests and tastes are probably quite different from a lot of the youngsters. That's not to say they don't overlap because they do. But the volume of music, volume of television and the type of programmes causes problems.

Petra Puddepha

Margot Metcalf argues that:

MM: Older women need to have their own space, yes, *they do*, because they need it to be quieter, they can't be bothered with the noise. You'll find that most older people, fifty plus, I should imagine the number one problem is with the noise. All we want is a bit of peace you know, peace and quiet.

You've got to realise that a lot of these young ones, there's a lot of trouble and most of the trouble is caused with drugs and lesbianism. But you know if I could choose, I would move on a different house with older people.

Margot Metcalf

Many elders sought out women of similar ages to provide them with the opportunity to talk about similar historical experiences of growing up in the 1950s, their grandchildren and great-grandchildren (Corston 1999; Evers 1983). Moreover, this gave them the opportunity to distance themselves from the drug culture and violence in prison.

Segregation is only a partial solution. What is needed is the flexibility of having accommodation and provision reserved for the elders without creating a separate prison or excluding elders from the main prison environment. If this was to happen, Wan-Nita Williams fears:

WW: I wouldn't go to a prison for *old people* because I feel I would grow older quicker. It's a bit like that already on the lifer house.

AW: Why's that?

WW: It's the land that time forgot. It's just as if it's a forgotten place over there. It is as if it's just forgotten. It's like a little jail within a jail.

Wan-Nita Williams

In this study the women were in favour of integration but with facilities and quiet rooms available for them to access. Aday, on the basis of 30 years of researching and working with elders in the criminal justice system, succinctly states: 'Like the elderly in the free world, they are familiar with life in the general population and perceive that it has a mark of independence' (2003:146).

Several scholars in the field have mooted the question of special programmes and facilities for elderly prisoners. An overriding theme is that the way forward is, as one elder wrote:

Not through segregation but through integration within a framework of tolerance, understanding and adaptability, which would reduce the pains of imprisonment that we as elders experience.

A central theme running throughout the book is that the proportion of the elderly in the general prison population has increased. However, research, policy initiatives and programmes targeted for the elderly criminal have not kept pace with this general movement. Age, in time, will be considered as one of the biggest issues that will continue to affect the criminal justice system and prison health care in the future. With the continued increase in criminal activity among the elderly population as a whole, learning more about crime and ageing, and about institutional adjustment, recidivism and release, will be an ever more important aspect of understanding and managing the older population within the criminal justice system.

Professionals in the field of gerontology and criminology can provide a greater awareness and understanding of the problems facing persons who encounter the criminal justice system in later life. It is only in the context of a heightened understanding of ageing in general that the problems of offending, prison adjustment and successful re-entry into society of the aged can be fully addressed. Policymakers will have to address the special needs of prisoners who will spend the remainder of their lives in prison as well as those who will be released in old age, in order to fulfil the prison statement of purpose.

Unlike the USA, the UK is still operating without a comprehensive plan to respond adequately to a pending crisis. The needs of elderly prisoners are substantial and can include physical, mental and preventative health care, custody classification to special housing considerations, educational, vocational, recreational, physical exercise, and rehabilitation programming, as well as dietary considerations and long-term geriatric and nursing care. As more cohorts enter the latter stages of life, the age revolution will significantly affect all facets of the criminal justice system. Women and men who are in later life and fall into the juridical system are often victimised by it. The elders found themselves in the criminal justice system which was for them traumatic and frightening where they were 'herded together' with 'lesbians', 'drug dealers', and 'prostitutes', into (in the words of one elder) local holding 'tanks'. Today we have family courts, juvenile courts and a large variety of special courts to handle specific problems. Along with the medley of juridical experts from child psychiatrists to social workers, will we in the future see court reports and parole boards informed by gerontologists who can advise the proper referral service for elders caught in the criminal justice system? Could we be accused of infantilising the older offender if we were to advocate a court which deals specifically with the older offender? The literature suggests the following initiatives, and this is not by any means an exhaustive list but it does raise various policy questions:

- Should an elderly person with no previous criminal conviction be given special consideration by the police or the courts?

- Should we change our sentencing structure to reflect probable years remaining in the offender's life?[2]

- Should older prisoners be segregated from the general prison population or should they be integrated into the mainstream of prison life?[2]

- Should both these options be available?

- How do we assist older offenders to ensure a successful transition into and out of prison?

- What type of end-of-life care should the criminal justice system provide for ageing prisoners who will certainly die in prison?

- What are the alternatives to imprisonment for this cohort (dependent on risk, nature of offence and time served)?

- What research is needed in order for the criminal justice system to respond better to the need of the ageing inmate?

The limited knowledge concerning the elderly, the absence of relevant policies and the lack of planning in this area, lead one to suggest that the criminal justice system should turn its attention to the following, if we are to respond to the growing number of elders who find themselves in the criminal justice system. A call for future research is necessary in order to understand the needs of elders in the criminal justice system. This research will need:

- to examine existing formal and informal practices regarding the elderly as the first step in developing an explicit and integrated set of policies and programmes to address the special needs of this group

- to begin to develop a comprehensive and gender-sensitive programme for elders that fosters personal growth, accountability and value-based actions that leads to successful reintegration into society

- to prepare all personnel of the criminal justice system to understand and appropriately address elder-specific topics and issues

- to address work-based prison programmes in order to develop and enable older prisoners to maintain their maximum levels of productivity and self-worth

- to have information on their health problems and needs so that prison and Health Service managers can plan to provide a standard of care equivalent to that available in the community.

In terms of being able to address the needs of elders in the criminal justice system, the Prison Policy Unit should:

- adopt the age of 50 as the chronological starting point in a definition of the older offender

- compile comprehensive data on the over-50s in the criminal justice system, from arrest to custody through to successful re-entry into wider society

- adapt and modify existing institutions to assure equitable treatment of the aged

- introduce specific programmes geared towards the needs of the elderly

- identify the costs of long-term incarceration of infirm prisoners and the potential risks of early release or extended medical furlough for this population

- involve the Home Office and organisations representing older persons (such as Better Government for Older People and Age Concern England and Wales), to create a consortium to formulate a national strategy for crime prevention programmes for the elderly.

Elderly crime will undoubtedly increase in the years ahead as the elderly population grows (Aday 2003; Flynn 2000). I hope this book has shown that crimes committed by elders are of sufficient importance to warrant increased research in this field. In order to understand the complex issues facing elders, a national study must look at the informal practices currently in use for this population. Further research in this area will inform best practice policies, from the time they encounter the criminal justice system at the point of arrest, to being released from prison.

Elders in prison are less likely to be a risk to society, and less likely to re-offend, and this allows for the possibility of designing future prisons/alternatives to prisons with the older female in mind. In a report produced by the Florida Corrections Commission (1999) they argued that elderly prisoners have the lowest recidivism rate of any group examined. Table 8.1 below shows that those over 50 are less likely to re-offend than their younger counterparts (source: Florida Corrections Commision 1999: 20).

Table 8.1 Age and recidivism	
Age	*Percentage who reoffend*
16–18	>70
45–49	26.6
50–64	22.1
65 and older	7.4

(Data cited in: http://www.fcc.state.fl.us/fcc/reports/final99/1eld.html)

While further research is needed to ascertain how these figures break down for the female and male prison population, one could certainly imagine a future in which imprisonment of elderly females was a rarity, reserved for those who are convicted of abnormally serious crimes of a nature indicating a continuing risk to society. Male and female prisoners are not comparable, they have different criminal profiles, both in terms of types of offences committed and previous offending history, and have different adjustment patterns to imprisonment. It is argued that a gender-specific policy based on substantive equality will improve the plight of women in prison across the life course (NACRO 1993, 1994a). By using this group to explore alternatives to imprisonment, what is certain is that there are savings to be made on both humanitarian and fiscal levels.

A good example of early release schemes is the Project for Older Prisoners (also known as POPS). This programme was founded in 1989, and is currently directed by law professor Jonathan Turley. POPS is the first and only organisation in the USA and Western Europe to work exclusively with the elderly to influence their early release. The Project for Older Prisoners is very selective and does not handle sex-offenders or first-degree murderers. POPS only helps 10 per cent of prisoners interviewed by volunteers. Candidates must be over 50 years of age, have already served the average time for their offences, and have been assessed as low risk and thus unlikely to commit further crimes in the future. Another unique requirement of this programme is that the victim, or the victim's family, must agree on early release. As a result of these strict standards, no prisoners released under the Project for Older Prisoners has ever returned to prison for committing another crime (Turley 1992). The programme helps them find employment and housing, and ensures that they receive their full entitlement to benefits. Such a scheme could beneficially be extended to include a large number of older women prisoners and, if successful, could foster a willingness within the penal system to consider shorter or non-custodial sentences for this low-risk group.

Because of the age of most prisoners, the design of the prison and the facilities available are geared towards young offenders. The potential risks of being visible in the prison environment led the majority of the elders to remain inside their cells, which further reduces their physical activity and reinforces their sense of isolation and otherness. Wilson and Vito (1986) found that older prisoners complained about the lack of privacy and continuous noise, which heightened the degree of anxiety and nervousness they suffered. Because of the lack of facilities, elders who are unable to work serve their entire sentence in idleness and isolation (Marquart *et al.* 2000). Their disengagement from the prison culture towards more solitary habits has at times caused misunderstanding between them, the officers and the younger women. This disengagement is sometimes interpreted as aloofness or as evidence that the elders are not coping with prison life, but in fact may be seen as a positive enactment of self, the best available adaptation in an environment that caters mainly for the younger prisoners.

In addition, some who have served an extremely long sentence in prison find that they have no family or social networks on the outside, and on this basis parole can be denied (HMIPP 2001; HMIP England and Wales 2002c). If society has little place for elders in general, it has even less place for the elderly prisoner or ex-convict. So what happens to the elderly offender who has nowhere to go?

Reflections on the research process

As the journey over this complex terrain of silences, fear and state-legitimated pain draws to an end, there are still unanswered questions about the methods I used and the questions I asked. For the readers I need to acknowledge to you my role in shaping the research process and what was produced. In the process of interpreting the research findings, I engaged in a process of making those whom I have called co-researchers and co-subjects, 'other'.

The dialogical narrative of the in-depth unstructured interviews represents a moment in time of the self-in-motion. I wonder what the elders would make of my interpretation of their words as I sit in my study, far away from them and their lives. Their names and identities have been replaced for the purposes of anonymity by pseudonyms, so they and their unique contributions will effectively be erased. Accordingly, although I make the claim of using the perspectives and words of the contributors to my research, in speaking for them does this in turn mean I am 'in the privileged position of naming and representing other people's realities'? (Mauthener and Doucet 1998:139). I have to admit that in some way I am 'appropriating their voices and experiences and further disempowering them by taking away their voice, agency and ownership' (Mauthener and Doucet 1998:139), because as a researcher I have to theorise their stories and place them within wider academic and theoretical debates. As far as possible I have tried to avoid reproducing and using the research in ways which re-inscribe inequality. The concern should always be for the person as an individual, who should:

1.　feel free to express themselves as and how they feel comfortable

2.　decide whether or not to be involved in the research

3.　feel able to reveal only what they want to.

In the process of revisiting the interviews, I find that they speak to me in a slightly different way, with different inflections, nuances and tone. This emphasises the liminal nature of the research. Furthermore this has indicated that a project such as this is posited in a particular time and space. These subtle changes demonstrate that, while I have had the opportunity to re-engage with the words of the elders, their words have remained frozen in time, subject to my shifting analysis. In this way the elders are unable to reconsider for themselves their experiences. This is, yet again, indicative of the unequal nature of the relationship between the elders and myself.

As I come to the end of writing this book, I am aware that by prioritising the needs of the elders, listening, observing and to a degree sharing the pain within their stories, I have not addressed in writing the effects the research has had on my personhood, but perhaps that is for another time. Nonetheless, in the sharing of the elders' pain, and being placed under the prison gaze, I observed, heard and experienced things that I would otherwise not have done (see Ward 1993). My sensibilities were pained and there were sights, voices and phrases that I will never forget.

Unless we begin to address the points raised in this book, older women in the criminal justice system will always be marginalised and they will be afforded the same lack of care that exists within the community at present. It is imperative that the prison system provides not only comprehensive opportunities whilst in prison and appropriate resettlement programmes, but also alternatives to the traditional custodial framework that older women find themselves growing old in. The ageing prison population poses a true dilemma, and deserves recognition both among those interested in the well-being of those in later life and those executing prison policy.

In this book I have attempted to navigate the women's experiences of the criminal justice system once in prison. The introduction promised you that I would 'begin at the beginning...and go on till [the] end: the[n] stop' (Carroll 1971). For these women this is not the end. Some want to fade into anonymity, others are raring to start living and some have nowhere and nobody to go to. The next stage of their journey (and this is for another book) is to chart the transition from prison to wider society and the complex issues surrounding through-care,[3] and adjustment patterns of elder offenders as they acclimatise to life in wider society. Prison does not stop at the prison gates (See Social Exclusion Unit 2002; HO 2001a; HMIP England and Wales 2002a). Women and men who leave bring with them the effects of a custodial sentence and, on release, they encounter suspicion, rejection and hostility as they make this transition from prison to an age-discriminatory society. So this is not the end and the final stage of their journey is yet to come.

Stern argues that in every country, 'there is a prison system for men, and women are everywhere tacked on in an awkward after-thought' (1998:141); unless this changes, female elders will remain in the shadows of prison life.

It is beyond the scope of this book to address all of the issues facing elders in the criminal justice system, but if at the end the reader feels a greater concern for elders in prison then this book will have achieved its overall aim.

Notes

1   Grendon prison was opened in 1962, as a unique experiment in the psychological treatment of offenders whose mental disorder did not qualify them for transfer to a hospital under Section 72 of the Mental Health Act 1959. Grendon is a category B training prison and may be described as a multi-functional establishment, accommodating three adult therapy wings which operate as therapeutic communities, an assessment and induction unit, and a treatment wing designed specifically for sex offenders (See Genders and Players 1995).

    HMP Latchmere House is a resettlement prison which holds male adult prisoners serving a sentence of four years or more, including up to 20 life-sentenced prisoners, and assists them to prepare for release.

2   Cristina Pertierra (1995) presents a series of cases brought to the American Court of Appeal in which elderly offenders, under the 8th Amendment, have claimed that, given their ages and life expectancies, the sentences imposed amount to life imprisonment, and are thus disproportionate to the crimes committed. For further details see *United States* v. *Angiulo*, 852 F. Supp. 54, 60 (D. Mass. 1994); see also *Alspaugh* v. *State*, 133, So. 2d 597, 588 (Fla. 2d Dist. Ct. App. 1961).

3   Through-care: The term will denote the assistance given to prisoners and their families by the prison, probation service and voluntary agencies. It includes training, education, work experience and preparation for release. It should help prisoners to fit back into society, get a job and a home, and cope with life without re-offending.

Examples of US Correctional Facilities for the Over-fifties

Several American States operate programmes specifically aimed at the elderly male offender, defining elderly offenders as 50 and over (Aday 1994a, 1994b; Goetting 1983; Steffensmeier 1987).

Alabama Department of Corrections maintains a 200-bed Aged and Infirm Unit in Hamilton, Alabama. This unit was opened to prevent victimisation of older prisoners and to respond to their special needs. The Hamilton facility is one of only a few in the States specialising in the care of aged and disabled prisoners.

North Carolina Department of Corrections – The McCain Correctional Hospital has been the leader in providing special housing and medical services for its ageing prison population for the last 17 years.

South Carolina Department of Corrections – State Park Correctional Centre opened for elderly prisoners in 1970. It is the only state that houses older females in a specialist geriatric facility. This correctional facility operates a pilot Modified Work Release Programme for older offenders, which is funded by the Job Training Partnership Act and offers training, employment and the opportunities similar to those afforded to younger work participants.

Florida Department of Corrections provide special services for older prisoners at the Lawtey Correctional Institution and the Hillsborough Correctional Institution. Female elders are placed at the Florida Correctional Institute (Adams 1995).

In 2000, Florida established a geriatric facility known as the River Junction Correctional Institution, which is for the healthy elderly offenders who can perform general work appropriate for their physical and mental condition.

Georgia Department of Corrections – Men's State Prison in Milledgeville houses the highest concentration of prisoners aged 50 and above. The facility has 24-hour medical care. It has specific programmes tailored for the elderly offender such as the talking-book service and Sit and Be Fit exercise, etc.

Minnesota Department of Corrections – The Minnesota Correctional facility – STW Senior Dormitory is designed to accommodate 23 self-sufficient men aged 50 and above. The older offenders in the Senior Dormitory go to meals before the general population to avoid the queues and rush in the dining hall.

Ohio Department of Corrections – The Hocking Correctional Facility, Nelsonville houses the country's oldest prison population. All staff attend special courses – for example, dealing with bereavement – which are also offered to prisoners. The facility has a two-part, pre-release programme specific to older prisoners – for prisoners returning to the workforce and for those who will retire.

Pennsylvania Department of Corrections – Laurel Highlands has an older prisoner facility.

Tennessee Department of Corrections provides medical attention, special diets, therapeutic programmes and counselling for older offenders. In addition it has a 50-bed unit at Wayne Correctional Annex for those assigned to minimum custody, who have minor medical needs and are capable of general work assignments.

Texas Department of Corrections – Geriatric ward at Texas' Estelle Unit was established to protect prisoners who are at least 60 years old from more hostile and aggressive prisoners. The Unit also accepts prisoners under 60 if they are disabled (*Abilene Reporter* – News, 9 December 1997). In many systems emphasis is placed not on age or diagnoses, but rather on functional assessment when determining integration versus segregation or the combing of sub-populations (Tennessee Department of Corrections 2001).

Virginia Department of Corrections – Deerfield Correctional Centre specialises in providing care to prisoners who need assisted living or skilled nursing-home care. The geriatric programme (Psychotherapeutic Support) operates within the Staunton Correctional Centre.

West Virginia Department of Corrections – provides care for 45 prisoners over the age of 50 who are housed in a medium security, protective custody dorm known as the 'Old Men's Colony'. They have another special dorm at Huttonsville Correctional Centre, which is adjacent to the infirmary. What is different about this facility is that no prison officers are posted there.

Aday (2003) in his seminal book argues that out of 51 States in America, only three have all six facilities (see below) for the older inmate, and 36 States have three or more of the facilities:

1.   grouped or in geriatric facilities

2.   programmes or recreational opportunities

3.   special work assignments

4.   hospice/end-of-life programmes

5.   medical or compassionate release

6.   early release planning.

What is developing in the States, is that a number of private companies are opening penal nursing homes: Just Care, Inc. was the first private company to open a facility, and others, such as National Corrections Corporation and Wackenhut Corrections Corporation, are exploring the possibility of opening facilities for the elderly (Beiser 1999). What is sure to follow (and harder to predict) is a time when this might become a feature in the criminal justice system in England and Wales. One certainty is that in the future there will be more and more prisons catering for the elderly offender.

Prison Information

At the time of writing there are 18 prisons in England and Wales which hold women. It is current policy for young women and girls to be held in prisons with adult women. The small number of prisons often means women are held long distances from families and friends, especially while on remand. On average women in prison are held more than 50 miles from home and a quarter are held more then 100 miles from home (Prison Reform Trust 2004). Three of these are units within larger male establishments. The lifer system consists of:

Main centres

There are two main centres in the female estate, Durham and Bullwood Hall. Few women lifers will spend more than three years at the main centre. The principal function of the main centre is a settling-in process, to help women lifers through the appeal process, and to come to terms with a life sentence.

Second stage

The ethos of the sentence changes noticeably in the second stage. Although some work on the offence and related behaviour will take place at the main centre, at the second-stage establishment the emphasis is geared towards the first parole board review. For some, this review may be up to seven or eight years away, but the variety of the population is such that on arrival lifers will be mixing with others about to move on to the third stage of their sentence as well as a whole range of determinate sentence prisoners.

Third stage

The transfer to an open establishment takes place only at the first formal review by the parole board. This final stage prepares women for life on the outside. Some prisons have their own pre-release hostels in the grounds of the main prison.

Incentive and Enhanced Privilege Scheme

(Source: Adapted and abridged from HM Prison Service Order 4000 (2001) *Incentives and Earned Privileges*, Issue 77, London: Home Office.)

Information sheet for prisoners: revised incentives and earned privileges assessment procedures

The Incentives and Earned Privileges system at HMP — follows national guidelines. These are:

1. that you are able to earn and lose access to privilege levels according to clear criteria

2. that the determination of privilege level is reached administratively through fair, equitable procedures

3. that local IEP schemes are integrated into other sentence planning and through-care schemes

4. that basic privilege levels do not fall below legal entitlements and minimum level of facilities.

In order to meet these national guidelines, there will be some changes to the way in which IEP Assessments are carried out. The main changes are as follows:

If you wish to be regraded, you must complete the new Form IEP. 1. This informs you very clearly of:

* the areas of compliance on which you will be assessed

* the members of staff required to provide an assessment (normally a Group Manager and a member of staff at your place of work)

* the documents which will be taken into consideration by the IEP Board when making a decision (your sentence plan, your history sheet and your adjudication record).

Assessment forms will be sent to your house/wing staff, Group Manager, and place of work.

There will be separate Boards for North Group and South Group. The board will consist of the IEP Governor, a Group Manager and your house officer or personal officer.

You will also be required to attend the Board; your house/personal officer will advise you of date and time.

The IEP Governor will explain the areas of compliance to you and will inform you how you measure up in each area, according to the assessment and the accompanying documents (sentence plan, history sheet, adjudication record). The IEP Governor will complete Form IEP.4 (Notification to Prisoner of IEP Assessment Board Decision) and you will later receive a photocopy of this form.

You will be informed of the Board's decision either immediately or later that day.

The areas of compliance against which your behaviour will be measured are as follows.

1.	Bullying	9. How you deal with grievances
2.	Offending Behaviour	10. Punctuality at Work
3.	Respect for others	11. Hygiene at Work
4.	Co-operation	12. Compliance with Rules at Work
5.	Compliance with Rules	13. Attention to Work
6.	Drugs	14. Co-operation and Flexibility at Work
7.	Hygiene	15. Respect for Others at Work
8.	Work	

If you feel that your behaviour measures up well against these areas of compliance, ask your officer for an application form (Form IEP. 1) for regarding. This form contains more information about the process. The standards required are high. Please remember that you can also be downgraded if your general behaviour is less than the standard required. Your house officers can also request an assessment if your behaviour is very good or very poor.

See below – HM Prison Service Order 4000 (2001) *Incentives and Earned Privileges*, Issue 77, London: Home Office.

Criteria	Earnable privileges	How to achieve this level
1. Not a bully and helps staff to address bullying issues. 2. Complies with sentence plan; addresses offending behaviour. 3. Always shows considerations for others. 4. Co-operates with staff. 5. No adjudications in the past two months. 6. Drug-free and encourages others to be drug-free. 7. Always well-groomed: keeps self and room in spotless condition. 8. Works and is committed, punctual and responsible. 9. Raises issues with staff in reasonable, mature manner and listens to advice.	1. Enhanced work and pay opportunities. 2. Enhanced weekly spending limits (unconvicted £30; convicted £15). 3. Access to enhanced visits on Sunday afternoons (sentenced only). 4. The opportunity to exchange every statutory VO for two PVOs (thus a maximum of 4 visits per month). 5. The opportunity to purchase up to £16 worth of phone-cards per week (subject to spending limits). 6. Above-average living accommodation. 7. Additional in-possession property as per Facilities List. 8. In-cell TV. 9. All standard association, exercise and gym facilities.	Maintain a clean record: no suspicion of bullying, no adjudications and no drugs - and - demonstrate substantial efforts to meet the other criteria. Apply on Form IEP.1 for regrading (Form available from office).
1. Not a bully but does not help staff to address bullying issues. 2. Complies with sentence plan. 3. Behaviour causes little or no concern to others. 4. Complies with rules; does as she is told. 5. No adjudications in the past month. 6. Does not use drugs. 7. Clean and tidy. 8. Works but not committed or unemployed but actively seeking work. 9. Does not seek or accept advice from staff.	1. Standard work and pay opportunities. 2. Standard association and exercise facilities. 3. Standard weekly spending limits (unconvicted £30; convicted £10). 4. Standard arrangements for visits. 5. The opportunity to exchange one statutory VO per month for two PVOs (thus a maximum of 3 visits per month). 6. Standard access to gym (at least once per week for adult prisoners and twice per week for young offenders). 7. The opportunity to purchase up to £16 worth of phone-cards each week (subject to spending limits).	All new prisoners are placed automatically on standard level. After that, it's up to you! You can move up – or you can move down.
1. Suspected of bullying. 2. Not meeting sentence plan targets or not addressing offending behaviour. 3. Shows no consideration to others or is noisy or offensive. 4. Unco-operative with staff or is slow to comply and requires constant reminders. 5. Has had more than one adjudication in the past month. 6. Suspected or proven to be using drugs. 7. Untidy or unclean and ignores advice. 8. Behaviour leads to dismissal from job or is unemployed but not trying to find work. 9. Constantly complains in a negative manner; does not heed advice and is often unreasonable.	1. No access to orderly jobs. 2. Basic association entitlement. 3. Basic exercise entitlement. 4. Basic weekly spending limits (unconvicted £15; convicted £2.50). 5. Basic canteen arrangements (limited to purchasing only one phone-card per week; spending on tobacco limited to £2.50 per week). 6. Basic VO entitlement (one statutory VO once per fortnight). 7. Basic visits facilities (30 minutes only for each visit). 8. Basic access to gym (no gym for adult prisoners and twice per week for young offenders).	Behave in such a way as to cause staff to believe that you are bullying others - or - collect a few warnings about your behaviour - or - collect a couple of positive MDT tests - or - make up your own combination of any of the above.
	HOW DO YOU MEASURE UP?	

Statistical Information

Table A1(a) Male population in prison in England and Wales under sentence by age, 2003[a]					
Age in years	*1998*	*1999*	*2000*	*2001*	*2002*
15–17	1627	1643	1786	2002	2037
18–20	5807	5633	5906	6313	5926
21–24	8780	8245	8700	8839	9918
25–29	10590	10080	10060	9881	10329
30–39	14109	14072	14454	14389	15596
40–49	5485	5552	5720	5976	6708
50–59	2608	2678	2750	2707	2857
60–69	768	890	946	1003	1128
70–79	120	153	183	190	225
80+	8	10	9	13	17
All ages	49902	48956	50514	51313	54741

[a]Including persons committed in default of payment of a fine.

(© Crown Copyright. Data provided by the Research, Development and Statistics Directorate of the Home Office.)

Table A1(b) Female population in prison in England and Wales under sentence by age, 2003[a]

Age in years	1998	1999	2000	2001	2002
15–17	62	67	65	67	104
18–20	210	224	265	324	357
21–24	425	427	458	486	596
25–29	501	491	563	579	684
30–39	709	798	862	897	1057
40–49	332	301	335	407	443
50–59	116	108	102	120	137
60–69	10	18	14	15	16
70–79	2	2	2	4	2
80+	0	0	0	0	0
All ages	2367	2436	2666	2899	3396

[a]Including persons committed in default of payment of a fine.

(© Crown Copyright. Data provided by the Research, Development and Statistics Directorate of the Home Office.)

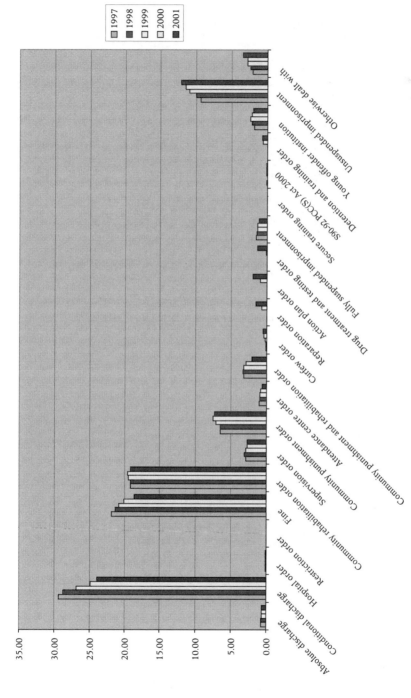

Figure A1 *Number of females of all ages sentenced at all courts for indictable offences, by type of disposal (© Crown Copyright. Data provided by the Research, Development and Statistics Directorate of the Home Office.)*

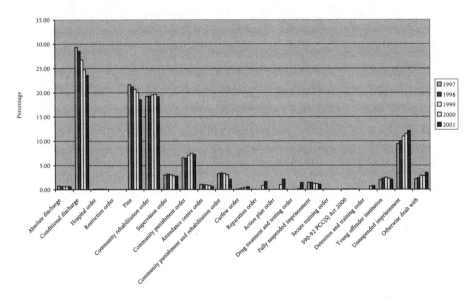

Figure A2 *Number of females aged 0 to 49 sentenced at all courts for indictable offences, by type of disposal (©Crown Copyright. Data provided by the Research, Development and Statistics Directorate of the Home Office.)*

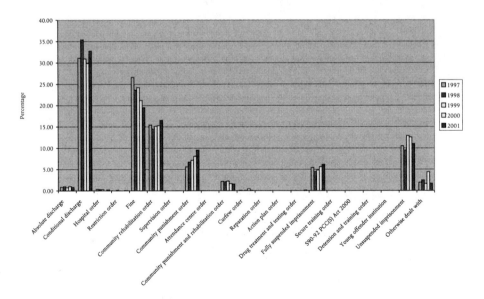

Figure A3 *Number of females aged 50 and above sentenced at all courts for indictable offences, by type of disposal (©Crown Copyright. Data provided by the Research, Development and Statistics Directorate of the Home Office.)*

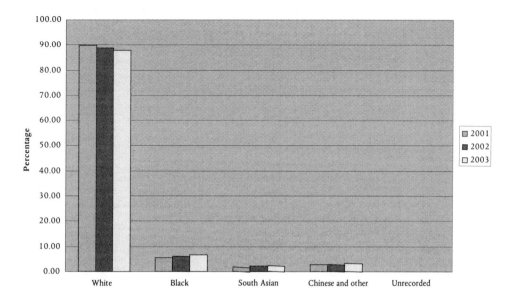

Figure A4 *Males over 50 in prison by ethnicity, years 2001–2003 (©Crown Copyright. Data provided by the Research, Development and Statistics Directorate of the Home Office.)*

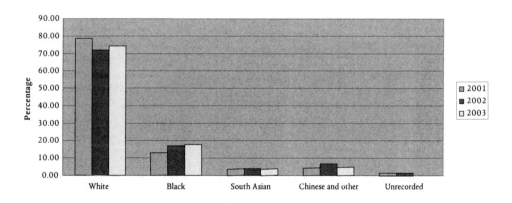

Figure A5 *Females over 50 in prison by ethnicity, years 2001–2003 (©Crown Copyright. Data provided by the Research, Development and Statistics Directorate of the Home Office.)*

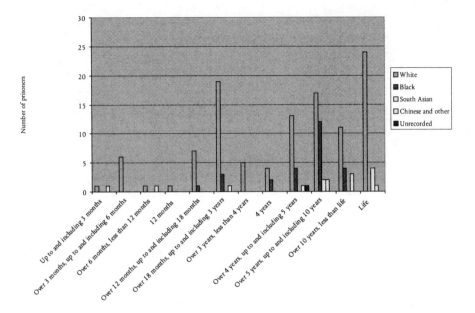

Figure A6 All females aged 50 and above by sentence length and ethnicity, 2002 (©Crown Copyright. Data provided by the Research, Development and Statistics Directorate of the Home Office.)

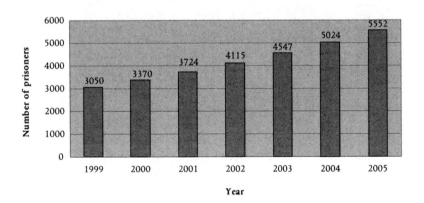

Figure A7 Projected standing population of inmates aged 50 and above (©Crown Copyright. Data provided by the Research, Development and Statistics Directorate of the Home Office.)

Table A2 Why and where? Nature of offence of women against establishment, 2003

Current establishment	Offence group								
	Burglary	Drug offences	Fraud and forgery	Offences not recorded	Other offences	Robbery	Sex offences	Theft and handling	Violence against the person
Askham Grange	0	2	0	0	1	0	0	0	6
Buckley Hall	0	3	0	0	0	0	0	0	0
Brockhill	0	0	1	0	0	0	0	0	0
Bullwood Hall	0	0	0	0	0	0	0	0	2
Cookham Wood	0	4	0	0	1	0	0	0	1
Drake Hall	0	6	1	0	1	0	0	2	1
Durham	0	0	0	0	0	0	2	0	3
Downview	0	7	0	2	1	1	0	1	0
East Sutton Park	0	2	1	0	1	0	0	1	0
Eastwood Park	0	1	0	0	2	0	0	1	1
Foston Hall	0	6	1	0	1	1	0	0	2
Highpoint	0	2	2	1	0	0	0	0	6
Holloway	1	7	2	0	2	0	0	2	4
Low Newton	0	0	0	0	0	0	0	0	1
Morton Hall	0	6	1	0	1	0	0	1	1
New Hall	0	3	1	0	1	0	0	1	6
Send	0	8	0	1	0	1	1	1	1
Styal	0	2	2	0	1	0	0	1	6
Winchester	0	2	0	0	0	0	0	2	1
Total	1	61	12	4	13	3	3	13	42

Sentence	Under 3 mths	3<6 mths	6<12 mths	12 mths	12<18 mths	18 mths <3 yrs	3<4 yrs	4 yrs	4<5 yrs	5<10 yrs	10<Life	Life	All
Table A3 Cross tabulations of age against sentence length for female inmates aged 50 and over (August 2003)													
Number of Prisoners	2	6	2	1	8	23	5	6	19	33	18	29	152

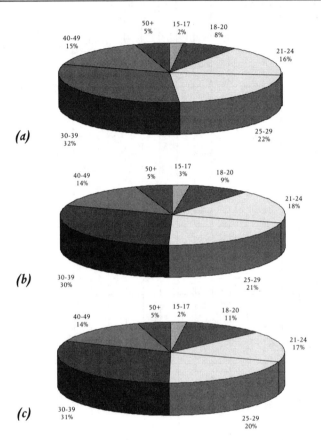

(a)

(b)

(c)

Figure A8(a) *Percentage of the sentenced female population by age (1995).* **(b)** *Percentage of the sentenced female population by age (1998).* **(c)** *Percentage of sentenced female population by age (2001) (© Crown Copyright. Data provided by the Research, Development and Statistics Directorate of the Home Office.)*

Figure A8 (a,b,c) relates to the sentenced female prison population from 1995 to 2001 broken down by age. The figures represent percentage proportions of the total sentenced female population. Perentages may not add up to 100 per cent due to figures being rounded independently. The pie-charts above show that although the actual numbers are rising the percentage of women over 50 has the stayed the same.

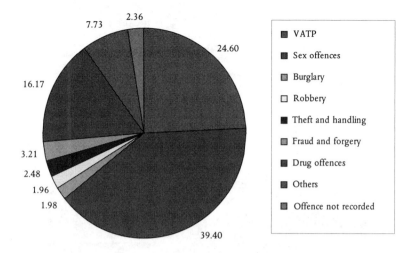

Figure A9 *Percentage of all offences across all sentence lengths for men and women over 50, 2003 (© Crown Copyright Data provided by the Research, Development and Statistics Sirectorate of the Home Office.)*

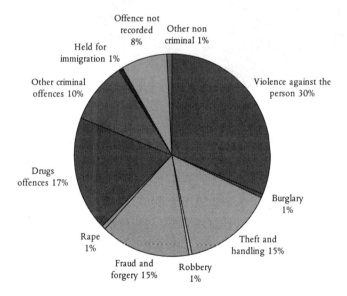

Figure A10 *Offence breakdown of all females in prison aged 50 and above, including remand, 2003. (©Crown Copyright. Data provided by the Research, Development and Statistics Directorate of the Home Office.)*

Note: Figures A9 and A10 show that the two biggest offence groups are violence against the person, and drugs offences, with violence against the person being almost twice as frequent as the second largest category.

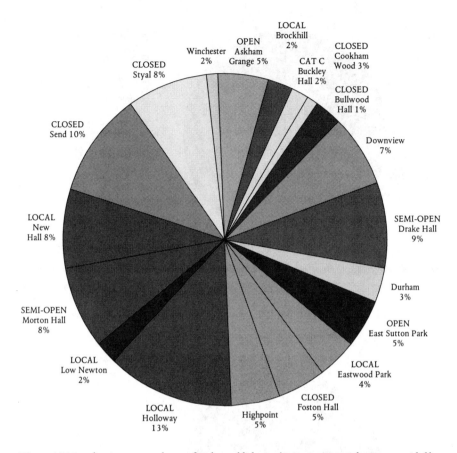

Figure A11 *Female prisoners over the age of 50 by establishment (© Crown Copyright. Data provided by the Research, Development and Statistics Directorate of the Home Office.)*

Bibliography

Achenbaum, W.A. (1978) 'Essay: Old Age and Modernisation.' In *The Gerontologist 18*, 307–312.

Achenbaum, W.A. (1995) 'Images of Old Age in America, 1790–1970.' In M. Featherstone and A. Wernick (eds) *Images of Aging – Cultural Representations of Later Life.* London: Routledge.

Acoca, L. (1998) 'Defusing the Time Bomb: Understanding and Meeting the Growing HealthCare Needs of Incarcerated Women in America.' In *Crime and Delinquency 44*, 49–70.

Adam, B. (1990) *Time and Social Theory.* Cambridge: Polity Press.

Adam, B. (1995) *Time Watch – A Sociological Analysis of Time.* Cambridge: Polity Press.

Adams, M.E. and Vedder, C. (1961) 'Age and Crime: Medical and Sociological Characteristics of Prisoners over 50.' In the *Journal of Geriatrics 16*, 177–180.

Adams, W. (1995) 'Incarceration of Older Offenders.' In *Nova Law Review 19*, 465–486.

Aday, R. H. (1984) 'Criminals.' In E. Palmore (ed.) *Handbook on the Aged in the United States.* Westport CT: Greenwood, pp.295–310.

Aday, R.H. (1988) *Crime and the Elderly – An Annotated Bibliography.* New York: Greenwood Press.

Aday, R. H. (1994a) 'Aging in Prison: A Case Study of New Elderly Offender.' In *International Journal of Offender Therapy and Comparative Criminology 1*, Part 38, 79–91.

Aday, R. H. (1994b) 'Golden Years Behind Bars: Special Programs and Facilities for Elderly Inmates.' In *Federal Probation 58*, 2, 47–54.

Aday, R. H. (1999) 'Responding to the greying of the American prisons: A 10 year follow up.' Unpublished report. Murfreesboro: Middle Tennessee State University.

Aday, R. H. (2002) 'Aging Prisoners: Issues and Solutions.' In *Summer Series on Aging*, July 8–10, 2002, Lexington Kentucky.

Aday, R. H. (2003) *Aging Prisoners: Crisis in American Corrections.* Westport CT: Praeger.

Aday, R. H., and Rosefield, H. A. (1992) 'Providing for the Geriatric Inmate: Implications for Training.' In the *Journal of Correctional Training 12*, 20, 14–16, Winter.

Aday, R. H. and Webster, E. (1979) 'Aging in Prison: The Development of a Preliminary Model.' In *Offender Rehabilitation 3*, 271–282.

Adler, P. and Adler, P. (1993) 'Ethical Issues in Self Censorship: Ethnographic Research on Sensitive Topics.' In C. Renzetti and R. Lee (eds) *Researching Sensitive Topics.* London: Sage Publications.

Adler, P. and Adler, P. (1994) 'Observational Techniques.' In K.N. Denzin and S. Lincoln (eds) *Handbook of Qualitative Research.* Thousand Oaks: Sage.

Age Concern (1997a) *Fifty Plus: Population and other Projections.* London: Age Concern.

Age Concern (1997b) *Pensions for People: Age Concern's Policy for an Adequate Income in Retirement.* London: Age Concern.

Age Concern (1998) *Pensioners Income.* Briefings Ref: 0898. London: Age Concern.

Age Concern (1999a) *National Insurance Contributions and Qualifying for a Pension. Fact sheet 20.* London: Age Concern.

Age Concern (1999b) *Your State Pension and Carrying on Working.* Fact sheet 19. London: Age Concern.

Age Concern (2003) 'Older People…In a Prison Somewhere Near You?' Unpublished report based on a special seminar on older offenders, March 2003.

Aiken, L.R. (1995) *Aging: An Introduction to Gerontology.* Thousand Oaks, CA: Sage Publications.

Allen, H. (1987) *Justice Unbalanced – Gender, Psychiatry and Judicial Decisions*. Milton Keynes: Open University Press.

Anderson, J.C. and Morton, J.B. (1989) 'Greying of the Nation's Prisons Presents New Challenges.' *Aging Connection 10*, 6–7.

Andrews, M. (1991) *Lifetimes of Commitment – Aging, Politics, Psychology*. Cambridge: Cambridge University Press.

Andrews, M. (1999) 'The Seductiveness of Agelessness.' In *Ageing and Society 19*. Cambridge University Press, 301–318.

Anno, B.J. (1991) *Prison Health Care: Guidelines for the Management of an Adequate Delivery System*. Washington, DC: National Institute of Corrections.

Arber, S. and Evandrou, M. (eds) (1993) *Ageing, Independence and the Life Course*. London: Jessica Kingsley Publishers (Ch. 1).

Arber, S. and Gilbert, N. (1983) 'Transitions in Caring: Gender, Life Course and the Care of the Elderly.' In B. Bytheway, T. Keil, K. Teresa, P. Allatt and A. Bryman (eds) (1989) *Becoming and Being Old – Sociological Approaches To Later Life*. London: Sage.

Arber, S. and Ginn, J. (eds) (1995a) *Connecting Gender and Ageing – A Sociological Approach*. Buckingham: Open University Press.

Arber, S. and Ginn, J. (eds) (1995b) *Gender and Elder Abuse in Connecting Gender and Ageing, A Sociological Approach*. Buckingham: Open University Press.

Armstrong, J.T. (1992) *Michel Foucault: Philosopher: Essays* (trans. from French and German). Hemel Hempstead; London: Harvester Wheatsheaf: XVi + 351.

Arrowsmith, P. (1970) *Somewhere Like This*. London: W.H. Allen.

Arrowsmith, P. (1983) *Jericho*. Worcester: Heretic Books.

Atherton, J.S. (1989) *Interpreting Residential Life – Values to Practice*. London: Tavistock, Routledge.

Atwood, M. (1997) *Alias Grace*. London: Virago.

Baars, M (1991) *The Challenge of Critical Gerontology: The Problem of Social Constitution in the Journal of Ageing Studies 5*, 3, 219–243.

Balfour, G. (2000) 'Feminist Therapy with Women in Prison: Working under the Hegemony of Correctionalism.' In K. Hannah Moffat and M. Shaw (eds) *An Ideal Prison: Critical Essays on Women's Imprisonment in Canada*. Halifax: Fernwood, pp.94–102.

Barak, Y., Perry, T. and Elizur, A. (1995) 'Elderly Criminals: A Study of the First Criminal Offence in Old Age.' In *International Journal of Geriatric Psychiatry 10*, 511–516.

Beiser, V. (1999) 'Pensioners or Prisoners: Private Penal Nursing Homes.' In *Nation 268*, 28.

Bell, V. (1992) 'Dreaming and Time in Foucault's Philosophy.' In *Theory, Culture and Society – Explorations In Critical Social Science: 11*, 2.

Bengston, V., Burgess, E. and Parrott, T. (1997) 'Theory, Explanation and a Third Generation of Theoretical Development in Social Gerontology.' In *Journal of Gerontology: Social Sciences 52* (B) 72–88.

Bengston, V. and Schaie, R. (1999) *Handbook of Theories in Gerontology*. New York: Springer.

Bennett, H., Parrot, J. and Macdonald, A. (1996) 'Psychiatric Disorder and Policing.' In *The Elderly Offender, Criminal Behaviour and Mental Health 6*, 241–252.

Bennett, T. and Wright, R. (1984) *Burglars on Burglary: Prevention and the Offender*. Aldershot: Gower.

Bergson, H. (1997) *Time and Free Will: An Essay on the Immediate Data of Consciousness* (trans. F.L. Pogson). London: R.A. Kessinger Publishing Co.

Bernard, M., Chambers, P. and Granville, G. (2000) 'Women Ageing: Changing Identities, Challenging Myths.' In M. Bernard and J. Phillips (eds) *Women Ageing – Changing Identities, Challenging Myths*. London: Routledge.

Bernard, M. and Meade, K. (1993) *Women Come of Age: Perspectives on the Lives of Older Women*. London: Edward Arnold.

Bernard, M. and Phillips, J. (eds) (2000) *Women Ageing: Changing Identities, Challenging Myths*. London: Routledge.

Bernard, M. and Strange, P. (eds) (1986) *Dependency and Independency in Old Age – Theoretical Perspectives and Policy Alternatives.* London: Croom Helm, 257–269.

Bernat, B. (1989) 'Dramatic Rise in Number of Elderly Prisoners Means Special Care Increased Costs.' In *National Prison Project Journal*, Washington, DC: American Civil Liberties Union Foundation, pp.9–11.

Berthelot, J. (1986) 'Sociological Discourse and The Body.' In *Theory Culture and Society 3*, 155–164.

Biggs, R. (1993) 'Biological Ageing in the Twentieth Century.' In J. Bond, P. Coleman and S. Peace (eds) *Ageing in Society* (1993) *An Introduction To Social Gerontology.* London: Sage.

Biggs, S. (1989) *Confronting Ageing.* London: CCETSW.

Biggs, S. (1990) 'Ageism and Confronting Ageing.' In *Journal of Social Work Practice 4*, 2, 49–65.

Biggs, S. (1993) *Understanding Ageing – Images, Attitudes and Professional Practice.* Buckingham: Open University Press.

Biggs, S. (1997) 'Choosing Not to be Old? Masks, Bodies and Identity Management in Later Life.' In *Ageing in Society 17*, 553–570.

Biggs, S. (1999) *The Mature Imagination Dynamics of Identity in Midlife and Beyond.* Buckingham: Open University Press.

Biggs, S. and Powell, J. (2001) 'A Foucauldian analysis of old age and the power of social welfare.' In *Journal of Aging and Social Policy 12*, 2, 93–111.

Bond, J. (1993) 'Living Arrangements of Elderly People.' In J. Bond, P. Coleman and S. Peace (eds) *Ageing in Society – An Introduction to Social Gerontology.* London: Sage.

Bond, J., Briggs, R. and Coleman, P. (1993a) 'The Study of Ageing.' In J. Bond, P. Coleman and S. Peace (eds) (1983) *Ageing in Society – An Introduction to Social Gerontology.* London: Sage.

Bond, J., Coleman, P. and Peace, S. (eds) (1993b) *Ageing in Society – An Introduction to Social Gerontology 5*, 1. London: Sage.

Booth, D.E. (1989) 'Health Status of The Incarcerated Elderly: Illness and Concerns in Institutions.' In *Journal of Custody, Care or Therapy*, 103–213.

Booth, T. (1985) *Home Truths – Old People's Homes and The Outcome of Care.* Aldershot: Gower.

Bornat, J., Phillipson, C. and Ward, S. (1985) *A Manifesto for Old Age.* London: Pluto Press.

Boswell, E. (2002), MSU–Bozeman Communication Services, 'Montana's Elderly Inmates Set Off National Survey', and 'Prisoner Care Leads to Collaboration.' Online 25 March 1999 at http://www.montana.edu/wwwpb/univ/inmate2.html.

Bosworth, M. (1999) *Engendering Resistance, Agency and Power in Women's Prisons.* Aldershot: Ashgate.

Bourdieu, P. (1978) 'Sport and Social Class.' In *Journal of Social Science Information 17*, 6, 819–840.

Bourdieu, P. (1990) 'Time Perspectives in the Kabyle.' In J. Hassard (ed.) *The Sociology of Time.* Basingstoke: Macmillan, pp.219–237.

British Medical Association, Royal Pharmaceutical Association of Great Britain (1999) *British National Formulary*, September 1999, *38*, 168.

Brogden, M. and Nijhar, N. (2000) *Crime, Abuse, and The Elderly.* Devon: Willan Publishing.

Brown, B. (1986) 'Women and Crime.' In *Economy and Society 3*, 15, 355–402.

Butler, J. (1987) *Bodies that Matter on the Discursive Limits of 'Sex'.* Oxford: Clarendon.

Butler, J. (1990) *Gender Trouble.* New York: Routledge.

Bytheway, B. (1983a) 'Ageing and Biography: The Letters of Linda and George.' In *Journal of The British Sociological Association 27*. No.1, February 1993, 153–165.

Bytheway, B. (1983b) 'Poverty, Care and Age: A Case Study.' In B. Bytheway, T. Keil, K. Teresa, P. Allatt and A. Bryman (eds) (1989) *Becoming and Being Old – Sociological Approaches to Later Life.* London: Sage.

Bytheway, B. (1994) *Ageism.* Buckingham: Open University Press.

Bytheway, B., Keil, T., Teresa, K., Allatt, P. and Bryman, A. (eds) (1983) *Becoming and Being Old – Sociological Approaches to Later Life.* London: Sage.

Bytheway, W.R. and Johnson, J. (1990) 'On Defining Ageism.' In *Critical Social Policy 27*, 27–39.

Cain, L. (1987) 'Elderly Criminals.' In *Journal of Contemporary Sociology 16*, 2, 209–210.

Cain, M. (1986) 'Realism, Feminism, Methodology and the Law.' In *The International Journal of the Sociology of Law 14* 255–267.

Caldwell, C. and Rosefield, J. (2001) 'Issues Impacting – Today's Geriatric Offenders.' In *Corrections Today 65*, 5, 112–114.

Cantor, D. and Cantor, S. (eds) (1979) *Designing for Therapeutic Environments: A Review of Research.* New York: John Wiley and Sons.

Carlen, P. (1983) *Women's Imprisonment: A Study in Social Control.* London: Routledge, Kegan and Paul.

Carlen, P. (1989) *Women's Imprisonment: A Strategy for Abolition – Prison.* London: Routlege.

Carlen, P. (2001) 'Death and the triumph of governance? Lessons from the Scottish Women's Prison.' In *Punishment and Society 3*, 4, 459–471.

Carlen, P. (2002) *Women and Punishment: The Struggles for Justice.* Cullompton: Willan.

Carlen, P., Hicks, J., O'Dwyer, J., Christina, D. and Tchaikovsky, C. (1985) *Criminal Women.* Cambridge: Polity Press.

Carlen. P. and Tchaikovsky, C. (1985) 'Women in Prison.' In P. Carlen, J. Hicks, J. O'Dwyer, D. Christina and C. Tchaikovsky (eds) *Criminal Women.* Cambridge: Polity Press.

Carlen, P. and Tchaikovsky, C. (1996) 'Women's Imprisonment in England and Wales at the End of the Twentieth Century: Legitimacy, Realities and Utopias.' In R. Matthews and P. Francis (eds) *Prisons 2000 An International Perspective on The Current State and Future of Imprisonment.* London: Macmillan Press.

Carlen, P. and Worrall, A. (eds) (1987) *Gender, Crime and Justice.* Milton Keynes: Open University Press.

Carpenter, E. (1905) *Prisons, Police and Punishment: An inquiry into the Causes and Treatment of Crime and Criminals.* London: A.C. Field.

Carroll, L. (1971) *Alice's Adventures in Wonderland* and *Through the Looking Glass.* London: Open University Press.

Castoriadis, C. (1997) *The Imaginary institution of Society.* Cambridge: Polity Press.

Cavadino, M. and Dignan, J. (1994) *The Penal System.* London: Sage (Intro, Chs 8–10).

Cavan, R.S. (1987) 'Is Special Treatment Needed for Elderly Offenders?' In *Criminal Justice Policy Review 2*, 3. Indiana, PA: IUP Imprint Series, 213–224.

Chaiklin, H. (1998) 'The Elderly Disturbed Prisoner.' In *Clinical Gerontologist 20*, 1. The Haworth Press.

Chaneles, S. (1987) 'Growing Old Behind Bars – The Aging of our Convict Population Brings with it Special Needs and Problems that Few of our Prisons are Ready to Handle.' In *Psychology Today,* October 1987: 47–51.

Chaneles, S. and Burnett, C. (eds) (1989) *Older Offenders: Current Trends.* New York: Haworth Press.

Christie, N. (1981) *Limits to Pain.* Oxford: Martin Robertson.

Clough, R. (1981) *Old Age Homes.* London: Allen and Unwin.

Cohen, S. (1985) *Visions of Social Control: Crime, Punishment and Classification.* Cambridge: Polity Press.

Cohen, S. and Scull, A. (eds) (1983) 'Social Control in History and Sociology.' In S. Cohen and A. Scull (eds) *Social Control and the State – Historical and Comparative Essays.* Oxford: Martin and Robertson.

Cohen, S. and Taylor, L. (1972) *Psychological Survival: The Experience of Long-Term Imprisonment.* Harmondsworth: Penguin.

Cohen, S. and Taylor, L. (1978) *Prison Secrets.* Briefing Paper. London: National Council for Civil Liberties and Radical Alternatives to Prison.

Cohen, S. and Taylor, L. (1992) *Escape Attempts – The Theory and Practice of Resistance to Everyday Life.* London: Routledge.

Cole, T., Achenbaum, W., Jokobi, P. and Kastenbaum, R. (1993) *Voices and Visions of Aging – Towards a Critical Gerontology.* New York: Springer Publishing Company.

Coleman, P. (1993) 'Adjustment in Later Life.' In J. Bond, P. Coleman and S. Peace (eds) *Ageing in Society – An Introduction to Social Gerontology.* London: Sage.

Coleman, P., Bond, J. and Peace, S. (eds) (1993) 'Ageing in the Twentieth Century.' In J. Bond, P. Coleman and S. Peace (eds) *Ageing in Society – An Introduction to Social Gerontology*. London: Sage.

Connor, S (1999) *Michel Serre's Five Seasons*. http://bbk.ac.uk/eh/eng/skc/5senses.htm.

Cook, F. (1998) *Hard Cell*. Liverpool: The Blue Coat Press.

Corbin, J. and Strauss, A. (1990) 'Grounded Theory Method: Procedures, Canons and Evaluative Criteria.' In *Qualitative Sociology 13*, 3–21.

Corston, M. (1999) 'The Time of Generations.' In *Time and Society 8*, 2, 249–272.

Councell, R. and Simes, J. (2002) *Projections of Long Term Trends in the Prison Population to 2009*. Home Office Statistical Bulletin No. 14/02.

Coyle, A. (1994) *The Prisons We Deserve*. London: HarperCollins.

Criminal Justice System (2001) *Criminal Justice: The Way Ahead*. London: The Stationery Office.

Cumming, E. and Henry, W. (1961) *Growing Old: The Process of Disengagement*. New York: Basic Books.

Dammer, H. (1994) 'The Problems of Conducting Ethnographic Research in American Prisons.' Paper Presented at Prison 2000 Conference: Leicester, England. (Unpublished Paper.)

Daniels, A.K. (1983) 'Self Deception and Self Discovery in Fieldwork.' In *Qualitative Sociology 6*, 195–214.

Davies, B. and Knapp, M.R.J. (1981) *Old People's Homes and the Production of Welfare*. London: Routledge, Kegan Paul.

Davis, K. (1990) *Women, Time and the Weaving of the Strands of Everyday Life*. Aldershot: Avebury.

Davis, P. (1995) *About Time – Einstein's Unfinished Revolution*. Middlesex: Penguin.

Deleuze, G. (1973) *Proust and Signs* (trans. from the French R. Howard). London: Lane.

Denzin, K.N. and Lincoln, Y. (1994a) 'Entering the Field of Qualitative Research.' In K.N. Denzin and S. Lincoln (eds) *Handbook of Qualitative Research*. Thousand Oaks: Sage Publications.

Denzin, K.N. and Lincoln, Y. (eds)(1994b) *Handbook of Qualitative Research*. Thousand Oaks: Sage Publications.

Denzin, K.N. and Lincoln, Y. (1998a) 'Introduction: Entering the Field of Qualitative Research.' In K.N. Denzin and Y. Lincoln (eds) *Collecting and Interpreting Qualitative Materials*. Thousand Oaks: Sage Publications.

Denzin, K.N. and Lincoln, Y. (eds) (1998b) *The Landscape of Qualitative Research – Theories and Issues*. London: Sage.

Denzin, K.N. and Lincoln, Y. (eds) (1998c) *Collecting and Interpreting Qualitative Materials*. Thousand Oaks: Sage Publications.

Department of Health (2000) *Health Survey for England 2000: The Health of Older People Summary of Key Findings*. London: Dept. of Health.

Department of Health (2001a) *Welcome to the Prison Health Policy Unit and Task Force website*. Prison Health Act: http://www.doh.gov.uk/prisonhealth/welcome.htm.

Department of Health (2001b) *National Service Framework for Older People*. London: Dept. of Health.

Department of Health/HM Prison Service (2001) *Changing the Outlook: A Strategy for Developing and Modernising Mental Health Services in Prison*. London: Dept. of Health.

Devault, M. (1990) 'Talking and Listening From Women's Standpoint: Feminist Strategies for Analyzing Interview Data.' In *Social Problems 37* No. 1, February 1990: 701–721.

Devlin, A. (1998) *Invisible Women*. Winchester: Waterside Press.

Dex, S. and Phillipson, C. (1986) 'Social Policy and the Older Worker.' In C. Phillipson and A. Walker (eds) (1986) *Introduction in Ageing and Social Policy, A Critical Assessment*. Aldershot: Gower.

Dickens, C. (1985) *American Notes for General Circulation*. Harmondsworth: Penguin, pp.146–147.

Dobash, R., Dobash, R.E. and Gutteridge, S. (1986) *The Imprisonment of Women*. Oxford: Blackwell.

Dollimore, J. (1999) *Death, Desire and Loss in Western Culture*. London: Penguin.

Donnelly, M. (1982) 'Foucault's Genealogy of the Human Sciences.' In *Economy and Society 11* No. 4: 363–380.

Donnelly, M. (1986) 'Foucault's Genealogy of the Human Sciences.' In M. Gane (ed.) *Towards a Critique of Foucault*. London: Routledge and Kegan Paul.

Dostoyevsky, F. *Notes From a Dead House*. Moscow, Union of Soviet Socialist Republic: Foreign Languages Publishing House (no date given: early edition).

Dostoyevsky, F. (1949) *Crime and Punishment*. London: William Heinemann Ltd.

Dreyfus, H. (1991) *Being-In-The-World: A Comment on Heidegger's 'Being and Time'*. Cambridge, MA: MIT Press.

Dreyfus, H. and Rabinow, P. (eds) (1982) *Michel Foucault: Beyond Structuralism and Hermeneutics*. Brighton: Harvester.

Duffee, D. (1984) 'A Research Agenda Concerning Crime Committed by the Elderly.' In E. Newman, D. Newman and M. Gewirtz (eds) *Elderly Criminals*. Oelgeschlager, Cambridge, MA: Gunn and Hain, Publishers, Inc.

Dugger, R.L. (1988) 'The Greying of American Prisoners: Special Care Considerations.' In *Corrections Today 50*, 3, 26–30, 34.

Dugger, R.L. (1990) 'Life and Death in Prison.' In *Prison Journal 7*, 1, 112–114.

Duncan, E. D. (1998) *The Calendar – The 5000-Year Struggle to Align the Clock and the Heavens – And What Happened to the Missing Ten Days*. London: Fourth Estate.

Durkheim, E. (1961) *The Elementary Forms of the Religious Life*. New York: Collier, Macmillan.

Durkheim, E. and Mauss, M. (1994) *Primitive Classification: The Argument and Its Validity*. New Jersey: Allen.

Eaton, M. (1986) *Justice for Women? Family, Court and Social Control*. Milton Keynes: Open University Press.

Edwards, S. (1994) 'The Social Control of Women in Prison.' In *Criminal Justice 12*: No 2.

Edwards, T. (1998) *The Aging Inmate Population: A Special Series Report of the Southern Legislative Conference*. Atlanta GA: The Council of State Governments Georgia.

Eliade, M. (1989) *The Myth of the Eternal Return – Cosmos and History*. Middlesex: Penguin.

Elias, N. (1978) *Civilising Process Revisited in Theory and Society 5*, 243–253.

Elias, N. (1992) *Time: an Essay*. Oxford: Blackwell.

Epstein, T. and Stuart, A. (1991) 'Quantitative and Qualitative Methods in the Social Sciences – Current Feminist Issues and Practical Strategies.' In M. Fonow and J. Cook (eds) *Beyond Methodology: Feminist Scholarship As Lived Research*. United States: Indiana University Press.

Erickson, E.H. (1983) *The Life Cycle Completed: A Review*. New York: Norton.

Estes, C. (1979) *The Ageing Enterprise*. San Francisco: Jossey–Bass.

Estes, C. (1993) 'The Ageing Enterprise Revisited.' In *Gerontologist 33*, 3, 292– 299.

Estes, C., Swan, J. and Gerand, L. (1982) 'Dominant and Competing Paradigms in Gerontology: Towards a Political Economy of Ageing.' *Ageing and Society 12*, 151–164.

Evers, H. (1983) 'Elderly Women and Disadvantage: Perceptions of Daily Life and Support Relationships.' In D. Jerome (ed.) *Ageing in Modern Society – Contemporary Approaches*. London: Croom Helm.

Fahey, C. and Holstein, M. (1993) 'Towards a Philosophy of the Third Age.' In T. Cole, W. Achenbaum, P. Jokobi and R. Kastenbaum (eds) *Voices and Visions of Aging – Towards A Critical Gerontology*. New York: Springer Publishing Company.

Falk, P. (1985) 'Corporeality and its fates in history.' In *Acta Sociologica 28*, 2, 115–136.

Falk, P. (1994) *The Consuming Body*. London: Sage.

Falk, P. (1995) 'Written in The Flesh.' In *Body and Society 1*, 1, 95–105.

Fattah, E.A. and Sacco, V.F. (1989) *Crime and Victimisation of the Elderly*. New York: Springer-Verlag.

Fazel, S., Hope, T., O'Donnell, I., Piper, M. and Jacoby, R. (2001) 'Health of Elderly Male Prisoners: Worse than the General Population, Worse than Younger Prisoners.' In *Age and Ageing 30*, 403–407.

Featherstone, M. (1982) 'The Body in Consumer Culture.' In *Theory, Culture and Society 1*, 18–33.

Featherstone, M. (1991) *Consumer Culture and Postmodernism*. London: Sage.

Featherstone, M. (1995) 'Post-Bodies, Ageing and Virtual Reality.' In M. Featherstone and A. Wernick (eds) *Images of Aging – Cultural Representations of Later Life*. London: Routledge.

Featherstone, M. and Hepworth, M. (1983) 'The Mid-life of George and Lynne.' In *Theory, Culture and Society 1*, 3, 85–92.

Featherstone, M. and Hepworth, M. (1989) 'Ageing and Old Age: Reflections on the Postmodern Life Course.' In B. Bytheway, T. Keil, K. Teresa, P. Allatt and A. Bryman (eds) *Becoming and Being Old – Sociological Approaches to Later Life*. London: Sage.

Featherstone, M. and Hepworth, M. (1991) 'The Mask of Ageing and the Postmodern Lifecourse.' In M. Featherstone, M. Hepworth and B. Turner (eds) *The Body, Social Process and Cultural Theory*. London: Sage.

Featherstone, M. and Hepworth, M. (1993) 'Images of Ageing.' in J. Bond, P. Coleman and S. Peace (eds) *Ageing in Society – An Introduction to Social Gerontology*. London: Sage.

Featherstone, M. and Wernick, A. (1995) Images of Aging – Cultural Representations of Later Life. London: Routledge.

Fennell, G., Phillipson, C. and Evers, H. (1993) *The Sociology of Old Age*. Milton Keynes: Open University Press.

Ferraro, K. (1997) *Gerontology Perspectives and Issues*. New York: Springer Press Company.

Fitzgerald, M. and Sim, J. (1982) *British Prisons*. Oxford: Blackwell.

Fleischer, M. (1989) *Warehousing Violence*. London: Sage.

Florida Corrections Commission (1999) *Elderly Inmates Annual Report*. http://www.fcc.state.fl.us/fcc/reports/final99/1eld.html.

Florida Corrections Commission (2001) *Annual Report Section 4: Status Report on Elderly Offenders*. Tallahassee FL: Florida Corrections Commission.

Flynn, E. (1992) 'The Greying of America's Prison Population.' In *Prison Journal 72*, No.s 1 and 2, 77–98.

Flynn, E. (2000) 'Elders as Perpetrators.' In M.B. Rothman, B.D. Dunlop and P. Entzel (eds) *Elders, Crime and the Criminal Justice System*. New York: Springer, pp.43–86.

Fontana, A. and Frey, H. J. (1991) 'Interviewing – The Art of Science.' In M. Fonow and J. Cook (eds) *Beyond Methodology – Feminist Scholarship as Lived Research*. Bloomington, Indiana University Press.

Fontana, A. and Frey, H.J. (1994) 'Interviewing – The Art of Science.' In M. Fonow and J. Cook (eds) *Beyond Methodology – Feminist Scholarship as Lived Research*. Bloomington, IN: Indiana University Press.

Ford, J. and Sinclair, R. (1987) *Sixty Years On – Women Talk About Age*. London: Women's Press.

Forsyth, C. and Gramling, R. (1988) 'Elderly Crime: Fact as Artifact.' In B. McCarthy (ed) *Older Offenders*. New York: Praeger.

Foucault, M. (1971) *Madness and Civilization: A History of Insanity in the Age of Reason* (trans. from the French R. Howard). London: Routledge.

Foucault, M. (1972) *The Archaeology of Knowledge* (trans. from the French A.M. Sheridan Smith). London: Tavistock.

Foucault, M. (1975) *I, Pierre Riviere, Having Slaughtered My Mother, My Sister, and My Brother, A Case of Parricide in the 19th Century*. Middlesex: Peregrine.

Foucault, M. (1976) *The Birth of The Clinic – An Archaeology of Medical Perception*. London: Routledge, Tavistock.

Foucault, M. (1977a) *History of Sexuality 1*. London: Penguin.

Foucault, M. (1977b) *Discipline and Punish – The Birth of the Prison* (trans. from the French A.M. Sheridan Smith). London: Allen Lane.

Foucault, M. (1978) *The History of Sexuality Volume 1*. New York: Pantheon.

Foucault, M. (1980) 'The Eye of Power.' In C. Gordon (ed.) *Power/Knowledge, Selected Interviews and Other Writings 1972–1977*. Brighton: Harvester Press.

Foucault, M. (1981) 'The Order of Discourse in Untying the Text.' In R. Young (ed.) *A Post-Structuralist Reader*. London: Routledge.

Foucault, M. (1982a) 'The Subject of Power.' In H. Dreyfus and P. Rabinow (eds) *Michel Foucault: Beyond Structuralism and Hermeneutics*. Chicago: University of Chicago Press.

Foucault, M. (1982b) 'The Subject and Power.' In *Critical Inquiry 8*, 777–795

Foucault, M. (1982c) 'Sexuality and Solitude.' In *Humanities Review 1*. New York: Cambridge University Press.

Foucault, M. (1986) 'Dream, Imagination, and Existence' (trans. F. Williams). In K. Hoeller (ed.) *Dream and Existence, Special Issue of Review of Existential Psychology and Psychiatry*. Seattle: Humanities Press.

Foucault, M. (1989) *Politics, Philosophy, Culture – Interviews and Other Writings 1977–1984*. London: Routledge.

Foucault, M. (1990) *The Care of the Self: The History of Sexuality Vol. 3*. London: Penguin.

Fountain, J. (1993) 'Dealing with Data.' In D. Hobbs and T. May (eds) *Interpreting The Field-Accounts of Ethnography*. Oxford: Oxford University Press.

Frank, A. (1990) 'Review Article – Bringing Bodies Back in A Decade Review.' In *Theory, Culture and Society 7*, 131–162.

Frank, A. (1991) 'For A Sociology of The Body: An Analytical Review.' In M. Featherstone, M. Hepworth and B. Turner (eds) *The Body: Social Processes and Cultural Theory*. London: Sage.

Friedan, B. (1983) *The Second Stage*. London: Abacus.

Friedan, B. (1992) *The Feminine Mystique*. London: Penguin.

Friedan, B. (1993) *The Fountain of Age*. London: Jonathan Cape.

Galford, E. (1984) *Moll Cutpurse – Her True History*. Scotland: Firebrand Books.

Gallagher, E. (1990) 'Emotional, Social, and Physical Health Characteristics of Older Men in Prison.' In *International Journal of Aging and Human Development 31*, 4, 251–265.

Gannon, L. (1999) *Women and Aging: Transcending the Myths*. London: Routledge.

Garland, D. (1990) *Punishment and Modern Society – A Study in Social Theory*. Oxford: Oxford University Press.

Garland, J. (1993) 'Environment and Behaviour: A Health Psychology Perspective.' In J. Bond, P. Coleman and S. Peace (eds) *Ageing in Society – An Introduction to Social Gerontology*. London: Sage.

Genders, E. and Player, E. (1987) 'Women in Prison: The Treatment, The Control and The Experience.' In P. Carlen and A. Worrall (eds) *Gender, Crime and Justice*. Milton Keynes: Open University Press.

Genders, E. and Player, E. (1994) 'Women Lifers: Assessing The Experience.' In *Corrections Research 6*, No. 1.

Genders, E. and Player, E. (1995) *A Study of a Therapeutic Prison*. Oxford: Oxford University Press.

Georgia Department of Corrections (2002) *Georgia's Aging Inmate Population* http://www. dcor.state.ga.us/research_reports/html/agingpop.html (Accessed 16 August 2002).

Gewerth, K. (1988) 'Elderly Offenders: A Review of Previous Research.' In B. McCarthy (ed) *Older Offenders*. New York: Praeger.

Giallombardo, R. (1966) *Society of Women: A Study of A Women's Prison*. New York: Wiley.

Giddens, A. (1981) 'Agency, Institution and Time-Space Analysis.' In K. Knorr-Cetina and A.V. Cicourel (eds) *Advances in Social Theory and Methodology Toward an Integration of Micro and Macro Sociologies*. Boston: Routledge and K.P, pp.161–174.

Giddens, A. (1984) *The Constitution of Society*. Cambridge: Polity.

Giddens, A. (1987) *Social Theory and Modern Sociology*. Cambridge: Polity (Ch. 6 – Time and Social Organisation).

Giddens, A. (1991a) *Modernity and Self-Identity: Self and Society in the Late Modern Age*. Cambridge: Polity.

Giddens, A. (1991b) 'Structuration Theory: Past, Present and Future.' In C. Bryant and D. Jary (eds) *Giddens' Theory of Structuration*. London: Routledge, pp.201–221.

Giddens, A. (1995) *A Contemporary Critique of Historical Materialism*. Houndmills: Macmillan.

Gilleard, C. and Higgs, P. (2000) *Cultures of Ageing: Self, Citizen and the Body.* London: Prentice Hall.

Gillespie, W.M. and Galliher, J. (1972) 'Age, Anomie, and the Inmate's Definition of Prison: an Explorative Study.' In P. Kent, D. Kastenbaum and S. Sherwood (eds) *Researching Planning and Action For The Elderly: The Power and Potential of Social Science.* New York: Behavioural Publications, pp.445–465.

Ginn, J. and Arber, S. (1995) *Connecting Gender and Ageing – A Sociological Approach.* Buckingham: Open University Press.

Ginn, J. and Arber, S. (1996) 'Ageing and Cultural Stereotypes of Older Women.' In J. Johnson and R. Slater (eds) *Ageing and Later Life.* London: Sage.

Glaser, B. and Strauss, A.L. (1967) *The Discovery of Grounded Theory; Strategies for Qualitative Research.* Chicago: Aldine de Gruyter.

Goetting, A. (1983) 'The Elderly in Prison: Issues and Perspectives.' In *Journal of Research in Crime and Delinquency 20*, 291–309.

Goetting, A. (1984) 'Prisons Programs and Facilities for Elderly Inmates.' In E. Newman, D. Newman and M. Gewirtz (eds) *Elderly Criminals.* Oelgeschlager, Cambridge, MA: Gunn and Hain, Publishers, Inc.

Goetting, A. (1992) 'Patterns of Homicide Among the Elderly.' In *Violence and Victims 7*, 203–215.

Goffman, E. (1961) *Asylum – Essays on the Social Situation of Mental Patients And Other Inmates.* Garden City, NY: Doubleday.

Goffman, E. (1963a) *Behaviour in Public Places – Notes on the Social Organisation of Gatherings.* New York: Free Press.

Goffman, E. (1963b) *Stigma – Notes on the Management of Spoiled Identity.* Englewood Cliffs, NJ: Prentice-Hall.

Goffman, E. (1971) *Relations in Public: Micro-studies of the Public Order.* London: Allen Lane, Penguin Press.

Goffman, E. (1983) 'The Interaction Order'– The American Sociological Association, 1982 Presidential Address in American Sociological Review. In *Official Journal of The American Sociological Association 48*, No 1, February 1983.

Goffman, E. (1990) *The Presentation of Self in Everyday Life.* London: Penguin.

Goldsmith, J. and Goldsmith, S. (1975) 'Crime and the Elderly: An Overview.' In J. Goldsmith and S. Goldsmith (eds) *Crime and the Elderly.* Washington, DC: Lexington Books, 1–7.

Gramling, R. and Forsyth, C. (1988) 'Elderly Crime: Fact and Artifact.' In B. McCarthy (ed) *Older Offenders.* New York: Praeger.

Grazia de, S. (1964) *Of Time Work and Leisure.* New York: Anchor Books.

Gregorio Di, S. (eds) (1987) *Social Gerontology: New Directions.* British Society of Gerontology. Kent: Croom Helm.

Guardian (1998) 'The Kick Inside.' 10 July.

Guardian (2001) 'The Jail for the Aged.' 30 January.

Gubrium, J. (1993) 'Voice and Context in a New Gerontology.' In T. Cole, W. Achenbaum, P. Jokobi and R. Kastenbaum (eds) *Voices and Visions of Aging – Towards a Critical Gerontology.* New York: Springer Publishing Company.

Gubrium, J. and Holstein, J.A. (1995) 'Individual agency, the ordinary, and postmodern life.' *The Sociological Quarterly 36*, 3, 555–570.

Gubrium, J. and Wallace, B. (1990) 'Who Theorises Age?' In *Ageing and Society 10*, 2,131–150.

Gurvitch, G. (1990) 'Varieties of Social Time.' In J. Hassard (ed.) *The Sociology of Time.* London: Macmillan, pp.67–87.

Gurvitch, G. (1990) 'The Problem of Time.' In J. Hassard (ed) *The Sociology of Time.* London: Macmillan, pp.35–47.

Gutting, G. (1989) *Michel Foucault's Archaeology of Scientific Reason.* Cambridge: Cambridge University Press.

Ham, J. (1976) *The Forgotten Minority: An Exploration of Long-term Institutionalized Aged and Aging Prison Inmates.* Washington, DC: National Institute of Law Enforcement, US Department of Justice.

Hamlyn, B. (2000) *Women Prisoners: A Survey of their Work and Training Experiences in Custody and on Release.* Home Office Research, Development and Statistics Directorate No 112.

Hamlyn, B. and Lewis, D. (2000) *Women Prisoners: A Survey of their Work and Training Experiences in Custody and Release.* London: Home Office Research Survey.

Hancock, R. and Sutherland, H. (1997) *Costs and Distributional Effects of Increasing the Basic State Pension.* London: Age Concern.

Harrison, J. (1983) 'Women and Ageing: Experience and Implications.' In *Ageing and Society 3*, Part 2, 208–235.

Harvey, D. (1990) 'Between Space and Time: Reflections on the Geographical Imagination.' *Annals of The Association of American Geographers 80*, 418–438.

Hassard, J. (1990a) 'Introduction: The Sociological Study of Time.' In J. Hassard *The Sociology of Time.* Basingstoke: Macmillan, pp.1–18.

Hassard, J. (1990b) *The Sociology of Time.* Basingstoke: Macmillan.

Hawking, S. (1988) *A Brief History of Time.* London: Batam.

Hearn, J. and Parkin, P.W. (1983) 'Gender and Organisations: A Selective Review and a Critique of a Neglected Area.' In *Organisational Studies 4, 219–242.*

Heidegger, M. (1978) *Being and Time.* Oxford: Blakewell.

Heidensohn, F. (1987) 'Women and Crime: Questions for Criminology.' In P. Carlen and A. Worrall (eds) *Gender, Crime and Justice.* Milton Keynes: Open University Press.

Heidensohn, F. (1989) *Crime and Society.* Basingstoke: Macmillan.

Heidensohn, F. (1994) 'Gender and Crime.' In M. Maguire, R. Morgan and R. Reiner (eds) *The Oxford Handbook of Criminology.* London: Clarendon Press.

Heidensohn, F. (1996) *Women and Crime.* Basingstoke: Macmillan.

Henderson, J. (1994) 'Ethnic and Racial Issues.' In J. Gubrium and A. Sankar (eds) *Qualitative Methods in Aging Research.* London: Sage.

Henwood, M. (1993) 'Age Discrimination in Health Care.' In J. Johnson and R. Slater (eds) *Ageing And Later Life.* London: Sage.

Hepworth, M. (1991) 'Positive Ageing and the Mask of Age.' In *Journal of Educational Gerontology 6, 2,* 93–101.

Hepworth, M. and Featherstone, M. (1982) *Surviving Middle Age.* Oxford: Blackwell.

Her Majesty's Chief Inspector of Prisons (1997) *Women in Prison: A Thematic Review. London: The Home Office.*

Her Majesty's Chief Inspector of Prisons (2001a) *Annual Report 1999–00, Inspectors' Report .* http://www.homeoffice.gov.uk/hmipris/ch2.pdf.

Her Majesty's Chief Inspectors of Prisons (2001b) *Report on a Full Announced Inspection of HMP Kingston,* 12–16 February 2001. Inspection Reports. http://www.homeoffice. gov.uk/hmipris/inspects/kingston01.pdf (accessed 3 August 2003).

Her Majesty's Inspectorate of Prisons for England and Wales (2001) *Follow-up to Women in Prison.* London: The Stationery Office.

Her Majesty's Inspectorate of Prisons for England and Wales (2002a) *Report of HM Inspectorates of Prison and Probation Conference: Through the Prison Gates.* London: The Stationery Office.

Her Majesty's Inspectorate of Prisons for England and Wales (2002b) *Annual Report of HM Chief Inspector of Prisons for England and Wales.* London: The Stationery Office.

Her Majesty's Inspectorate of Prisons for England and Wales (2002c) *Report on an Unannounced Follow-up of Inspection of HM Prison Kingston.* London: The Stationery Office.

Her Majesty's Inspectorate of Probation (1991) *Women Offenders and Probation Service Provision: A Thematic Report.* London: The Home Office.

HM Inspectorates of Prisons and Probation (2001) *Through the Prison Gate: A Joint Thematic Review.* London: HMIP.

HM Prison Service (1990) *Lifer Manual*. London: The Home Office.

HM Prison Service Order 4000 (2001) *Incentives and Earned Privileges*. Issue 77. London: Home Office.

HM Prison Service/NHS Executive (1999) *The Future Organisation of Prison Health Care*. London: The Stationery Office

HMP Kingston–Portsmouth (1996) *An Introduction for Lifers to the Older Prisoner's Unit*. Portsmouth: HMP Kingston.

Hockey, J. (1983) 'Just A Song At Twilight: Residents' Coping Strategies Expressed in Musical Form.' In D. Jerome (ed.) *Ageing in Modern Society – Contemporary Approaches*. London: Croom Helm.

Hockey, J. (1989) 'Residential Care and the Maintenance of Social Identity: Negotiating the Transition to Institutional Life.' In M. Jefferys (ed.) *Growing Old in The Twentieth Century*. London: Routledge, pp.201–218.

Holman, J.R. (1997) 'Prison Care: Our Penitentiaries are Turning into Nursing Homes. Can we Afford It?' *Modern Maturity 40*, 30–36.

Holtzman, J.M., Brauger, A. and Jones, C. (1987) 'Health Care of Older Women and minorities: Implications for Education and Training Programmes.' In G. Lesnoff-Caravagua (ed.) *Handbook of Applied Gerontology*. New York: Human Service Press, Inc.

Home Office (1966) *Report of the Inquiry into Prison Escapes and Security by Admiral of the Fleet, the earl Mountbatten of Burma*. London: HMSO. Cmnd 3175.

Home Office (1991) *The Sentencing of Women. A Section 95 Publication*. The Research and Statistics Directorate, Research Findings No. 58. London: HMSO.

Home Office (1993) *Lifer Manual – A Guide For Members of The Prison and Probation Services Working With Life Sentence Prisoners*. London: HMSO.

Home Office (1994) *Does the Criminal Justice System Treat Men and Women Differently?* Research Findings No. 10, London: HMSO.

Home Office (1995a) *Managing the Needs of Female Offenders*. London: Home Office.

Home Office (1995b) *Prison Service Annual Report and Accounts*. April 1994–March 1995. London: Home Office.

Home Office (1997a) *Understanding the Sentencing of Women Research Study 170*. London: The Research and Statistics Directorate.

Home Office (1997b) *The Prison Population in 1997: A Statistical Review*. Research Findings No. 76. London: HMSO.

Home Office (1997c) *Projections of Long Term Trends in the Prison Population to 2005*. London: HMSO.

Home Office (1999) *Statistics on Women and the Criminal Justice System*. Home Office Publication Under Section 95 Of The Criminal Justice Act 1991.

Home Office (2001a) *The Government's Strategy for Women Offenders: Consultation Report*. London: Home Office.

Home Office (2001b) *Home Office Prison Population Brief June 2001*. http://www.homeoffice.gov.uk/rds/pdfs.

Home Office (2001c) *Statistics on Women and the Criminal Justice System*. Home Office Publication Under Section 95 of the Criminal Justice Act. London: Home Office.

Home Office (2002) *Statistics on Women and the Criminal Justice System*. Home Office Publication Under Section 95 of the Criminal Justice Act. London: Home Office.

Howe, A. (1994) *Punish and Critique: Towards a Feminist Penality of Analysis*. London: Routledge.

Howson, A. (1998) 'Embodied Obligation – The Female Body and Health Surveillance.' In S. Nettleton and J. Watson (eds) *The Body In Everyday Life*. London: Routledge.

Hoy, D.C. (1986) *Foucault: A Critical Reader*. Oxford: Blakewell.

Hutter, B. and Williams, G. (1981) 'Controlling Women: The Normal and the Deviant.' In B. Hutter and G. Williams (eds) *Controlling Women*. London: Croom Helm.

James, M. (1992) 'Sentencing of Elderly Criminals.' In *American Criminal Law Review 29*, 1025–1044.

Jaques, E. (1982) 'The Enigma of Time.' In J. Hassard (eds) *The Sociology of Time*. London: Macmillan, pp.21–34.

Jayaratne, E.T. and Stewart, J.A. (1991) 'Quantitative and Qualitative Methods in The Social Sciences: Current Feminist Issues and Practical Strategies.' In M. Fonow and J. Cook (eds) *Beyond Methodology – Feminist Scholarship As Lived Research.* Bloomington, IN: Indiana University Press, pp.1–16.

Jerrome, D. and Young, A. (1983) *Ageing in a Modern Society.* London: Croom Helm.

Johnson, J. and Bytheway, B. (1993) 'Concepts and Values, Ageism: Concept and Definition.' In J. Johnson and S. Robert (eds) (1993) *Ageing in Later Life.* London: Sage.

Johnson, J. and Robert, S. (eds) (1996) *Ageing in Later Life.* London: Sage.

Johnson, P. (1996) *Sharing in the Prosperity of the Nation-Uprating Pensions.* London: Age Concern.

Johnson, W. (1989) 'If Only, the Experience of Elderly Ex-Convicts.' In the *Journal of Gerontological Social Work* 14, 191–208.

Johnson, W. and Alozie, B.O. (2001) 'The Effect of Age on the Criminal Processing: Is there an Advantage in Being 'Older'? *Journal of Gerontological Social Work 35,* 47–62.

Katz, S. (1996) *Disciplining Old Age: The Formation of Gerontological Knowledge.* Charlottesville, VA: Virginia University Press.

Kelly, J. (1967) *When The Gates Shut – Governor of Holloway Prison 1959–1966.* London: Longman, Green and Co Ltd.

Kelly, L. (1988) *Surviving Sexual Violence.* Cambridge: Polity Press.

Kerbs, J. (2000) 'The Older Prisoner: Social, Psychological and Medical Considerations.' In M. Rothman, B. Dunlop and P. Entzel (2000) *Elders, Crime and The Criminal Justice System – Myth, Perceptions, and Reality in the 21st Century.* New York: Springer Publishing Company.

Kercher, K. (1987) 'The Causes and Correlates of Crime Committed by the Elderly.' *Research in Ageing 9,* Part 2, 256–280.

King, R. and Mauer, M. (2001) *Aging Behind Bars: Three Strikes. Seven Years Later in the Sentencing Project.* Washington DC, The Sentencing Project.

King, R.D., Raynes, N.V. and Tizard, J. (1971) *Patterns of Residential Care.* London: Routledge and Kegan Paul.

Knight, B. (1986) 'Geriatric Homicide – Or The Darby and Joan Syndrome.' In *Geriatric Medicine 13,* 205–230.

Krajick, K. (1979) *Growing Old in Prison. Corrections Magazine 5,* 1, 32–46.

Krane, J. (1999) *Death and Mourning Inside the Walls: Funerals becoming a part of Prison Life.* www.apbonline.com/cjsystem/behindbars/old–prisoners, pp.1–4.

Kratcoski, P. (1990) 'Circumstances Surrounding Homicides by Older Offenders.' In *Criminal Justice and Behaviour 17,* 420–430.

Kratcoski, P. and Babb, S. (1990) 'Adjustment for Older Inmates: An Analysis by Institutional Structure and Gender.' In *Journal of Contemporary Criminal Justice 6,* 139–156.

Krebs, J.J. (2000) 'The Older Prisoner: Social, Psychological, and Medical Considerations.' In M.B. Rothman, B.D. Dunlop and P. Entzel (eds) *Elders, Crime and the Criminal Justice System.* New York: Springer, pp.207–228.

Lash, S. (1984) 'Foucault/Deleuze/Nietzsche.' In *Theory Culture and Society 2,* 2, 1–17.

Lash, S. and Urry, J. (1994) *Economies of Space.* London: Sage.

Layder, D. (1993) *New Strategies In Social Research.* Oxford: Polity Press (Chs 1–5).

Leech, M. (2003) *The Prisons Handbook.* Manchester: MLA Press.

Levi, P. (1996) *If This Is A Man – The Truce.* London: Abacus.

Levi, P. (1998) *The Drowned and The Saved.* London: Abacus.

Lewis, D.J. and Weigart, L. (1990) 'The Structures and Meanings of Social Time.' In J. Hassard (ed.) *The Sociology of Time.* London: Macmillan, pp.47–77.

Liebling, A. (1992) *Suicides in Prison.* London: Routledge.

Lombroso, C. and Ferrero, W. (1895) *The Female Offender.* New York: Philosophical Library.

Lyon, J. and Coleman, J. (1996) *Understanding and Working with Young Women in Custody: Information Pack.* London: Trust For The Study of Adolescence.

Macdonald, B. and Rich, C. (1984) *Look Me in the Eye: Old Women, Ageing and Ageism.* London: The Women's Press.

MacKenzie, D. (1987) 'Age and Adjustment to Prison Interactions with Attitudes and Anxiety.' In *Criminal Justice and Behaviour 14, 4, pp. 427–447.*

Maher, L. (1997) *Sexed work: Gender, race and resistance in a Brooklyn drug market.* Oxford: Oxford University Press.

Malinchak, A.A. (1980) *Crime and Gerontology.* Englewood Cliffs, NJ: Prentice Hall.

Mandaraka-Sheppard, A. (1986) *The Dynamics of Aggression in Women's Prisons in England.* Aldershot: Gower.

Mandela, N. (1994) *Long Walk To Freedom – The Autobiography of Nelson Mandela.* London: Little Brown and Company.

Manthorpe, J. (1983) 'With Intent to Steal in the New Age.' In *Journal of Offender Counselling Services and Rehabilitation 13* (Spring) 25–28.

Markus, T. (1993) *Buildings and power: freedom and control in the origin of modern building types.* London: Routledge.

Marquart, J.W., Merianos, D.E., Herbert, J.L. and Carroll, L. (1997) 'Health Condition and Prisoners. A Review of Research and Emerging Areas of Inquiry.' In *Prison Journal 77,* 184–208.

Marquart, J.W., Merianos, D.E. and Doucet, G. (2000) 'The Health Related Concerns of Older Prisoners: Implications for Policy.' *Aging and Society 20,* 79–96.

Marx, K. and Engels, F. (1976) *Collected Works Volume 5 April 1845–April 1847.* London: Lawrence and Wishart (Capital, *1,* p.129) (translation amended).

Marshall, C. and Rossman, G.B. (1989) *Designing Qualitative Research.* London: Sage Publications.

Mauthener, L. and Doucet, A. (1998) 'Reflections on a Voice Central Relational Method: Analysing Maternal and Domestic Voices.' In R. Edwards and J. Ribbens (eds) *Feminist Dilemmas in Qualitative Research – Public Knowledge and Private Lives.* London: Routledge, pp.119–146.

McCarthy, B. (1988) *Older Offenders.* New York: Praeger.

McCarthy, B. and Langworthy, R. (1988) 'Elderly Crime and The Criminal Justice System Response: Conceptualisation the Problems.' In B. McCarthy *Older Offenders.* New York: Praeger, pp.xxi–xxviii.

McDonald, D.C. (1995) *Managing Prison Health Care and Costs.* Washington, DC: National Institute of Justice, US Department of Justice.

McQuaide, S. and Ehrenreich, J.H. (1998) 'Women in Prison: Approaches to Understanding the Lives of a Forgotten Population in Affilia.' In *Journal of Women and Social Work 13,* 233–246.

McShane, M.D. and Williams, F.P. III (1990) 'Old and Ornery: The disciplinary experiences of elderly prisoners.' In *International Journal of Offender Therapy and Comparative Criminology 34,* 3, 197–212.

McVicar, J. (1974) *McVicar by Himself.* London: Hutchinson and Co. Ltd.

Melossi, D. and Pavarini, M. (1981) *The Prison and the Factory. The Origins of The Penitentiary System.* London: Macmillan.

Merquior, G.J. (1985) *Michel Foucault.* Paris: Paraguine Books.

Midwinter, E. (1997) *Pensioned Off Retirement and Income Examined.* Buckingham: Open University Press.

Mies, M. (1993) 'Towards a Methodology for Feminist Research.' In M. Hammersley (ed.) *Social Research Philosophy, Politics and Practice.* London: Routledge.

Miller, J. (1990) 'Carnivals of Atrocity: Foucault, Nietzsche, Cruelty.' In *Political Theory 18,* 474.

Moberg, D. (1953) 'Old Age and Crime.' In *Journal of Criminal Law 43,* 773–782.

Moore, E.O (1989) 'Prison Environment and the Impact on Older Citizens.' In *Journal of Offending and Counselling, Services and Rehabilitation 13,* 175–192.

Morton, J. (1992) *An Administrative Overview of the Older Inmate.* Washington DC: US Department of Justice National Institute of Corrections.

Moser, A.C. and Kalton, G. (1971) *Survey Methods in Social Investigation.* London: Heinemann Educational.

NACRO (1992a) *Women and Criminal Justice.* NACRO Briefing No. 94 (August). London: NACRO.

NACRO (1992b) *Women and Criminal Justice: Some Facts and Figures.* NACRO Briefing No. 91 (August). London: NACRO.

NACRO (1992c) *Women in Prison.* NACRO Briefing No.33 (October). London: NACRO.

NACRO (1993) *Women Leaving Prison.* London: NACRO.

NACRO (1994a) *Prison Overcrowding – Recent Developments.* NACRO Briefing No. 28 (July). London: NACRO.

NACRO (1994b) *Imprisonment in England and Wales; Some Facts and Figures.* NACRO Briefing No. 24 (August). London: NACRO.

Neeley, L.C., Addison, L. and Moreland-Craig, D. (1997) 'Addressing the needs of elderly offenders.' *Corrections Today 59,* 120–124.

Neugarten, B. (1996) *The Meanings of Age: Selected Papers.* Chicago: The University of Chicago Press.

Newman, D. (1988) 'Forword.' In B. McCarthy *Older Offenders.* New York: Praeger, pp.xv–xix.

Newman, E. (1984) 'Elderly Offenders and American Crime.' In E. Newman, D. Newman and M. Gewirtz *et al., Elderly Criminals.* Cambridge, MA: Oelgeschlager, Gunn and Hain, Publishers, Inc.

Newman, E. Newman, D. and Gewitz, M. (1984) *Elderly Criminals.* Cambridge, MA: Oelgeschlager, Gunn and Hain, Publishers, Inc.

Nietzsche, F. (1996) *On The Genealogy of Morals.* Oxford: Oxford University Press.

Nyland, C. (1990) 'Capitalism and the History of Work Time Thought.' In J. Hassard (ed) *The Sociology of Time.* London: Macmillan, pp.131–154.

Öberg, P. (1996) 'The Absent Body – A Social Erotological Paradox.' In *Ageing and Society 16,* 701–719.

O'Dwyer, J., Wilson, J. and Carlen, P. (1987) 'Women's Imprisonment in England, Wales and Scotland: Recurring Issues.' In P. Carlen and A. Worrall (eds) *Gender, Crime and Justice.* Milton Keynes: Open University Press.

Ohio Department of Rehabilitation and Corrections (1999) *A Comprehensive Approach to Addressing the Needs if Aging Prisoners.* Ohio: Columbus.

Olesen, V. (1994) 'Feminisms and Models of Qualitative Research.' In K.N. Denzin and S. Lincoln (eds) *Handbook of Qualitative Research.* London: Sage.

Olsen, T. (1980) *Tell Me A Riddle.* London: Virago, p.110.

Opie, A. (1992) 'Qualitative Research, Appropriation of the "Other" and Empowerment.' In K. N. Denzin and S. Lincoln (eds) *Handbook of Qualitative Research.* London: Sage, pp.273–285.

Osborne, P. (1995) *The Politics of Time – Modernity and Avant-Garde.* London: Verso.

Ovrebo, B. and Minkler, M. (1993) 'Voices and Visions of Aging: Towards a Critical Gerontology.' In R.T. Cole (ed.) *Voices and Visions of Aging Towards a Critical Gerontology.* New York: Springer.

Parsloe, P. and Stevenson, O. (eds) (1993) 'A Power House for Change: Empowering Users.' In J. Johnson and R. Slater (eds) *Ageing and Later Life.* London: Open University.

Patai, D. (1991) 'U.S. Academics and Third World Women: is Ethical Research Possible?' In S.B. Gluck and D. Patai (eds) *Women's Words: The Feminist Practice Of Oral History.* New York: Routledge.

Pawelczynska, A. (1980) *Values and Violence in Auschwitz – A Sociological Analysis.* Berkeley: University of California Press.

Peace, S. (1986) 'The Forgotten Female: Social Policy and Older Women.' In C. Phillipson and A. Walker (eds) *Ageing and Social Policy – A Critical Assessment.* Aldershot: Gower, pp.61–87.

Penal Affairs Consortium (1996) *The Imprisonment of Women: Some Facts and Figures.* London: Penal Affairs Consortium.

Penhale, B. (1993) 'The Abuse of Elderly People: Considerations for Practice.' In *British Journal of Social Work 23,* 2, 95–112.

Peralyla, A. (1998) 'Reliability and Validity in Research Based on Transcripts.' In D. Silverman (ed.) (1998) *Qualitative Research – Theory, Method and Practice.* London: Sage.

Pertierra, J.C. (1995) 'Do the Crime: Do the Time: Should Elderly Criminals Receive Proportionate Sentences?' In *Nova Law Review,* Winter, 1–25.

Phillips, J. (1996) 'Crime and Older Offenders.' In *Practice 8,* 1, 43–55.

Phillips, J., Worrall, A. and Brammer, A. (2000) 'Elders and The Criminal Justice System in England.' In M. Rothman, B. Dunlop and P. Entzel (2000) *Elders, Crime and The Criminal Justice System – Myth, Perceptions and Reality in the 21st Century.* New York: Springer Publishing Company.

Phillipson, C. (1982) *Capitalism and the Construction of Old Age.* London: Macmillian.

Phillipson, C. (1991) 'The Social Construction of Retirement: Perspective From Critical Theory and Political Economy.' In M. Minkler and C. Estes (eds) *Critical Perspectives on Ageing.* Amityville, N.Y: Baywood.

Phillipson, C. (1993) 'The Sociology of Retirement.' In J. Bond, P. Coleman and S. Peace (eds) *Ageing in Society – An Introduction to Social Gerontology.* London: Sage.

Phillipson, C. (1997) 'Editorial Review – Social Relationships in Later Life: A Review of The Research Literature.' In *International Journal of Geriatric Psychiatry 12,* 505–512.

Phillipson, C. (1998) 'Reconstructing Old Age.' *New Agendas in Social Theory and Practice.* London: Sage.

Phillipson, C. and Biggs, S. (1998) 'Modernity and Identity: Themes and Perspectives in the Study of Old Adults.' In *Journal of Ageing and Identity 3,* 1, 11–23.

Phillipson, C. and Walker, A. (eds) (1986) *Ageing and Social Policy, A Critical Assessment.* Aldershot: Gower.

Pollak, O. (1941) 'The Criminality of Old Age.' In *Journal of Criminal Psychotheraphy 3,* 213–235.

Postone, M. (1978) 'Necessity, Labor, And Time: A Reinterpretation of The Marxian Critique of Capitalism.' In *Journal of Social Research 45,* 739–788.

Postone, M. (1996) *Time, Labor, and Social Domination a Reinterpretation of Marx's Critical Theory.* Cambridge: Cambridge University Press.

Priestley, P. (1989) *Jail Journeys: The English Prison Experience 1918–1990.* London: Routledge.

Prins, H. (1980) *Offenders, Deviants Or Patients? An Introduction to the Study of Socio-Forensic Problems.* London: Tavistock.

Prior, L. (1997) 'Following in Foucault's Footsteps; Text and Context.' In D. Silverman (ed.) *Qualitative Research – Theory, Method and Practice.* London: Sage.

Prison Reform Trust (1995) *Education in Prisons: A National Survey.* London: Prison Reform Trust.

Prison Reform Trust (2003) *Growing Old in Prison: A Scoping Study on Older Prisoners.* London: Prison Reform Trust.

Prison Service Institution (2003) *Prison healthcare: new financial reproting arrangements.* Issue 13. London: Home Office.

Probyn, W. (1977) *Angel Face: The Making of a Criminal.* London: Allen and Unwin, pp.109–110.

Punch, M. (1986) *The Politics and Ethics of Fieldwork.* Newbury Park: Sage.

Puner, M. (1978) *To the good long life. What we know about growing old.* London: Sage.

Rabinbach, A. (1992) *The Human Motor – Energy, Fatigue, and the Origins of Modernity.* Berkeley: University of California Press.

Rabinow, P. (1986) *The Foucault Reader.* Toronto: Peregrine.

Rafter, N. (2000) *Encyclopedia of women and crime.* Phoenix, AZ: Oryx Press.

Reary, D. (1996) 'Inside Perspectives or Stealing The Words Out of Women's Mouths: Interpretation.' In *The Research Process in Feminist Review 53,* Summer, 57–73.

Reed, M.B. and Glamser, F.D. (1979) 'Ageing in a Total Institution: The Case of Older Prisoners.' In *Gerontologist 19,* 4, 354–360.

Reinharz, S. (1983) 'Experiential Analysis: A Contribution to Feminist Research.' In G. Bowles and R.D. Kein (eds) *Theories of Women's Studies.* London: Routledge.

Reinharz, S. (1992) *Feminist Methods in Social Research.* New York: Oxford University Press.

Renzetti, C. and Lee, R. (eds) (1993) *Researching Sensitive Topics.* London: Sage.

Rose, N. (1990) *Governing the Soul.* London: Routledge.

Rose, N. (1996) 'Identity, Genealogy, History.' In S. Hall and P. Gay (eds) *Questions of Cultural Identity.* London: Sage. (Ch. 8: pp.130–147).

Roseneil, S (1993) 'Greenham Revisited: Researching Myself and My Sisters.' In D. Hobbs and T. May (eds) *Interpreting the Field.* Oxford: Oxford University Press, pp.177–208.

Rosenthal, E. (ed.) (1990) *Women, Aging, and Ageism.* London: Haworth Press.

Roth, E. (1992) 'Elders Behind Bars in Perceptions.' In *Ageing 21,* 28–31.

Rothman, M.B., Dunlop, B.D. and Entzel, P. (2000) *Elders, crime and the Criminal Justice System.* New York: Springer.

Rouse, J. (1994) 'Power/Knowledge.' In G. Gutting (ed.) *The Cambridge Companion to Foucault.* Cambridge: Cambridge University Press.

Roy, D. (1990) 'Time and Job Satisfaction.' In J. Hassard (ed.) *The Sociology of Time.* London: Macmillan, pp.155–167.

Ruberstein, D. (1984) 'The Elderly in Prison: a Review of the Literature.' In E. Newman, D. Newman, M. Gewirtz *et al.* (1984) *Elderly Criminals.* Cambridge, MA: Oelgeschlager, Gunn and Hain, Publishers Inc., pp.153–168.

Sapsford, R. (1983) *Life Sentence Prisoners – Reaction, Response and Change.* Milton Keynes: Open University Press.

Schichor, D. (1984) 'The Extent and Nature of Lawbreaking by the Elderly: A Review of Arrests Statistics.' In E. Newman, D. Newman, M. Gewirtz *et al.* (1984) *Elderly Criminals.* Cambridge, MA: Oelgeschlager, Gunn and Hain, Publishers, Inc., pp.17–29.

Scraton, P., Sim, J. and Skidmore, P. (1991) *Prisons Under Protest.* Milton Keynes: Open University Press.

Serge, V. (1963) *Memoirs of a Revolutionary, 1901–1941.* London: Oxford University Press.

Serge, V. (1977) *Men in Prison.* London: Writers and Readers.

Shapiro, J. (1993) 'Osteoporosis in Women.' In J. Johnson and S. Robert (eds) (1996) *Ageing in Later Life.* London: Sage.

Shilling, C. (1993) *The Body and Social Theory.* London: Sage.

Sim, J. (1990) *Medical Power in Prisons, the Prison Medical Service in England 1774–1989.* Milton Keynes: Open University Press.

Sim, J. (2002) 'The Future Organisation of Prison Health Care: A Critical Analysis.' In *Critical Social Policy 22,* 2, May, 300–323.

Smart, B. (1983) 'On Discipline and Social Regulation: A Review of Foucault's Genealogical Analysis.' In D. Garland and P. Young (eds) *The Power to Punish.* Hampshire: Gower.

Smart, B. (1985) *Michel Foucault.* London: Routledge.

Smart, C. (1981) 'Law and the Control of Women's Sexuality: The Case of the 1950's.' In B. Hotter and G. Williams (eds) *Controlling Women.* London: Croom Helm.

Smart, C. (1989) *Feminism and the Power of The Law.* London: Routledge.

Smart, C. (1995) *Law, Crime and Sexuality – Essays in Feminism.* London: Sage.

Smyer, T., Graget, M.D. and LaMere, S.H. (1997) 'Stay Safe! Stay Healthy! Surviving Old Age in Prison.' In *Journal of Psychosocial Nursing 35,* 9, 10–17.

Social Exclusion Unit (2002) *Reducing Reoffending by Ex-prisoners.* London: Social Exclusion Unit.

Sorokin, P. and Merton, R. (1990) 'Social-time: A Methodological and Functional Analysis.' In J. Hassard (ed.) *The Sociology of Time.* London: Macmillan, pp.56–66.

Steffensmeier, D. (1987) 'Invention of the New Senior Citizen – An Analysis of Crime Trends of Elderly Males And Elderly Females, 1964–1984.' In *Research on Aging 9,* 2, June, 281–311.

Steffensmeier, D. and Allan, E. (1995) 'Age Inequality and Property Crimes: The Effects of Age-Linked Stratification and Status-Attainment Process on Patterns of Criminality Across the

Life Course.' In J. Hagan and R. Peterson (eds) (1995) *Crime and Inequality*. California: Stanford University Press.

Steffensmeier, D. and Moti, M. (2000) 'Older Women and Men in the Arms of Criminal Law; Offending Patterns.' In *Journal of Gerontology 6*, 5141–5151.

Stern, V. (1989) *Bricks of Shame – Britain's Prisons*. London: Pelican.

Stern, V. (1998) *A Sin Against The Future – Imprisonment in The World*. London: Penguin.

Stone, N. (1997) *A Companion Guide to Life Sentences*. Ilkley: Owen Wells.

Strauss, A. (1987) *Qualitative Analysis for Social Scientists*. Cambridge: Cambridge University Press.

Strauss, A. and Corbin, J. (1990) *Basics of qualitative research: granded theory procedures and techniques*. Newbury Park, Calif: Sage Publications.

Swift, S. (1989) 'The Elderly in Prison: in The Prison Service.' *Chaplaincy Review*, Issue 6.

Sykes, G. (1958) *The Society of Captives: A Study of a Maximum Security Prison*. Princeton, NJ: Princeton University Press.

Taft, B. and Wilkinson, R. (1999) *A Comprehensive Approach to Addressing the Needs of Aging Prisoners*. Department of Rehabilitation and Corrections. Ohio: U.S. Department of Justice.

Taylor, P. and Parrott, J. (1988) 'Elderly Offenders – A Study of Age Related Factors Among Custodial Remanded Prisoners.' In *British Journal of Psychiatry 152*, 340–346.

Tennessee Department of Corrections (2001) *Special Needs Offenders: an Overview of Housing Issues*. Nashville, TN.

Thane, P. (1983) 'The History of Provision for the Elderly to 1929.' in D. Jerrome and A. Young (eds) *Ageing in Modern Society – Contemporary Approaches*. London: Croom Helm.

Thomas, I.W. (1923) *The Unadjusted Girl*. New York: Harper and Row.

Thompson, E.P. (1967) 'Time, Work – Discipline and Industrial Capitalism.' In *Past and Present 38*, 51–68.

Thompson, P. (1992) 'I Don't Feel Old: Subjective Ageing and the Search for Meaning in Later Life.' In *Ageing and Society 12*, 23–47.

Thrift, N. (1990) 'The Making of Capitalist Time Consciousness.' In J. Hassard (ed.) *The Sociology of Time*. London: Macmillan, pp.105–147.

Times Educational Supplement (1998) 'Cuts Will Sentence More to Ignorance.' 10 April, 5.

Tinker, A. (1997) *Older People in Modern Society*, Harlow, Essex: Longman.

Toch, H. (1992) *Living In Prison: The Ecology of Survival*. Washington, DC: American Psychological Association.

Townsend, P. (1962) *The Last Refuge – A Survey of Residential Institutions and Homes for the Aged in England and Wales*. London: Routledge and Kegan Paul.

Townsend, P. (1981) 'The Structured Dependency of the Elderly: Creation of Social Policy in the Twentieth Century.' In *Ageing and Society 1*, 5–28.

Tseëlon, E. (1995) *The Masque of Femininity: the Presentation of Women in Everyday Life*. London: Sage.

Turley, J. (1990) 'Long-Term Confinement and the Aging Inmate Population.' *Alternative Solutions* U.S. Department of Justice, Federal Bureau of Prisons, Form on Issues in Corrections, Vol 5, 23–28.

Turley, J. (1992) 'A Solution to Prison Overcrowding.' In *USA Today Magazine 121*, November, 80–81.

Turner, B. (1988) 'Ageing, Status Politics and Sociological Theory.' In *British Journal of Sociology 40*, 4, 589–605.

Turner, G.S. and Champion, D.J. (1989) 'The Elderly Offender and Sentencing Leniency.' In *Journal of Offender Counselling, Services and Rehabilitation 13*, 125–140.

Twigg, J. (2000) *Bathing: The Body and Community Care*. London: Routeldge.

Urry, J. (1991) 'Time and Space.' In C. Bryant, D. Jarry and A. Giddens (eds) *Theory of Structuration*. London: Routledge, pp.160–175.

Urry, J. (2000) *Sociology Beyond Societies Mobilities for the Twenty-first Century*. London: Routledge.

Victor, R.C. (1987) *Old Age in Modern Society – A Textbook of Social Gerontology*. London: Croom Helm.

Victor, R.C. (1991) 'Continuity or Change: Inequalities in Health in Later Life.' In *Ageing and Society 11*, 23–39.

Victor, R.C. and Evandrou, M. (1983) 'Does Social Class Matter in Later Life?' In S. Di Gregorio (ed.) (1987) *Social Gerontology: New Directions* – British Society of Gerontology. London: Croom Helm.

Vito, G.F. and Wilson, D.G. (1985) 'Forgotten People: Elderly Inmates.' In *Federal Probation 49*,1, 18–24.

Wahidin, A. (2000) 'Life behind the shadows: Women's experiences of prison in later life.' In R. Horn and S. Warner (eds) *Issues in Forensic Psychology, Positive Directions for Women in Secure Environments.* Leicester: The British Psychological Society.

Wahidin, A. (2002) 'Reconfiguring Older bodies in the Prison Time Machine.' In *Journal of Aging and Identity 7*, 3, 117–193.

Wahidin, A. (2003) 'Women, old age and the prison system.' In *Criminal Justice Matters 53*, 38–40.

Wahidin, A. (2004) 'Reclaiming Agency – Managing aging bodies in prison.' In E. Tulle (ed) *Old Age and Human Agency.* New York: Nova Science Publishers.

Wahidin, A. and Powell, J. (2001) 'The Loss of Aging and Identity: Social Theory, Old Age, and the Power of Special Hospitals.' In *Journal of Aging and Identity 6*, 1, March 131–148.

Ward, J. (1993) *Ambushed My Story.* London: Vermillion.

Weber, M. (1930) *The Protestant Ethic and the Spirit of Capitalism.* London: Urwin Hyman.

White, L. (1991) 'Subordination, Rhetoric, Survival Skills and Sunday Shoes: Notes on Mrs G.' In M. Fineman and N. Thompsen (eds) *At the Boundaries of the Law: Feminism and Legal Theory.* New York: Routledge.

White, P., Woodbridge, J. and Flack, K. (1999) *Projections of Long Term Trends in the Prison Population to 2006.* Home Office Statistical Bulletin Issue1/99, 20 January.

Whitrow, J.G. (1972) *The Nature of Time.* Middlesex: Penguin.

Wildeblood, P. (1955) *Against The Law.* London: Weidenfeld & Nicolson.

Willcocks, D. (1986) 'Residential Care.' In C. Phillipson and A. Walker (eds) *Ageing and Social Policy – A Critical Assessment.* Aldershot: Gower, pp.146–163.

Willcocks, D., Peace, S. and Kellaher, L. (1983) 'A Profile of Residential Life: A Discussion of Key Issues Arising Out of Consumer Research in One Hundred Old Age Homes.' In D. Jerome (eds) *Ageing in Modern Society: Contemporary Approaches.* London: Croom Helm.

Willcocks, D., Peace, S. and Kellaher, L. (1987) *Private Lives in Public Places: A Research Based Critique of Residential Life In Local Authority Old People's Homes.* London: Tavistock.

Wilmott, Y. (1996) *Understanding and Working with Young Women in Custody: Trust for the Study of Adolescents.* London: HM Prison Service.

Wilson, D.G. and Vito, G.F. (1986) 'Imprisoned Elders. The Experiences of one Institution.' *Criminal Justice Policy Review 1*, 399–421.

Wilson, G. (2000) *Understanding Old Age – Critical and Global Perspectives.* London: Sage.

Women's National Commission (1992) *Older Women, Myths and Strategies – An Agenda For Action.* London: WNC.

Wood, D. (1989) *The Deconstruction of Time.* USA: International Humanities Press.

Woodward, K. (1988) 'Youthfulness as a Masquerade.' In *Journal of Discourse 11*, 1120–1142.

Worrall, A. (1990) *Offending Women.* London: Routledge.

www.doh.gov.uk/prisonhealth Department of Health. Accessed 26 July 2003.

Yates, J. and Gillespie, W. (2000) 'The Elderly and Prison Policy.' In *Journal of Aging and Social Policy 11*, 2–3, 167–175.

Zerubavel, E. (1990) 'Private Time and Public Time.' In J. Hassard (ed.) *The Sociology of Time.* London: Macmillan, pp.168–178.

Subject Index

Author Index